Lawrence Kohlberg's Approach to Moral Education

D0937283

Critical Assessments of Contemporary Psychology
A Series of Columbia University Press
Daniel N. Robinson, Series Editor

Lawrence Kohlberg's Approach to Moral Education

**F. Clark Power,
Ann Higgins,
Lawrence Kohlberg**

Columbia University Press
New York

Library of Congress
Library of Congress Cataloging-in-Publication Data

Lawrence Kohlberg's approach to moral education / F. Clark Power . . . [et al.].
p.   cm.—(Critical assessments of contemporary psychology)
Bibliography: p.
Includes index.
ISBN 0-231-05976-0
1. Moral education—United States—Case studies. 2. Moral
development—United States—Case studies. 3. Student ethics—United
States—Case studies. 4. Community—Case studies. 5. Kohlberg,
Lawrence, 1927–1987. I. Power, F. Clark. II. Series.
LC311.L38 1989
370.11'4'0973—dc19   88-18970
CIP

Columbia University Press
New York   Guildford, Surrey
Copyright © 1989 Columbia University Press

Casebound editions of Columbia University Press books are
Smyth-sewn and printed on permanent and durable acid-free paper

Book designed by Ken Venezio

Contents

Preface

This book is the product of a close working relationship among the authors that goes back to 1975 when we used to pile into Lawrence Kohlberg's car for the short hop to Cambridge Rindge and Latin High School. There we observed the weekly democratic community meetings of the Cluster School, the first of the experimental just community high schools. Those meetings were the heart of the just community approach to moral education, and Kohlberg spent long hours preparing himself and the faculty for them. By the time of the meeting he was bristling with anticipation. In his view, each meeting presented a unique opportunity for Cluster staff and students to develop as community based on principles of justice and care.

As interested as he was in the decisions made in a meeting, Kohlberg was far more concerned about the way in which they were made. Like Dewey and Piaget, he believed that students learned only by doing. Therefore, in the meetings he did all that he could to encourage their full participation. Often he would prod them with questions; sometimes he would advocate a position, speaking for the ideals of the community.

Kohlberg had the knack of relating as comfortably to a tough street kid as to a distinguished academic. Disarming in appearance with his two flannel shirts, baggy trousers, his hair tousled, glasses askew, and briefcase overstuffed, he was equally disarming in manner. He listened so intently and responded to thoughtfully that all who encountered him, even briefly, felt valued and understood.

The Cluster community meetings were scheduled with a lunch break in the middle. Typically Kohlberg spent that time scurrying between faculty and student cafeterias, in an effort to reach some closure before adjournment for afternoon classes. The end of a meeting signaled the beginning of the "research," as Kohlberg typically launched into an analysis of the previous meeting and looked ahead to the next week's agenda. Kohlberg's theory of moral education developed out of these community meetings and research discussions and those that followed at just community programs in Scarsdale and the Bronx. As a result of his experience in Cluster and the Scarsdale Alternative School, he came to believe strongly that democratic schools provide a rich context for collaborative theory-building. Even his own early work on moral discussion began to strike him as having fallen prey to the "psychologist's fallacy" of deriving a theory of education from psychological research.

In acknowledging the contribution of teachers and students to the development of the just community approach, we are conscious, of course, of the indispensible role that Kohlberg played in helping all of us to integrate theoretical, practical, and research-based insights. His contribution to moral education has been a most auspicious one, as he almost singlehandedly revived serious social science inquiry into this area after it had been virtually devastated by the publication of the Hartshorne and May Character Inquiry over a half a century ago. We are indeed privileged to have worked so closely with him.

This book was substantially completed before Lawrence Kohlberg's death in January 1987, and so we feel a keen and deep disappointment that he will not be sharing the celebration of its publication, a celebration of our cherished friendship and colleagueship with him. It is our hope that this book will testify not only to his intellectual contribution to the theory of moral education but also to his passion for justice and love for the young.

Acknowledgments

The research that is reported here was funded by a grant from the Ford Foundation. We are deeply grateful to the Foundation for their assistance and for the advice that we received when we began our study. We would also like to express our gratitude to the Joseph P. Kennedy, Jr. Foundation and especially Eunice Kennedy Shriver for supporting the establishment of the Center for Moral Education at Harvard and our early work in Cluster, the first just community school. Finally, special thanks is due to the Danforth Foundation, which provided funding for moral education programs in Cambridge and Brookline. The Foundation's representatives, Geraldine Bagby and Freeman R. Butts, were particularly helpful during their visits with us.

Of all those with whom we worked on this research, there are a few individuals whose work deserves particular recognition. Chris Mackin organized the early interviewing at Cluster in 1974 and 1975, and his copious notes on the establishment of the Discipline Committee were most helpful for our later writing. Joseph Reimer was the Director of the Ford Foundation Project beginning in 1976. He oversaw the data collection and the development of the research methodology, wrote the major portion of the first three chapters, and reviewed the others. The fifth original member of the Ford Project, Marvin Berkowitz, collaborated in the data collection and the preliminary research analysis. Anat Abrahami, Eileen Gardener, and Dan Hart were involved in the data collection and helped to construct a manual for the coding of moral atmosphere interviews.

Virtually all of the research associates and graduate students of the

Center for Moral Education between the years 1974 and 1979 participated in the data collection for this research. Most of them also commented at one time or another on our ideas as they took shape. In particular, we are most appreciative of the time and talent provided by Cheryl Armon, Charles Blakeney, Ronnie Blakeney, Daniel Candee, Anne Colby, Andrew Garrod, John Gibbs, Carol Gilligan, Fredrick Gordon, Charles Heckshire, Alexandra Hewer, Robert Howard, William Jennings, Marlena Johnson, Marcus Lieberman, Nona Lyons, Robert Kegan, Nancy Richardson McCaskey, Mordecai Nisan, Gil Noam, Fritz Oser, Sally Powers, William Puka, Laura Rogers, Betsy Rulon, Peter Scharf, Robert Selman, John Snarey, Betsy Speicher, and Elsa Wasserman. They helped to make the Center a genuine intellectual community.
community.

We are deeply grateful to those who helped to write, edit, and type this manuscript. Judy Codding, the former coordinator of the Scarsdale Alternative School, collaborated in writing chapter 6. Phyllis Brethols and Betsy Grady from the Cluster School assisted in writing the postscript to chapter 5. Ralph Mosher contributed to chapter 7 through many conversations and his publications on School-Within-A-School. Elsa Wasserman's dissertation on the history of the first two years of Cluster School was an invaluable resource for chapters 4 and 5. Robert Kenney's dissertation on the Democracy Project at Brookline High School and many conversations with Robert McCarthy, the former headmaster of that school, were most helpful to us in composing chapter 10. Sarah Lawrence Lightfoot provided guidance for the writing of the middle chapters and Georg Lind and Daniel Lapsely commented on our data analyses in chapters 8 and 9. Steve Fallon took time from his Milton studies for innumerable editorial consultations during the final drafting of the manuscript. We would also like to thank Karen Blackburn for her editorial assistance, as well as Cheryl Reed, Forestine Blake, Nila Gerhold, and Nancy Kegler of Notre Dame, who typed the many revisions of this manuscript.

David and Kara Power gave their father times to write and joy in between. Ann Power endured the travel and endless meetings that coauthorship demanded, and offered invaluable critical comments and suggestions during the numerous drafts of the book. Her husband has been singularly graced by her patience, tenderness, understanding, and love.

The authors would also like to thank their parents, their first moral teachers.

Finally we must thank the anonymous coauthors of Kohlberg's just community approach to moral education: the faculty and students of Cluster, School-Within-A-School, and Scardsdale Alternative High School. It was through observing and interviewing them that we learned the importance of participatory democracy and community in the education of young people.

Introduction

"**A**nything that reduces the effectiveness of moral education, whatever disrupts patterns of relationships, threatens public morality at its very roots" (Durkheim 1925/1973:3). With these words Durkheim introduced his lectures on moral education. He claimed as his audience not only professional educators, but all concerned citizens of his nation. He recognized that the justice and vitality of the civic community depended upon the citizenship education that only the school could provide. Although we have written this book from within what may loosely be called the cognitive developmental "paradigm" of educational psychology, we raise issues which go far beyond the boundaries of descriptive social science. The issues we address cannot and should not be regarded as technical questions, reserved for the expertise of psychologists, educators, and sociologists. These issues properly belong to the broader political domain and must be resolved through public moral discussion.

In writing a book about "just community schools," we propose an educational renewal of our democratic society, which is threatened as never before by a rapidly growing privatizing culture. Our approach to moral education is simple and direct. We have attempted to establish schools that do more than teach about democratic citizenship, that are themselves democratic societies. Instead of relying on clubs, sports, and various extracurricular activities to promote student relationships of friendship and care, we have tried to build community throughout the entire school day.

While democracy and community are familiar notions for most readers, high schools organized as direct participatory democracies (staff members and students each have one vote) and explicitly dedicated to a communitarian or *Gemeinschaft* ideal are rarely, if ever, encountered in this country. Because the schools we describe are cultural oddities, we present them in some detail. The chapters of this book are sequenced in such a way that the reader can think through our educational theory, the just community approach, as it developed out of our experiences in schools. We start in the first chapter with a review of Kohlberg's theory of moral development and what led him into moral education and democratic schooling. In the second chapter we trace his practical efforts to apply these ideas beginning with classroom moral discussion and culminating in the "just community prison." Here we see Kohlberg juggling his stage 6 moral, philosophical view of the just society with his cognitive developmental moral psychology and his adaptation of Durkheim's practical insights into communitarian education. Although he did not then have a comprehensive theoretical model that integrated these insights, he did have a living model of such an integration—a democratic Israeli kibbutz, which he visited in 1969. Through his acquaintance with that kibbutz, Kohlberg became convinced of the value and the possibility of an approach to moral education focused on the moral issues arising in the day-to-day concerns of staff and students, governed by democracy, and motivated by an altruistic commitment to community.

In chapters 3 through 7 we describe three experimental, alternative high schools that have in the literature (Kohlberg 1981, 1985; Mosher 1978, 1980) been referred to as just community schools: Cluster School in Cambridge, Massachusetts; Scarsdale Alternative High School (the A School) in Scarsdale, New York; and School-Within-a-School (S.W.S.) in Brookline, Massachusetts. All three of these schools have certain common features, such as small size (from sixty to a hundred students), direct participatory democracy, consultation from university professors and graduate students, and a concern, shared in varying degrees by the staff, for promoting moral development. They may be contrasted as follows:

First, Cluster and S.W.S. are both "schools within schools," that is, they are housed within larger public high schools and the students in those schools take at least half of their courses in the larger high school.

The A School is virtually a self-contained program with its own building on the grounds of the parent high school.

Second, the Cluster School, an urban school, has by far the most diverse student population of the three. By its fourth year the population was almost half black and half white, half privileged by social class background and half disadvantaged. The A School, located in an affluent suburb of New York City, and S.W.S., situated in a semi-urban town bordering on Boston, have predominantly white, upper- to upper-middle-class student populations.

Third, Kohlberg, who consulted in Cluster and the A School, and Mosher, who consulted in S.W.S., had somewhat different intervention models, based on their respective views about community.

In chapter 3 we outline the beginnings of Cluster School, Kohlberg's first attempt to establish a just community alternative high school. There we present the major institutions and practices that make up the organizational structure of the just community approach. We also include substantial excerpts from the transcripts of democratic meetings to flesh out that structure. Through these transcripts and our commentary the reader will come to know what a typical week in the life of Cluster was like. A qualification is in order here. We do not present the details of Cluster's curriculum or the curriculum of any of the schools that we have studied. This is not to say that we regard what takes place in the classroom to be superfluous, uninteresting, or disconnected with democratic governance or the communitarian values of the school. Dewey (1916/1966) writes eloquently about the importance of having the curriculum encompass the needs and interests of the students and the reality beyond the confines of the school walls. We believe that the experimental schools we present made considerable progress in the direction envisioned by Dewey.[1] Yet a critical analysis of their curricular achievements awaits future research. The focus of our study is on the norms and values that regulate discipline and social relationships in schools—what is sometimes called the "hidden curriculum" of moral education. The democratic processes that we describe are aimed toward making that curriculum more visible so that together students and staff can deliberate and change it to reflect more adequately principles of justice and care.

1. See Mosher (1978) and Codding and Arenella (1981) for examples of some of the curricular innovations undertaken in the experimental schools.

In chapter 4 we shift from a practical perspective on the just community approach to a research and evaluational perspective on the effectiveness of that approach in transforming Cluster into a just community over a period of four years. Just as we present the just community intervention as evolving out of prior theory and research, so too do we present our research on the moral atmosphere, more specifically the moral culture, as evolving out of antecedent theory and research on the effects of institutions on moral reasoning competence and performance. Our methodology for assessing the moral culture of schools grew almost entirely out of longitudinal analysis of Cluster's community meetings. In this chapter we reconstruct the steps we took in developing that methodology. Here the reader can see how the goals of the intervention helped to concretize and delimit what dimensions of school culture we think make up its specifically "moral" character.

In chapter 5 we apply our method for assessing moral culture to the study of the specific norms and values that we tried to promote throughout Cluster's first four years. Although organized to present the findings of our early research on Cluster, this is much more than a data analysis and results chapter. It is a selective history of the Cluster School that highlights how staff and students responded to problems of stealing, skipping class, racial tensions, and alcohol and marijuana use. The reader will learn how Kohlberg and the teachers framed these problems within a just community context and how they were consequently discussed and resolved. While these problems did not disappear, we shall witness Cluster responding to them ever more successfully and from the perspective of our scoring system ever more adequately.

In chapter 6 we introduce a second just community school, Scarsdale Alternative High School (the A School). Although illustrating the same intervention approach as Cluster and having almost identical democratic structures, the A School encountered a rather different set of problems. In the A School issues of the rights of the minority, faculty intimidation, cheating, and an honor code constituted the focus of discussion and decision making. The A School's history is also of interest because, unlike Cluster, it began in the early seventies as a part of the free school movement in alternative education. Later staff members, sensing that it had not lived up to their expectations as a "democratic school," turned to Kohlberg for help.

We describe the third of the experimental schools, School-Within-a-

School (S.W.S.), in chapter 7. Like the A School, S.W.S. was founded in the heyday of the free school movement and later became affiliated with the just community approach. Strictly speaking, however, S.W.S. is better described as being a democratic rather than a just community school; that is, its students, staff, and consultant, Mosher, do not claim to be implementing Kohlberg's approach, taken as a whole. Comparing S.W.S. with Cluster and the A School leads us to contrast Mosher's ideas about democratic community with Kohlberg's. This we do after a brief presentation of S.W.S.'s history.

In chapters 8 and 9 we present research data comparing the three experimental schools with their parent high schools. In chapter 8 we analyze differences in the moral cultures of these schools, as assessed by a standardized school dilemmas interview. The school dilemmas interview and coding system were derived from the methodology outlined in chapter 4. In our view a school's moral culture may be thought of as a variable mediating between its organizational structure, including its educational practices, and individual student outcomes. According to the just community approach, a school's organizational structure and pedagogical practices should be directed primarily at promoting a positive school culture defined in terms of its embodiment of the principles of justice and community. We theorized that the better the culture, the greater the likelihood that the organizational structure of school would function more effectively and the greater the likelihood that the students would develop morally. We present the research data on individual sociomoral development in chapter 9.

We conclude in chapter 10 with a discussion of the future of the just community approach. We focus on attempts to adapt an approach developed in small alternative settings to large, traditional schools. Our interest in extending the just community approach to other types of schools stems not from a false sense of confidence or optimism, based on our experiences within a few experimental schools, but from a heightened awareness of the failure of most schools to provide an environment conducive to the development of moral judgment and action. John Dewey's critique of schools at the turn of the century is as valid now as it was then:

I believe that much of present education fails because it neglects this fundamental principle of the school as a form of community life. It conceives of the school as a place where certain information is to be given, where certain lessons are to be learned, or where certain habits are to be formed. . . . I believe that the moral education centers upon this conception of the school as a mode of social life, that the best and deepest moral training is precisely that which one gets through having to enter into proper relations with others in authority of work and thought. The present educational systems, so far as they destroy or neglect this unity, render it difficult to get any genuine regular moral training. (1897/1959: 23–24)

If our schools are to help renew our democratic way of life and commitment to such principles as freedom, justice, and fellowship, then we must be willing to marshal our intellectual resources and spiritual energies into developing "the best and deepest moral training" we can offer. Through this book we hope to make a modest contribution to that effort.

1

From Moral Discussion to Democratic Governance

with Joseph Reimer

W here do we begin in telling the story of the just community? As authors we view the Cluster School, the first application of the just community approach, as part of a trend within the tradition of developmental moral education. Thus our story will open in this chapter with that tradition. The prehistory to be reviewed consists of the attempts— in theory and in practice—to apply the work of Lawrence Kohlberg on the stages of moral development to the field of moral education. The question to be addressed is why from the perspective of developmental moral education it made sense to think of running a democratically governed school-within-a-school as a means toward the end of promoting student moral development.

KOHLBERG: FROM MORAL DEVELOPMENT TO MORAL EDUCATION

Lawrence Kohlberg stands, inevitably, at the center of our story. He authored the theory of moral development and articulated the philosophy of moral education on which the just community approach was based. He was also a founder of the Cluster School and its main

Table 1.1.
The Six Stages of Moral Judgment

Level and Stage	Content of Stage		
	What is right	*Reasons for doing right*	*Social perspective of stage*
LEVEL I. Pre-conventional Stage 1: heteronomous morality	Avoiding breaking rules backed by punishment; obedience for its own sake; to avoid physical damage to persons and property.	Avoidance of punishment, and the superior power of authorities.	*Egocentric point of view.* Doesn't consider the interests of others or recognize that they differ from the actor's; doesn't relate two points of view. Actions are considered physically rather than in terms of psychological interests of others. Confusion of authority's perspective with one's own.
Stage 2: Individualism, instrumental purpose, and exchange	Following rules only when it is to someone's immediate interest; acting to meet your own interests and needs and letting others do the same. Right is also what's fair, an equal exchange, a deal, an agreement.	To serve your own needs or interests in a world where you have to recognize that other people have their interests too.	*Concrete individualistic perspective.* Aware that everybody has his own interest to pursue and these conflict, so that right is relative (in the concrete individualistic sense).
LEVEL II. Conventional Stage 3: Mutual Interpersonal expectations, relationships, and interpersonal conformity	Living up to what is expected by people close to you or what people generally expect of people in your role as son, brother, friend, etc. "Being good" is important and means having good motives, showing concern about others. It also means keeping mutual relationships, such as trust, loyalty, respect, and gratitude.	The need to be a good person in your own eyes and those of others. Your caring for others. Belief in the Golden Rule. Desire to maintain rules and authority which support stereotypically good behavior.	*Perspective of the individual in relationships with other individuals.* Aware of shared feelings, agreements, and expectations which take primacy over individual interests. Relates points of view through the concrete Golden Rule, putting yourself in the other guy's shoes. Does not yet consider generalized system perspective.

Stage	Content	Reasons for doing right	Social perspective of stage
Stage 4: Social system and conscience	Fulfilling the actual duties to which you have agreed. Laws are to be upheld except in extreme cases where they conflict with other fixed social duties. Right is also contributing to society, the group, or institution.	To keep the institution going as a whole, to avoid the breakdown in the system "if everyone did it," or the imperative of conscience to meet your defined obligations (easily confused with stage 3 belief in rules and authority).	*Differentiation of societal points of view from interpersonal agreement or motives.* Takes the point of view of the system that defines roles and rules. Considers individual relations in terms of place in the system.
LEVEL III. Post-conventional or principled Stage 5: Social contract or utility and individual rights	Being aware that people hold a variety of values and opinions, that most values and rules are relative to your group. These relative rules should usually be upheld, however, in the interest of impartiality and because they are the social contract. Some nonrelative values and rights like *life* and *liberty*, however, must be upheld in any society and regardless of majority opinion.	A sense of obligation to law because of your social contract to make and abide by laws for the welfare of all and for the protection of all people's rights. A feeling of contractual commitment, freely entered upon, to family, friendship, trust, and work obligation. Concern that laws and duties be based on rational calculation of overall utility, "the greatest good for the greatest number."	*Prior-to-society perspective.* Perspective of a rational individual aware of values and rights prior to social attachments and contracts. Integrates perspectives by formal mechanisms of agreements, contract, objective impartiality, and due process. Considers moral and legal points of view; recognizes that they sometimes conflict and finds it difficult to integrate them.
Stage 6: Universal ethical principles	Following self-chosen ethical principles. Particular laws or social agreements are usually valid because they rest on such principles. When laws violate these principles, one acts in accordance with the principle. Principles are universal principles of justice: the equality of human rights and respect for the dignity of human beings as individual persons.	The belief as a rational person in the validity of universal moral principles, and a sense of personal commitment to them.	*Perspective of a moral point of view* from which social arrangements derive. Perspective is that of any rational individual recognizing the nature of morality or the fact that persons are ends in themselves and must be treated as such.

SOURCE: Kohlberg 1984:174–176.

educational consultant. Let us begin our review, then, with his work.

1. In 1958 Kohlberg completed his doctoral dissertation, which was an extension of Piaget's (1932/1965) work on children's moral judgment. Working with a sample of boys aged ten to sixteen, Kohlberg showed, from their responses to hypothetical moral dilemmas, that the reasoning used to justify their moral positions could be classified as fitting six distinct patterns of moral judgment. These patterns are age-related, though not age-dependent, and can be characterized as levels of moral judgment.

2. To test whether these identified levels of moral judgment would meet the Piagetian criteria of stages, Kohlberg initiated a longitudinal study of his original subjects, interviewing them every four years to test their level of moral judgment. By the late 1970s a twenty-year study had been completed (Kohlberg, Gibbs, and Lieberman 1983; Colby and Kohlberg 1987).

3. During the 1960s Kohlberg (1969) elaborated a "cognitive-developmental theory of moralization" that attempts to account for (a) how these stages develop from an interaction between an individual and his environment; (b) how an individual passes from one stage to the next; (c) why some individuals develop further than others; and (d) what the relation is between these cognitively based structures and an individual's moral feelings and actions. The theory has been based on a mix of solid empirical evidence (Rest 1980) and theoretical speculation. It has been highly controversial, giving rise to critics and supporters (e.g., Modgil and Modgil 1985), as well as many studies by other researchers on social and moral development (e.g., Damon 1977; Selman 1980; Turiel 1983).

At the heart of Kohlberg's developmental work has been the delineation of the stages of moral judgment. This has proven to be a long and arduous task (Colby 1978), but has culminated in an extensive manual for scoring moral judgment interviews (Colby et al. 1987). As it is beyond the scope of this chapter to do more than list the six stages (see table 1.1), readers not familiar with these stages are recommended to look elsewhere for their description.[1] Much of what follows assumes such familiarity.

Given both the generative and controversial nature of Kohlberg's

---

1. For a good introduction to Kohlberg's stages see Reimer, Paolitto, and Hersh (1983).

theory of moral development, there is little doubt he could have spent his whole career within the field of developmental psychology. But by the late 1960s his attention seems to have increasingly turned to applying his theory of development to educational practice. A second phase of his career—as a theoretician and practitioner of moral education—began with the work of one of his graduate students, Moshe Blatt.

BLATT: THE FIRST APPLICATION

Blatt hypothesized on the basis of research by Elliot Turiel (1966) and James Rest (1968), that if children were systematically exposed to moral reasoning one stage above their own, they would be positively attracted to that reasoning, and would, in attempting to appropriate the reasoning as their own, be stimulated to develop toward the next higher stage of moral judgment. To test this hypothesis, Blatt set up a pilot project for a class of sixth-grade students in a Jewish Sunday School. He reasoned that the most effective and least artificial way to "expose" children to moral judgment one stage above their own would be to have a group discussion of moral dilemmas in which group members who were at different stages would hear one another's resolutions to the dilemmas. In trying to convince one another of why their resolutions were best, children would thereby expose the others to their stages of reasoning.

Blatt began by initially testing the students for their stages of moral judgment and then met with them as a class group once a week for twelve weeks. He would present a moral dilemma and then ask the group to propose solutions and explain why their solutions were best.

As these arguments developed, the experimenter would take the "solution" proposed by a child who was one stage above the majority of the children . . . and clarify and support the child's argument. The experimenter elaborated this solution until he felt that the children understood its logic and seemed convinced that its logic was reasonable or fair. The experimenter made it a point to leave as much of the argument to the children as possible; he stepped in to summarize the discussion, to clarify, add to the argument and occasionally present a point of view himself. (Blatt and Kohlberg 1975:133)

At the conclusion of the twelve weeks Blatt retested the students and found that 64 percent of them had developed one full stage in their moral reasoning. Encouraged by the results, Blatt attempted to replicate the findings in four public school classrooms, two sixth and two tenth grades. These students were divided into three groups: those who met with Blatt for teacher-led moral discussions for eighteen sessions, those who met in peer-led moral discussions for the same time period, and those in a control group who received no treatment. At the end, the teacher-led group showed an average gain of one-third of a stage, while the other groups showed almost no change. In a follow-up testing one year later, the teacher-led group maintained its lead over the others.

Although the second experimental attempt led to less stage change than did the first, the cumulative effect of Blatt's educational experiment was ground breaking and made, as Kohlberg retrospectively reports, a marked impression on Blatt's thesis adviser.

I was skeptical that Blatt's verbal discussion of purely hypothetical dilemmas would lead to genuine moral stage change. But Blatt persisted in spite of my pessimism and found "the Blatt effect" . . . that one-fourth to one-half of the students in one semester of such discussion groups would move (partially or totally) to the next stage up—a change not found in the control groups. Blatt's venture launched cognitive-developmental moral education. (1978:4)

THE CONDITIONS FOR MORAL GROWTH

What Blatt "launched" was a process by which Kohlberg's theory of moral development could be applied practically to educational (classroom) practice. His study demonstrated three points essential to the endeavor of developmental moral education.

1. The development of moral judgment is amenable to educational intervention; the movement from one stage to the next, which naturally occurs over a span of several years (Colby and Kohlberg 1987), can be effected in a concentrated period of time.

2. The stimulated development is not a temporary effect of learning "right answers," but, as measured a year later, is as lasting as is "natural" development and is generalized to new dilemmas not covered in the classroom.

3. The stimulated development occurs when the intervention sets up the conditions which promote stage progression. These involve providing opportunities for cognitive conflict, moral awareness, role-taking, and exposure to moral reasoning above one's own stage of reasoning.

Blatt took as the objective of his educational intervention the stimulating of students' level of moral judgment from one stage to the next. His success in achieving that objective could, though, have been called into question were it not for the follow-up testing a year later. By showing that the gains achieved remained constant without any reinforcement from the intervention, he could rebut potential criticism that what accounted for the change was students' learning from the teacher the content of the higher-stage arguments. Were the change due to content learning, rather than structural transformation, it is more likely that it would have been reversed in a year's time.

Since Blatt's pioneering research on moral discussion, there have been a large number of studies which have replicated his findings. These have been reviewed by Lockwood (1978), Higgins (1980), Leming (1981), Enright, Lapsley, and Levy (1983), Enright, Lapsley, Harris, and Shauver (1983), Schläfli, Rest, and Thoma (1985), and Lapsley, Enright, and Serlin (in press). Unfortunately there has been very little research conducted to clarify what are the critical conditions in these discussion programs that promote development (Schläfli, Rest, and Thoma 1985). The process analysis of moral discussion undertaken by Berkowitz and his colleagues (Berkowitz, Gibbs, and Broughton 1980) is the most significant and promising approach in this area. Berkowitz and Gibbs (1979, 1983) analyzed the moral discussions of thirty dyads of college students according to a manual categorizing eighteen transactive types. They found that certain of these transactive types, which they called operative, predicted to moral stage change. Operative moral transacts are exchanges in which the discussants do not simply assert their own opinions or paraphrase the opinions of the other, but rather engage each other's reasoning in an ongoing dialectic.

A second promising line of research that should help to clarify further the conditions for promoting stage development has been undertaken by Walker (1983), who focused on the impact of various cognitive conditions on moral development. He presented fifth- to seventh-grade children with a thirty-minute moral discussion between two adults in which they were exposed to one of the following treatment conditions: supportive and conflicting opinions at reasoning one stage above the (subject pro/con + 1 reasoning); conflicting opinions supported by reasoning one stage above the subject (con + 1 reasoning); supportive opinions at reasoning one stage above the subject (pro +1 reasoning); conflicting and supportive opinions at subject's own stage of reasoning (pro/con 0); a neutral treatment condition, that is, control supportive opinions at the subject's own stage of reasoning (pro 0); and a no-treatment control condition. Surprisingly for such a brief intervention, subjects in all of the treatment conditions developed. This study indicated that exposure to conflicting moral reasoning one stage above the subject's own (the pro/con + 1 and the con + 1 conditions) was the most effective. It also showed that conflict in the absence of higher stage reasoning (pro/con 0) brought about change. In interpreting the success of these treatments, note that Walker's subjects included only those with certain cognitive and role-taking prerequisites.

TOWARD A PHILOSOPHY OF DEVELOPMENTAL MORAL EDUCATION

Though Kohlberg's writing about education began before Blatt's experiment (Kohlberg 1966), the success of that experiment focused his theoretical attention much more on issues of education. From 1970 Kohlberg's writings deal at least as much with issues of moral education as with the definition of the stages of moral judgment. But as we will see, there was more breadth to the educational ideas that Kohlberg articulated than to the educational practices initiated by Blatt. There arose an imbalance between what Kohlberg advocated in writing and what initially became identified as developmental moral education. That imbalance would in part be "corrected" by Kohlberg's introduction of the just community approach.

Kohlberg's educational writings (1966, 1967, 1970a, 1970b, 1971c) begin with basic questions: how should we think about values and about the teaching of values? By what right do teachers teach values to their students? If by values a teacher means that which is relative to each person—that which each person esteems as a result of his own individuality—by what right can such values be taught to others? To teach values would then involve teaching the teacher's own values to students who have developed or should be developing values of their own. If by values a teacher means that which is transmitted by the society to all its members, then how does the teacher legitimately decide which of all the values transmitted by the society are the ones to be taught to the students? Given the diversity of values available in a modern society, how do teachers decide which are the most basic ones to be taught in school?

Kohlberg raises these age-old questions to indicate that teachers cannot properly assume that teaching values is any less a thought-provoking activity than is teaching reading or mathematics. Yet he believes that at least in American public schools teachers have the responsibility to *teach* values, though they do not have the right to impose their own, or any, set of values on their students. "It is clear that the Constitution and the law of the land compose or imply 'a value system' or body of norms. . . . The school, like the government, is an institution with a basic function of maintaining and transmitting . . . the consensual values of society. The most fundamental are termed moral values, and the major moral values, at least in our society, are the values of justice" (Kohlberg 1967:165).

As Kohlberg reads the Constitution, it is not only a historical or a legal document, but also a moral document. It spells out the basic moral values on which our society is founded and which, therefore, schools ought to be transmitting to students. But Kohlberg is not advocating a literal teaching of the Constitution. Rather, he sees the Constitution as representing the moral principle of justice and claims that it is by teaching "justice" that the schools can legitimately transmit "the consensual values of society." For justice, seen from the perspective of moral development theory, is not a given value, which can be concretely transmitted to or imposed on children, but is the basic valuing process that underlies each person's capacity for moral judgment. It is that native sense of fairness which at each stage of development gives form to how individuals make judgments of right and wrong. To "teach justice," then, involves helping students to develop an increasingly more adequate sense of fairness.

Kohlberg's position provides a way out of the bind of how to teach moral values without imposing them on children. By promoting the development of their native sense of fairness, the teacher is not imposing any value content on the students, but is preparing them to better comprehend and then appropriate the principle of justice on which the moral philosophy of the Constitution is based. Furthermore, because justice is a universal moral principle that any morally mature person in any society should use as a basis for making moral judgments, the aim of the developmental approach is not limited to the goals of American education, but extends to include the goals of global citizenship.

DEVELOPMENT AS THE AIM OF EDUCATION

In an essay coauthored by Rochelle Mayer, Kohlberg (1972) explores three prevailing educational ideologies to which educators could turn in searching for a deliberate approach to moral education. He refers to them as the "romantic," "cultural transmission," and "developmental" or "progressive" approaches. To clarify the differences between these approaches and to argue for the greater adequacy of the developmental approach, Kohlberg and Mayer review how each approach conceptualizes the aims of values education. They suggest four possible conceptions of aims based on the three ideologies:

1. to develop in students values and skills that will contribute to achieving a psychologically healthy and self-fulfilling life-style (romantic);
2. to teach students behaviors and attitudes that reflect the traditional values of their society (cultural transmission);
3. to teach students skills in order to live more effectively and successfully as members of their society (cultural transmission);
4. to promote the development of students' capacities in areas of cognitive, social, moral, and emotional functioning (developmental).

The argument for choosing the developmental approach rests on two primary assumptions: that educational aims should be justifiable in terms of their intrinsic worth, and that human capacities that develop consistently and expansively over time should be seen as having more worth than behaviors, attitudes, or skills that are limited in scope and subject to being extinguished or reversed.

To concretize the first assumption, imagine three successful educational programs: the first teaches students to clarify their values, the second teaches students leadership skills, and the third promotes the development of students' moral judgment. Few people would contest that clarifying one's values or learning to lead a group effectively has functional worth to those who learn these skills. Yet we can still ask to what end these are being learned; for learning the use of these skills does not define how they will be used. One may clarify what one's values are, but still have values that are not (from a philosophic perspective) rationally justifiable. Or one may become an excellent group leader, but lead a group to immoral ends. In contrast, developing to a higher stage of moral judgment is a process that contains its own moral ends. It has intrinsic worth; for although the students might not act on their newly developed highest stage, were they to act by its logic, they would make a more adequate moral decision than if they were to act on the basis of lower-stage reasoning.

Thus what Kohlberg and Mayer argue is not that the aims of values clarification (romantic approach) or group leadership skills (cultural transmission) are not worthy of pursuit, rather, that they should be incorporated as objectives within a program whose final goal is to promote moral development. Then students and teachers could together examine to what moral ends they should be putting their newly acquired personal and social skills.

To concretize the second assumption, imagine a program designed to teach children to act more in accordance with the value of honesty and altruism. The program incorporates elements of modeling and behavior modification and is successful in getting students to act more honestly and altruistically toward one another. While in this case there is little contest about the intrinsic worth of this learning, Kohlberg would point to any number of social psychological studies that throw doubt on the durability of such learning. These studies show that people's acting honestly or altruistically is not a stable, traitlike characteristic, but varies with the conditions of the situations in which they find themselves (Hartshorne and May 1928/1930; Brown and Herrnstein 1975). Thus this program runs the serious risk of teaching sets of behavior that in other settings might not prove to be transferable or lasting.

In contrast, when a program aims to promote students' development of moral judgment, the objective is to change not simply a set of behaviors, but a structural capacity. That structural capacity—as Colby and Kohlberg's (1987) longitudinal and Blatt and Kohlberg's (1975) follow-up studies show—is rarely reversible. Once a person develops a new structural capacity, she "has" it, though its performance will be subject to situational variance. The durability of developmental gains leads Kohlberg and Mayer to advocate that educational programs be measured for worth against a long-term yardstick: to what extent do they contribute not only to immediately observable changes in behavior, attitude, or values, but also to developmental changes that will accompany the student in his or her future life?

Kohlberg and Mayer close their essay with two further points that should be kept in mind. The first corrects a misapprehension that the aim of developmental education is stage acceleration: getting children to move as quickly as possible through the stages of development. There is no educational value, they remind us, in speeding up the natural course of development, for there are probably normative-optimal points of developmental transition within particular cultures. For example, in our culture preadolescence is a normative point of transition between stage 2 and stage 3, and there would be no real reason to try to get children to stage 3 before that age. However, developmental education does aim to avoid stage retardation. Thus with a group of adolescents who are still operating at a primarily stage 2 level, it would be appropriate to aim to promote their development to the next stage, which is the level at which they could and should be operating.

A second important aim of developmental education that gets little attention is to foster *decalage*—the spreading out of a cognitive operation across a range of basic physical and social activities. The concern here is for the breadth and depth of development rather than for its rate of progression. For example, in moral development an adolescent who has reached a stage 3 level of judgment in reasoning about issues of law, life, and property may yet reason about issues of interpersonal relations —and particularly sexual relations—at a lower, stage 2 level. There would in this case be an educational concern not to move his reasoning up to stage 4, but to spread his stage 3 capacities to include the more complex issues of sexual relations (Gilligan, Kohlberg, Lerner, and Belenky, 1971).

Decalage as an aim of developmental education reminds us that though we are dealing with a theory of *cognitive* development, there has to be an ever-present concern in developmental education for the *whole person*—for feelings and thinking alike. Though affective or ego development remains the underdeveloped pole of this theory, Kohlberg and Mayer are aware of and concerned about an overly cognitive, overly stimulative interpretation of the goals of developmental education.

Finally, we need to note that in the realm of ego-development a focus on "horizontal *decalage*" rather than acceleration is especially salient. The distinc-

tion reflects . . . an educational focus upon "healthy" passage through stages . . . [for] cognitive-developmental theory would agree that a premature development of a higher ego stage without a corresponding *decalage* throughout the child's world and life presents problems. In psychoanalytic maturational terms, the dangers of uneven or premature ego development are expressed as defects in ego-strength with consequent vulnerability to regression. In cognitive-developmental terms, inadequate "horizontal *decalage*" represents a similar phenomenon. (1972:492)

Some successors to Blatt have integrated psychological and moral education into cohesive programs that take a developmental perspective on issues of both morality and mental health (Mosher and Sullivan 1976; Sprinthall 1980). That integrative approach becomes increasingly important as the developmental tradition grows and expands (Noam 1985; Selman 1980).

LIMITATIONS OF THE APPROACH

For all that the work of Blatt and his successors excited in Kohlberg's imagination and stimulated in his thinking and writing about the implications of the cognitive-developmental approach for educational practice, one can also read in Kohlberg's essays of the early 1970s a note of limitation. Though developmental moral education was proving successful in meeting its objectives—promoting the development of individuals' moral judgment—it did not fully address the everyday school issues of student behavior and discipline. "It must be noted that these procedures should not constitute a full-fledged program of moral education. Methods emphasizing a rational discussion approach should be part of a broader, more enduring involvement of students in the social and moral functioning of the schools" (Kohlberg and Turiel 1971:456). No matter how eloquently he argued in theory for the intrinsic worth of promoting student moral judgment, Kohlberg acknowledged what a reviewer later wrote.

Even if there were agreement that the development of moral reasoning is a desirable educational aim, teachers and policy makers are unlikely to find it alone to be a fulfilling goal. . . . Researchers would provide an important service by identifying the extent to which changes in moral reasoning are associated with changes in the behavioral, affective and cognitive realms. (Lockwood 1978:361)

About the relation between changes in moral reasoning and moral behavior Kohlberg had to be cautious. Blatt (Blatt and Kohlberg 1975) had administered pre and post experimental cheating tests to his subjects, but found that even those who advanced in moral reasoning were not significantly more likely to resist the temptation to cheat than they had been before the program began. This finding made theoretical sense: Blatt's subjects were moving up to stage 3 and stage 4, and other studies (Kohlberg 1969) showed that consistent noncheating begins only at stage 5. But the finding made it difficult to make strong claims for the practical effects of such programs on student behavior.

From Kohlberg's perspective, however, the main limitation of Blatt's approach is not this finding. For even were a researcher to find a successful way to change students' behavior along with their reasoning, the focus would still be limited to individual change. Though he authored a theory of individual development, Kohlberg is explicit in stating that the *social value* of a developmental approach lies beyond its effect on individual behavior.

The unit of effectiveness of education is not the individual but the group. An individual's moral values are primarily important for society as they contribute to a moral social climate, not as they induce particular pieces of behavior. . . . Moral discussion classes . . . are limited, not because they do not focus on moral behavior, but because they have only a limited relation to the "real life" of the school and the child. (1971a:82)

The aim of developmental moral education has to be a change in the life of the school as well as in the development of individual students. For the teaching of justice, as the teaching of reading or arithmetic, is set in a *context* of a classroom and a school, and how the students experience the life of the classroom and school will have a shaping effect on what they learn from what the teacher teaches.

To get a conceptual handle on the school as a context for learning, Kohlberg (1970b) turned outside of developmental theory (with its focus on the individual organism) to the sociology of education. He was particularly attracted to the work of Durkheim (1925/1973), Dreeben (1968), and Jackson (1968). From their view, the school is seen primarily by the role it plays in providing the setting and the occasion for the child's first formal entry into the society at large. It is the first public institution to which the child is sent not as a member of his family, but as an individual with an emerging identity of his own. The school thus represents the larger society to the child; by going to school, the child learns to fill the expected public roles of a member of his society.

Coming from a home in which she is accustomed to being a center of attention for adults who are personally invested in her care and well-being, the child has a lot of learning to do to adjust to school life, which, by necessity, is arranged quite differently from home life. Jackson has termed this learning process the "hidden curriculum," and he specifies its content in terms of the child's learning to deal with "the crowds, the praise and the power." The child has to learn to be one among a crowd of peers in a classroom that is run by a relatively impersonal authority figure who gives orders and has the power to wield praise and blame. What the child learns about how to handle "the crowds, the praise and the power" will, from this point of view, give shape to her public morality: her conception of how one ought to act to get along and even prosper in the public domain.

While Kohlberg maintains a philosophic distance from this sociological perspective (a distance we will explore), he is in full agreement that a complete approach to moral education would have to address the hidden curriculum. For even if the values of justice were discussed in classes, if the students perceive that getting along in school runs by a quite different set of norms, they will tend to perceive the latter as the real rules of the game and the former as nice talk one engages in with teachers. To avoid reinforcing a split such as this between students' principles and their practices, educators have to provide an educational context in which there is a felt congruence between the values of the school and the norms of action.

DEALING WITH THE HIDDEN CURRICULUM

There are two existing models to which Kohlberg (1970a; 1971e) points for how to deal explicitly with the hidden curriculum. One is the "romantic" model of A. S. Neill's *Summerhill* (1960), and the other is the "cultural transmission" model of Emile Durkheim's *Moral Education* (1925/1973).

Neill's approach is to replace the hidden curriculum with a curriculum of freedom. If schools run into trouble by trying to covertly shape the behavior of students while overtly claiming not to be imposing values on them, then let educators give up their efforts at moral influence: "A child is innately wise and realistic. If left to himself without adult suggestion of any kind he will develop as far as he is capable of developing." (p. 4)

While Kohlberg appreciates Neill the educator, with his great moral energy and unfailing belief in the potential of students' development, he finds unconvincing the romantic assumption, common to free schools, that authority can be replaced by an ethic of freedom. He points to an incident cited in *Summerhill* to show that when the chips are down, Neill ends up unwittingly resurrecting the hidden curriculum, though in seemingly amoral terms.

We had two pupils arrive at the same time, a boy of seventeen and a girl of sixteen. They fell in love with each other and were always together. I met them late one night and stopped them. "I don't know what you two are doing," I said, "and morally I don't care for it isn't a moral question at all. But economically, I do care. If you, Kate, have a kid my school will be ruined.

You have just come to Summerhill. To you it means freedom to do what you like. Naturally, you have no special feeling for the school. If you had been here from the age of seven, I'd never have had to mention the matter. You would have such a strong attachment to the school that you *would* think of the consequences to Summerhill. (pp. 57–58)

There is little question where "the power and the praise" lies in Summerhill. In Kohlberg's view no matter whether Neill exercises his power in economic or moral terms, the fact remains that in dealing with a conflict between the rights of the individual and the interests of the school, Neill puts the latter first. While as headmaster he may have the right as well as the need to do so, he is being neither honest with himself nor helpful to the students by denying that a conception of moral authority is at play here. Kohlberg's preference would be to make that conception explicit and share it openly with the students as a moral problem.

If Neill wishes to throw out the hidden curriculum, Durkheim wants to embrace it, make it explicit, and use it for purposes of moral education. He is not concerned, as Neill is, with "civilization and its discontents," for he sees *anomie*—or the lack of moral order—as being more problematic for modern society than the repression of instincts. Thus his concern is for the school to implicitly initiate children into the moral order of their society. This is accomplished by beginning not with the individual student and his behavior, but with the class and its group behavior. Durkheim suggests that the teacher take the dull routines of classroom discipline and invest them with moral meaning by treating the classroom as a small society with its own rules, obligations, and sense of social cohesion.

> Morality is respect for rule and is altruistic attachment to the social group. . . . That which is essential to the spirit of discipline, respect for the rule, can scarcely develop in the familial setting, which is not subject to general impersonal immutable regulation, and should have an air of freedom. But the child must learn respect for the rule; he must learn to do his duty because it is his duty, even though the task may not seem an easy one. Such an apprenticeship must devolve upon the school. Too often, it is true, people conceive of school discipline so as to preclude endowing it with such an important moral function. Some see in it a simple way of guaranteeing superficial peace and order in the class. Under such conditions, one can quite reasonably come to view these imperative requirements as barbarous, as a tyranny of complicated rules. In reality, however, school discipline is not a simple device for securing superficial peace in the classroom; it is the morality of the classroom as a small society. (p. 148)

Though Durkheim's conception of morality—with its emphasis on respect for society's transmitted rules and attachment to the group—is different from Kohlberg's developmental conception, Kohlberg is quite attracted by Durkheim's vision of an explicit use of the hidden curriculum to create a moral society in the classroom. He agrees more with Durkheim than with Neill that schools cannot get rid of authority in classrooms, for societies depend on schools to socialize children into a sense of attachment and obligation. The problem with the hidden curriculum is not that there is a curriculum, but that it is hidden. Durkheim is on target when claiming that as long as school rules are seen as "a simple way of guaranteeing superficial peace and order," the hidden curriculum will remain hidden. The serious work of deliberate moral education entails, as Kohlberg learned from Durkheim, opening up that process and dealing with the ways everyday rules of behavior are made and enforced. For it is those rules that define the moral atmosphere—the context for moral learning—in the school.

A CURRICULUM OF JUSTICE

The attraction for Kohlberg of the Durkheim model—"It is in my opinion the most philosophically and scientifically comprehensive, clear and workable approach to moral education extant" (Kohlberg 1970b:

108)—could not obviate the philosophic difficulties it posed for his developmental-progressive ideology.

Durkheim has simply taken to its logical conclusion a justification of the hidden curriculum which many teachers vaguely assume, that the discipline of group life directly promotes moral education. When, however, this line of thinking is carried to its logical conclusion, it leads to a definition of moral education as the promotion of collective national discipline which is consistent neither with rational ethics nor the American constitutional tradition. (Kohlberg 1971e:28)

Durkheim's model may well be effective in creating a cohesive group of students who operate dutifully by a code of conventional morality, but it is not likely to stimulate student development to the postconventional stages of principled morality. Given a conflict between the interests of the collective and the rights of the individual, such students would probably be so over-committed to the collective's perspective that they would undervalue even the legitimate claims of the individual. Kohlberg's philosophic commitment to universal moral principles left him finally dissatisfied with the otherwise attractive Durkheimian model.

If reading Durkheim (as well as Dreeben and Jackson, whose sociological approach derives from Durkheim) led Kohlberg to take seriously the problem of context raised by the hidden curriculum, he chose to deal with the problem from the developmental-progressive perspective.

The crowds, the praise, and the power are neither just nor unjust in themselves. As they are typically used in the schools, they represent the values of social order and of individual competitive achievement. The problem is not to get rid of the praise, the power, the order, and the competitive achievement, but to establish a more basic context of justice which gives them meaning. In our society authority derives from justice, and in our society learning to live with authority should derive from and aid learning to understand and to feel justice. (Kohlberg 1970b:122)

What Kohlberg sought was a way to transform the hidden curriculum into a curriculum of justice. He envisioned extending the types of moral discussions initiated by Blatt to the rules, regulations, and social relations that define the process of schooling. Why limit discussions to hypothetical travelers in a desert when questions of whether the teacher is acting fairly and who has been stealing from the lockers are always present and waiting to find expression? Once raised, these questions could lead to a different form of school governance: to a decision-making process in which the rights of the students—as well as those of the teachers—are taken seriously and the value of justice or fairness, rather than the value of adult authority, is given primacy. "To extend classroom discussions of justice to real life is to deal with issues of justice in the school. Education for justice, then, requires making schools more just, and encouraging students to take an active role in making the school more just" (Kohlberg 1971e:82).

The wheel of this intellectual journey turns back from Durkheim to Dewey—from a conception of the school as the initiator of the youth into the existing moral traditions of the society to a conception of the school as the context in which students learn with teachers the process by which rules and regulations are created in a just society. "In regard to ethical values, the progressive ideology adds the postulates of *development* and *democracy*. The notion of educational democracy is one in which justice between teacher and child means joining in a community in which value decisions are made on a shared and equitable basis" (Kohlberg and Mayer 1972:474).

To learn "to understand and to feel justice," students have to be both treated justly and called upon to act justly. For Kohlberg that means *educational democracy:* schools in which everyone has a formally equal voice to make the rules and in which the validity of the rules are judged by their fairness to the interests of all involved. If the best learning is learning by doing, then students can best learn justice not only by discussing its claims in the abstract, but also by acting on its claims in the here and now of the school day.

The return to the progressive ideal of educational democracy is accompanied, though, with a new appreciation for the issues of the hidden curriculum. Democracy cannot be a surface maneuver—a gesture to fairness that leaves the traditional authority structure in place. If students are asked to play at democracy while the teachers go on making the real decisions, little is gained while the good name of democracy is lost. There is a need to carefully think through how to implement a democratic process of governance that gains the acceptance and participation of both teachers and students as partners in a common endeavor.

There is also a need to view democratic governance from a developmental perspective. Simply instituting a formal democracy—everyone gets one vote, etc.—is no more likely to stimulate students' moral development than is simply having moral discussions. The concern for creating the conditions for moral growth has to be transferred to educational democracy if it too is to become stimulating to moral development.

FROM MORAL DISCUSSION
TO DEMOCRATIC GOVERNANCE

What we have seen in this review of the intellectual prehistory of Cluster's opening is a kind of dialectical process at work.

1. Kohlberg authors a theory of moral development that Blatt applies to educational practice. Blatt empirically demonstrates that a developmental educational intervention can promote moral stage change, and Kohlberg supplies a philosophic justification for the process Blatt launched.

2. By reading Durkheim, Dreeben, and Jackson, Kohlberg finds that both Blatt's work and his own thinking about developmental moral education is limited by not taking into account the problems of context raised by the hidden curriculum.

3. Kohlberg attempts to integrate Durkheim's with Dewey's progressive ideology and discovers in educational democracy a way of addressing the hidden curriculum while still promoting both individual moral development and a progressive view of the schools as serving the cause of justice.

DEMOCRACY AND AUTONOMY

In describing the route from moral discussion to democratic governance, we have taken a historical point of view and focused on developments within Kohlberg's theorizing that led him to the notion of democratic community. We conclude this chapter by reflecting on the general question of why high schools should become democratic. There are basically two kinds of arguments that can be made: a practical pedagogical one, that the democratic process is a valuable means of promoting development, teaching about the political system, and securing order and harmony in the school; and a moral philosophic one, that the inclusion of adolescents in democratic decision making respects their autonomy as moral persons.

Since by now the reader is familiar with some of our pedagogical reasons for choosing democracy as a means to moral development, we will only summarize the practical argument and give greater attention to the philosophic one. The first of the practical considerations is that because democratic meetings deal with real-life problems and resolutions, they may more effectively promote moral development than discussions of hypothetical dilemmas. Second, democracy, by equalizing power relations, encourages students to think for themselves and not to depend upon external authorities to do their thinking for them. Third, if we accept the Deweyan principle of learning by doing, then the most effective way of teaching students the democratic values of our society is to give them the opportunity to practice them. Fourth, as Mill noted, errors are more likely to be corrected in a democratic society that encourages open expression and examination of opinions than in a closed, authoritarian society. This means that administrators and teachers are more likely to make wiser decisions if they include students in the process. Fifth, democracy can help to overcome the breach between adult and peer cultures in the school by creating a shared sense of ownership of and responsibility for the school rules. Finally, democracy encourages students to follow the rules of the school. Having publicly voted for rules, individuals experience personal and social pressure toward consistency in their actions.

As compelling as these practical considerations for democratic schools may appear, we believe the more decisive considerations are based on morality as justice. The linkage of democracy to morality depends upon how one interprets the fundamental moral principle of respect for persons. In the Kantian moral tradition, respect for persons entails a respect for their free and rational nature.

Etymologically, autonomy implies self-governance. Kant took autonomy to mean that persons are the subjects or constructors of the moral law. He contrasted it with heteronomy or being governed by an external will or object. Feinberg (1973) elucidates one meaning of autonomy by differentiating it from anomie, or being "virtually out of control." Autonomy implies self-control according to self-chosen principles. However, we must be careful here, as Feinberg (1973) and Rawls (1971) warn, not to confuse autonomy with the relativistic authenticity of the existentialist hero. The Kantian notion of autonomy presupposes that moral agents are bound by rationally objective moral principles. These principles are objective in the sense that we would expect any moral agent to adopt them freely from an impartial point of view. We should also be careful not to equate autonomy with psychological independence. Although the notion of autonomy presupposes that selves make choices that do not depend on the will of others, this does not imply that selves make those choices in isolation from others. We agree with Piaget (1932/1965), who maintained that cooperation is necessary for autonomy. In analyzing how children developed their understanding of the game of marbles, he noted that they acquired a new conception of rules as they applied them in a cooperative way. They learned that rules did not depend on the fiat of an external and inscrutable authority but on mutual agreement among equals. Through discussion children are able to contrast their point of view with others and reach a reasonable consensus. Heteronomy, on the other hand, depends upon a relationship of unilateral constraint. Insofar as children experience rules as imposed on them from the outside, they remain locked within the bounds of their egocentrism or subjectivity. Piaget thought that as long as children are constrained by heteronomous relationships, they are egos, but they are not real "selves" or personalities. Personality is constituted through relations of mutual respect. The autonomous self is a social self.

Piaget's linkage of autonomy with cooperation cuts through the dichotomy between dependence and independence or attachment and separation. The autonomous self is in a sense created and sustained through dialogue with other autonomous selves. Kohlberg's concept of stage 6 helps to elucidate in the context of making moral decisions how autonomy and dialogue presuppose one another. Stage 6 is a process of reversible role taking or "moral musical chairs" that leads to consensus. In the process, parties having a conflict of interest are required to consider each other's claims from their point of view until they reach a solution that they can agree on. Although this process of reversible role taking is epitomized in moral dialogue, there are substantial obstacles to achieving such a dialogue. For example, the persons involved in a dispute may refuse to examine impartially each other's claims, or they may attempt to manipulate an agreement through some form of coercion. At best, real-world moral dialogues approximate but never fully actualize the ideal conditions of stage 6 reversibility. Thus Kohlberg describes the stage 6 role-taking process as an imaginative one. It should not displace moral discussion, but it may be necessary as a corrective when discussion becomes distorted or as a substitute when it breaks down or becomes impossible (Kohlberg, Boyd, and Levine 1986).

For the sake of brevity we will presume that our readers are amenable to the notion that respect for autonomous persons ordinarily will require democratic forms of decision making. What is far more controversial is whether children and adolescents have a claim or a right to democratic participation in their schools. There are two ways of approaching this issue: one is to establish whether they possess the requisite competencies to qualify as autonomous moral agents. A second is to determine whether democratic participation is necessary as a means to the end of promoting their development to autonomy.

Given that the process of socio-moral development from childhood through adolescence appears relatively continuous, "slippery slope" arguments for and against the competency of minors are readily available. At one end of the continuum infants and preschoolers appear utterly dependent and incompetent. Yet from the earliest years of life they begin to develop interests, talents, and a sense of fairness. At the other end, eighteen-year-olds appear quite competent. Legally they are adults. They are permitted to vote, serve on juries and in the military, marry, and enter into legally binding contracts. Yet according to cognitive developmental research, few, if any, have attained stages of autonomous judgment in terms of their reasoning about justice and the good life (Armon 1984; Colby and Kohlberg 1987; Fowler 1981; and Loevinger 1976). Most are scored at the midpoint of these developmental scales.

As long as we are willing to treat those age eighteen and older equally, we must be willing to adopt a minimalistic definition of the competence necessary for moral personhood. If we look to cognitive developmental theory for guidance, there are two reasons why stage 3 might be considered a baseline for mature moral judgment. First, most eighteen-year-olds reason either at stage 3 or at the transition between stages 3 and 4. Few are found either at pure stage 2 or pure stage 4 (Colby and Kohlberg 1987). Second, the development from stage 2 to stage 3 is perhaps the single most important transition in the entire sequence of moral stages. It may be characterized as a shift from a premoral point of view in which justice is based on reciprocal exchange to the beginning of a genuine moral point of view in which justice is based on the Golden Rule. Since some children reason at stage 3 as early as age ten and most are at least in transition to stage 3 by junior high school, we would be hard put from a purely cognitive standpoint to regard high school students as ethically incompetent.

In presenting moral principles that should guide paternalistic interventions, Rawls argues that paternalism is justified only when defects of reason or will are "evident" (1971:250). Competence must be presumed until proof to the contrary can be established. Given the difficulties in clearly establishing the cognitive incompetence of adolescents, it seems plausible that they have a justifiable claim that their liberties be respected. Of course there may be other cognitive and noncognitive grounds for judging them to be incompetent; for example, they may lack the power or will to act reasonably. We will not examine those here. Suffice it to say that our experience suggests that they do not suffer from any serious defects of reason or will that render them "incapable" of rational democratic participation.

Although adolescents may not be qualitatively less competent than young adults, they have not yet reached the time in their life cycle when they are expected to make crucial choices that will define their identities. Feinberg (1980) argues that before adulthood certain paternalistic interventions may be necessary for the sake of fostering development and keeping the future open. He notes that such paternalistic interventions limit children's immediate exercise of autonomy for the sake of promoting more meaningful autonomy in their adulthood.

Our approach to democratic high schools grants that teachers have the primary responsibility to determine the curriculum of the school and that they ought to act as advocates in democratic discussions that deal with noncurricular issues. As developmentalists, we agree with Dewey (1938/1963) that educators must not simply cater to what immediately gratifies students but must provide experiences that lead beyond themselves to further growth. From a developmental view, respecting the autonomy of the young may still allow teachers in designing a curriculum to override certain of students' preferences if these are inconsistent with their long-range development. Nevertheless, if classroom education is not to be indoctrination, it must be an interactive process that enlists the cooperation of students. Teachers have a moral responsibility not only to help students to understand the rationale behind what they are teaching but also to develop their power to evaluate it critically.

While our approach to schooling allows a certain paternalism in curricular matters, it bars it elsewhere. We believe that decisions involving discipline and student life ought to be made democratically, with students and teachers having an equal vote. This process respects students as having the right, given the capabilities they already possess, to participate in certain decisions that affect them in the school. Furthermore, democracy promotes their development to greater autonomy through practice.

What are the moral grounds for virtually excluding students from all decision making if it can be shown that they have competence to make certain decisions that would not in any significant way conflict with their own interests or the rights of others? Perhaps one could argue that their long-term interests and autonomy would be *better* served in an authoritarian context. However, this would have to be demonstrated. It seems more likely that an authoritarian context militates against the development of autonomy. Piaget (1932/1965) held this in making his classic distinction between the heteronomous morality of authoritarian constraint and the autonomous morality of democratic cooperation. His point was simply that adults can subvert the process of moral education by ignoring the capacity of children for self-government. Piaget goes too far in the direction of a laissez-faire approach in suggesting that the best role the teacher could play would be as a "comrade" to the children (p. 364). We think that teachers can exercise a benign leadership role, as advocates, speaking for the ideals of the community while accepting the formal constraints of democratic procedures.

Nevertheless, Piaget's critique of authoritarian practices seems basically on target. How can students learn to be autonomous if they are not allowed to make meaningful choices about the rules and practices that govern a good portion of their daily lives? What encouragement is there for rational moral judgment if the principal governs unilaterally and is the only court of appeal? How are students to discover the intrinsic worth of virtuous conduct if discipline depends upon adult-enforced rewards and punishments? The point is that children and adolescents cannot develop as morally autonomous persons without opportunities to participate in decision making. As Piaget put it, "Since cooperation is a method, it is hard to see how it could come into being except through its own exercise" (1932/1965:98).

Of course it is a great deal to ask of teachers and principals to put aside the security of being in a position of unquestioned authority and to open themselves up to the vicissitudes of democratic decision making.

Fears of a "mobocracy" or a "tyranny of the student majority" are to be expected when patterns of authoritarian governance and student alienation are ingrained. In arguing for democracy as a way of respecting and fostering the autonomous personhood of students, we by no means share the romantic assumption that all will be well once adolescents are delivered from the bondage of adult control. The kind of high school democracy that we envision demands considerable courage, intelligence, and patience from both staff and students. Democracy means more than giving everyone a vote. It is a process of "moral communication" that involves assessing one's own interests and needs, listening to and trying to understand others, and balancing conflicting points of view in a fair and cooperative way. We continue in the next chapter with an account of how this understanding of democracy was joined with a communitarian ethic to form the just community approach on which Cluster was founded.

2

The Just Community Approach: Democracy in a Communitarian Mode

with Joseph Reimer

Our brief review in chapter 1 of the theory and practice of developmental moral education left us at the point of Kohlberg's turning to democratic education as the developmental-progressive response to the problems raised by the hidden curriculum. But the described embrace of democracy was purely theoretical, a vision of possibility rather than a concrete program for action. Yet by the opening of the Cluster School in 1974 Kohlberg had a democratic program in place. Describing how that democratic program took shape is the aim of this chapter. It is an intellectual course that involves a reconsideration of Durkheim and takes us on a visit to an Israeli kibbutz and a democratically run unit in a Connecticut prison. It may seem an odd journey, but it is the one that led to the formulation of the just community approach and the founding of the Cluster School.

BACK TO BLATT

The route from moral discussion to democratic governance, described on a theoretical plane in the last chapter, ran a practical course as well.

There is much in what Blatt and his successors achieved that set the foundations for the democratic education programs that followed, and there are practical limitations to the moral discussion programs that called for moving on to more ambitious endeavors.

Blatt's moral discussion curriculum had a more profound effect on its adolescent participants than could be summarized in the statistical table of mean gains in moral maturity scores. Hypothetical dilemmas, when well chosen and well crafted, opened up new vistas of imagined experience for students. Frank discussions of moral issues such as euthanasia, sexual and interpersonal relations, and racial discrimination challenged and stretched the minds of students and allowed them to explore with one another questions they would otherwise rarely discuss. The tone set by Blatt and the other leaders (who were often trained counselors) encouraged the exploration of feeling along with reasoning. Discussions that began on an abstract plane would often, through the students' interjection of concrete examples, become personal and emotionally moving. The resulting dynamics would be of a group, led by a trained leader, that would be eager to express personal opinion, supportive of divergent viewpoints, and willing to share and debate points of reasoning and to explore the feeling side of what it meant to be in a hypothetically described situation in which one's values and convictions were being challenged by a difficult-to-resolve conflict.

Moral discussion programs have continued to the present, long after Blatt the originator left the field. In addition, more ambitious programs have been piloted that have incorporated the principles and techniques of moral discussion into the curriculum for social studies, English literature, and psychological education. Yet, for all their ability to effect positive change in students, these programs have the limitation mentioned in chapter 1, of directing attention to the realm of the hypothetical rather than to the realm of the everyday. Their success depends on the student's capacity to operate cognitively and emotionally on the plane of the imagined. While this strategy works well most often for middle-class high school students, interventionists who have worked with working- and lower-class students or with younger students have found that their success often depended on the ability to connect with the concrete world of everyday events (Hickey 1972; Paolitto 1975). Even with middle-class students, some have wondered if the furthered expansion of the imaginative capacities has not been achieved at the cost of glossing over some more immediate problems. As Kohlberg retrospectively reports: "In 1969 . . . Blatt was conducting a program of classroom dilemma discussion in a Boston area junior high school. . . . I was a visitor to the program . . . [when] the school principal raised a familiar objection . . . 'Why is Blatt doing his science-fiction dilemma discussion when I need help with real behavior problems in the school?' " (1978:8).

The philosophic response, that programs like this would help stimulate more mature moral judgment that would in time lead to more ethically responsible behavior, would be small comfort for a junior high principal faced daily with the all-too-evident immature behavior of thirteen-year-old students. Though at the time neither Blatt nor Kohlberg had much to offer in the way of direct help, Kohlberg was already thinking of other possible approaches.

I replied to his request . . . by saying, "Helping you would mean dealing with real life dilemmas, i.e. school dilemmas. And dealing with behavior means not only asking what's fair or just, but encouraging action to make the school more just. That means trying to promote fairness in teacher and administrative behavior as well as student behavior." . . . Luckily, the principal did not call my bluff, since I had no idea how I would do what I proposed. *(Ibid.)*

The importance of developing an alternative to the hypothetical moral discussion approach became most evident after Kohlberg and Fenton had concluded a rather large-scale project training social studies teachers to lead hypothetical dilemma discussions. Research done on the effectiveness of the moral discussion classes showed significant student moral judgment development (Colby et al. 1977). Kohlberg and Fenton were elated at the prospect of further, more ambitious dissemination of the moral discussion approach. Yet a year after the project ended, when they returned to classrooms of the teachers that they had so successfully instructed, not one had continued to lead moral discussions. Kohlberg (1980) later quipped, "The operation was a research success but the research patient died." Subsequent conversations with the teachers indicated that they lacked the motivation to use an approach so disconnected with their particular curricular goals and with classroom discipline. Although Kohlberg and Fenton did not abandon the moral discussion approach but tried to make it more relevant to the formal curriculum, the need to move moral education more directly into the life and discipline of the school was apparent.

If developmental education were to aim to change student behavior as well as judgment, there would first have to be a shift in the focus of discussions from the hypothetical to the everyday. Students would be encouraged to raise problems from their daily experiences in school and learn to frame those problems in terms of their moral dimensions. They would learn that there are moral components to commonplace school conflicts that they had never thought of before in those terms. The problems would then be open to group discussion, using the method pioneered by Blatt to achieve the same results as he did. But there would be the added possibility, since the discussions dealt with real-life issues, of encouraging students to act on what they decided during the group discussion.

Paolitto (1975) applied this discussion method with some success. Yet, as Kohlberg anticipated in his response to the junior high school principal noted above, problems arose in this approach that moral discussion leaders had never before had to face: some of the protagonists to the dilemmas were real people in the school whose attitudes and behaviors affected directly the outcomes of the dilemma discussions. For example, if the students agreed among themselves in the discussion that a given school policy was unfair and ought to be changed, the principal's reaction to their objectives would matter greatly. If he treated the discussion as simply a class exercise and was not in a serious way willing to enter the discussion, there would be little point in continuing to have the discussion. It would only lead to aggravating the split in the school between the "explicit" and the "hidden" curriculum and to making the students less, rather than more, trusting of the school administration. Therefore, in responding to the junior high principal, Kohlberg warned that without the teachers and administrators joining in as participants in the moral discussion and being willing to change their behavior along with the behavior of the students, there would be little chance of any such program significantly affecting student behavior or making the school a more just institution.

The move, then, from what Blatt and his successors accomplished to what Kohlberg envisioned as the aim of a full-fledged developmental moral education program would involve far more than a shift in the focus of discussions. It would have to involve a redefinition of the role of authority in the school and of the relation between students and teachers. As those are among the hardest elements of the school culture to change (Sarason 1971), Kohlberg was indeed lucky that the principal did not call his bluff in 1969. But Kohlberg was to go that summer on a trip to an Israeli kibbutz, which would initiate the evolution of a workable model for involving school authorities in a program that could affect both student moral judgment and moral action.

A TALE OF TWO CULTURES

Before going on to the kibbutz let us recall James Coleman's (1961) landmark study on the adolescent society of American high schools. Coleman leaves little doubt that the springs of behavior are not primarily in the hands of teachers or school administrators, but in the hands of the dominating peer groups that set up particular social climates in these schools. A social climate is oriented in distinct value directions, and Coleman's statistical charts convince us that most students (whom we would assume operate at the second and third stages of moral judgment) act in ways quite consistent with those value directions.

Bronfenbrenner (1967) makes a similar point in comparing children in the Soviet Union with those in America and England. He notes that Soviet children identify more strongly with adult standards of behavior than do American or English children. Furthermore, the Soviet children find peer support for adult-approved behavior, while American and English children experience peer pressure that conflicts with the adult norms. For example, in a comparative study with twelve thirteen-year-olds he found that American and English children were likely "to go along with the gang" and cheat, neglect a sick friend, and break parental rules, while their Soviet counterparts were likely "to go along with the gang" and do the opposite.

Bronfenbrenner attributed this difference to an explicit concern in the Soviet Union for utilizing the peer group as a socializing agent and suggests that educators in America can learn from them: "In the light of increasing evidence for the influence of the peer group on the behavior and psychological development of children and adolescents, it is questionable whether any society, whatever its social system, can afford to leave largely to chance the direction of the influence, and realization of its high potential for fostering constructive development for the child and his society" (1967:206).

The task, then, of affecting the rational behavioral choices of high school students involves giving shape to the social climate created by their peer groups. The problem, as Coleman points out, is that in most American high schools peer expectations run along lines that are determined not by mature moral considerations, but by the trends of commercial advertisements. Being popular and getting ahead have to do more with the car one drives, the persons one dates, and the athletics in which one excels than in one's cognitive or moral achievements.

Gaining control of that part of the hidden curricula (the "crowds") and turning it around to work for the ends of "justice" or "intellectual excellence" seems a very tall order, Coleman's and Bronfenbrenner's practical suggestions notwithstanding. Yet on a smaller scale—that of a small alternative school—it may be a more feasible project.

Kohlberg's dream—which went well beyond Blatt's program and which he began to reveal to the junior high school principal—was to be able to create a school climate or atmosphere which would encourage adolescent peer groups, at their own operative stage levels, to choose to live by the ideals of fairness or justice. This would have to involve creating a new relationship between adults and adolescents by which the adults could create expectations for behavior that the adolescents could as a group rationally and affectively endorse. This dream began taking shape with his visit to the kibbutz.

THE KIBBUTZ VISIT

As a kibbutz—or an Israeli collective settlement—runs by a set of operating principles quite different from those of a capitalist society, it may be a logical place to begin in a search for an alternative way of educating youth to becoming responsible members of their society. This is especially so since the kibbutz is a self-consciously moral society that has created a collective system of education that deliberately uses the hidden curriculum to advocate for collective rather than individual achievement, equal rather than stratified social relations, and democratic rather than hierarchical decision making.

During the summer of 1969, at the invitation of the Youth Aliyah Organization, Kohlberg spent time observing and interviewing at one (left-wing) kibbutz that had attracted his attention. This kibbutz was unusual in having established a high school program that had as its main objective bringing lower-class adolescents from the cities of Israel to the kibbutz and educating them—alongside a smaller number of kibbutz-born adolescents—to become future members of the kibbutz. With an Israeli colleague, Miriam Bar Yam, Kohlberg conducted a cross-sectional study of these adolescents' levels of moral reasoning to test how effective the kibbutz program was in promoting their moral development. The results (Kohlberg 1971a) were very positive, with the kibbutz-placed youth showing significantly higher scores than a comparable sample of Israeli urban youth.

Even before the results of the study were tabulated, Kohlberg was drawn to what he observed on this kibbutz and learned from interviewing the *Madrich,* or educator, who was in charge of the high school program. Having read descriptions of Russian collective education, Kohlberg seemed surprised to discover how different from that was kibbutz education.

The youth sector of the kibbutz looks to the tourist much more like A. S. Neill's Summerhill hippie commune than like the Russian school just described. The young people know the *Madrich* only by the first name, they have never called him anything else. In the group each student is relaxedly working on his own. The *Madrich* is a consultant, not an authority, and orders are seldom given, speeches or lectures seldom made, voices seldom raised. On closer view, however, one sees that the youth life in a kibbutz is about as much like a Summerhill hippie commune as is youth life in the Israeli army. The informality, the flexibility, the democracy of youth life in the kibbutz is a function of the Israeli talent for dispensing with frills and rules and harshness, not of a permissive individualistic educational ideology.

Underneath the informality of the *Madrich* there is a considerable amount of iron, and this iron is based on the theory of collective education. By the theory of collective education I do not mean indoctrination into a collectivist ideology. In spite of all talk of ideology, the tourist sees little real striving for ideological purity and ideological indoctrination in the kibbutz. . . . With regard to ideology, the *Madrich* tells us, "I demand high values. What I mean by high values are certain social values. I am not talking about the kibbutz, socialism or some other generality. I am talking about living within a society." The iron kibbutz education, then, is not kibbutz ideology, but the iron of the welfare of the peer group and of the kibbutz in which it is embedded. (1971a:358)

Here was an educational system that, though informal and democratic in its style of operation, was not a Summerhillian free school with a romantic view of school life, but a collectivist enterprise demanding "high values" of its "disadvantaged" youth. The values demanded were the values of the kibbutz, but they were not taught in the abstract. Rather, the youth were to learn them by seeing them in practice in the (adult) kibbutz society and by putting them into practice in their own "youth society."

"Living within a society" is the hallmark of kibbutz living and education. As a collective society, the kibbutz keeps the eyes of its members directed toward the society as a whole, discouraging focus on the self as the center of the universe. On a kibbutz one learns that the questions of everyday living ("Where shall I work," "What shall I eat," "Where shall I live," "How much shall I earn") are not answered primarily by reference to the desires of the self, but by reference to the needs and demands of the society. One works where one is needed, lives where accommodations are available, eats what is served to everyone, and earns the same as everyone else. Not that the desires of the self are ignored; they simply weigh in second to the needs of the collective.

To be educated on a kibbutz means learning that one lives in a society and by its norms. These norms are clear and their public violation brings disapproval not only from adults, but also from peers. If everyone is supposed to have a roughly equal amount of clothing (supplied by the kibbutz), a boy who receives several new and fashionable shirts from an aunt in the city is going to hear about the newly created inequality from his peers. If everyone is supposed to work for two hours in the afternoon on the kibbutz (on the farm or in a service branch) and someone is regularly playing her guitar during that time, she will soon enough hear about it from her friends. For in a collective living situation, everyone has a stake in everyone else's living by the same norms of conduct.

In addition, the *Madrich* enforces certain rules which, though perhaps at variance with the norms of youth culture, the kibbutz requires of its youth.

Our *Madrich* tells us that he sometimes rigidly enforces arbitrary rules because it is necessary for the maintenance of the solidarity of the group. The *Hashomer* code prohibits smoking, drinking, and social dancing for the youth. This is not because such actions are believed to be sins according to a Puritan ethic. As our *Madrich* explains these rules: "I myself can't believe smoking or social dancing are crimes. All over the world children dance and here not. Originally it was part of the youth code, like the scouts. . . . but now it is something else. The 'no dancing' may be the only way to keep one within the society, here, to keep the youth society together. Because if a boy wants to be with a girl on more than friendship terms and have sexual intercourse or at least a real sexual life, they withdraw from the group; it destroys the social life of the group. In my own response to the sexual life in the group, I may close my eyes to it; it depends upon which couple and upon the total picture of the group life."

Our *Madrich*, then, is willing to enforce rules about smoking or social dancing or sexual restriction, but not for their own sake, not as rigid matters of morality, discipline, or ideology. They are to be enforced only if their violation threatens the solidarity of the group or its willingness to be guided by the *Madrich*. (1971a:359)

However we as outsiders evaluate this kibbutz code of adolescent conduct—and by today's kibbutz standards it is quite outdated (Reimer 1977)—the interest for Kohlberg here is not the particular content of the code, but the spirit with which it is enforced. From the developmental perspective discussed in the last section, having a clear and enforceable set of rules is a helpful, if not necessary, component of morally educating adolescents operating at a stage 2 or stage 3 level. If they are to learn to act consistently on their judgment, they need to know there are specifiable expectations that are being enforced by a caring and reliable authority. But the kibbutz is not interested in their adolescents' observing these rules to please the adult authority. Rather the youth are being asked to make sacrifices of personal pleasure (not smoking, dancing, or having sex) to keep their group strong and cohesive.

Few educators on left-wing kibbutzim would even pretend to believe that smoking or having sex is in itself wrong. It is, rather, inappropriate for this age group. The demands of collective cohesion are greater during high school than they will be later when one has his or her own room to live in and own social life to lead. This educational process requires an extra dosage of collective discipline during adolescence so one will learn to feel from within the demands of the collective. The rules are an expression of those demands and derive their meaning from what they contribute to a sense of group discipline and cohesion.

Our *Madrich* tells us in the most honest way that kibbutz education depends upon the solidarity of the group: "Our methods of education depend upon the group. For 24 hours the adolescent lives with other members of the group. He has to be affected by the group if we are to succeed. Examples: For instance, do you know about the system of studying here? The system is no examinations, no punishment. Note also that we don't punish, because in itself punishment by the adult has no meaning, it is nothing. The most we can do is to throw a ward out, and that only really happens when he wishes to be thrown out, when he doesn't want to belong to the group anymore, when he doesn't fit in. So we have no real punishment if the child doesn't study or learn. We can come to a person and tell him, 'go and study, go and learn.' He says, maybe not in these words, but he can say to me, 'if I don't study, what are you going to do to me?' And I say, 'nothing, what can I do to you?' So I have to use the group. I can go to the group and say, 'look, this one, and one or two others, they don't study, they don't participate in class, they are slowing down the progression of the whole group in learning; and he can say to me I don't care,' but the group can put the pressure on him. If he cares for the group and has a good relationship with the others, he might change his ways. This works in some groups, it doesn't work in others; it depends on the group; if the group is strong and has solidarity, it works; if the group is not, it doesn't work." (1971a: p. 360)

The value of group solidarity is that it allows the peer group to function as a moral authority for its members. There are rules and norms which the *Madrich* knows he cannot himself enforce. Unlike in most American or Israeli schools, kibbutz schools do not put much weight on grades. There are few tests in classes and not much pressure from parents or teachers to excel in a purely academic sense. Yet there is a need, as in any nonindividualized study situation, for the students to keep up with the work so the class can progress together in its discussion of the material. When individuals do not keep up, the *Madrich* describes how he turns the issue over to the group to inquire if they care that their progress is being impeded by some members not studying. If they do care, and if they have among themselves a coherent set of expectations, they can effectively put pressure on the reluctant students and get them back on track (which often requires helping them to catch up on lost work). But without sufficient normative cohesion, the group will be divided and unable to deal effectively with the problem.

For the peer group to work as a normative force, the *Madrich* has a crucial role to play. It is he who has to find a balance between making clear the demand for high values and allowing those values to take shape as the norms of the group. Similarly, he has to know when to give the group room to work out its own solution and when to more actively intervene to support a faltering group. He also has to make it clear that in acting as educator, he is not acting on his own behalf alone or expressing only his values, but representing the kibbutz society to the youth. In all this, he has to be in control of his own self, limiting it sufficiently to give room to the expression of others and yet being sufficiently present as a person so the youth can identify with him personally as the kind of person and kibbutz member they would like to become.

Were the kibbutz educational system aimed solely at getting these youth to become good members of their groups and eventually of the kibbutz, it would—like the Durkheimian model it resembles—be seen by Kohlberg as a successful but limiting means of socializing adolescents into a particular way of life and system of values. What saves it from being this and what accounts for its ability to promote moral development beyond stage 3 are the quality of its educators and its commitment to democracy and the rights of the individual.

As a human being, what the *Madrich* values is not a "mere conformist," not even "a good member of the kibbutz," but an autonomous or a morally-principled person like himself. While in one sense he espouses the same moral education ends as the author of the Russian moral education textbook, he sounds very different about these ends. The Russian textbook is written from an unabashed Stage 4 Law and Order moral perspective. What the *Madrich* calls "mere conformism" the Russian glories in as "scrupulous discipline," "acceptance of the authority of the teacher, her word is law," "doing the best work" (as the teacher defines it), etc. Our *Madrich* rejects such a Stage 4 concept of morality and moral education, though he partly accepts the necessity of acting in a Stage 4 Law and Order way toward the wards as part of the method of collective education. Even his acceptance of collective education theory, or ideology, is limited, however.
He says, "I don't have any ideology behind me, I pick things because I feel for it. I don't believe I have the right to demand. . . . I have to work in a more democratic way." (1971a:361–62)

Though Kohlberg can only report on the one *Madrich* he interviewed, his observation has validity more generally for the kibbutz movement (Reimer 1977). The kibbutz exists in a tension between its commitment to the universal values of justice, equality, and brotherhood and a felt reality that calls for tight, collective (and national) discipline. This tension affects many aspects of kibbutz life, including education. While it is a hard tension to resolve, there is a dual commitment to do what is necessary to preserve the collective discipline (the stage 4 perspective), but yet do so in a way that remains democratic and respectful of individual difference. The voice of individual and subgroup dissent is never silenced on a kibbutz, and, as never could be true in a really conformist society, demonstrations for more individual rights are continually part of the public discourse. Since that voice is genuinely respected, it is incorporated as well into the educational system. Individual students are encouraged to write, to dance, and to make music according to their own tastes, as they are equally encouraged to work hard on common projects. They are told to call their educators by their first names, to visit them at home, argue with and vote against them at group meetings, while they are also told to respect the rules they insist upon. Autonomy and collectivity coexist in this tension, and that makes the kibbutz, as Kohlberg noted, an exciting place in which to grow up.

Lessons from the Kibbutz

Kohlberg concludes the article on kibbutz education with the following observation: "Right now, Youth Aliyah Kibbutz youth group practice seems *better than anything we conceive from our theory*, and it is not revisions in practice, but revisions of the way of thinking about it that I am suggesting" (1971a:370; emphasis added).

This formulation is striking, for it means that Kohlberg's kibbutz visit led him to realize that he would *not* be able to derive the model for moral education that he sought entirely from his own developmental theory. Rather, he would have to "combine the principles of moral discussion with some of the psychological principles of collective education" (1971a:369). Particularly, he would need to derive from the principles of collective education a *model of group practice* that could serve to affect student action along with moral judgment and involve educators in a new relationship with their adolescent students.

Kohlberg did not at the time specify the model that he derived from the kibbutz educational system; however, as he moved toward the just community approach, he slowly put together the following model of group practice that helped transform his conception of developmental moral education and give shape to his ideas about educational democracy.

A Model of Group Practice

1. Though from its inception developmental moral education had utilized a group context for the discussion of moral dilemmas, the initial model did not view the group as having a normative role in itself. Group participants developed no normative expectations of one another other than participating in the discussion. The participants were simply fellow classmates for an hour or two a week.

In contrast, the kibbutz model places group membership and group consciousness at the forefront of the educational experience. A student's social place, and therefore social identity, is defined by the group to which he belongs and by the quality of his membership in that group. There are clear normative expectations that arise from living with others in a group, and each member knows both what is expected of him and what he may expect of others in terms of appropriate group behavior.

2. In the kibbutz model, the group exercises discipline in relation to its members. The members realize their common lives depend on common understandings being upheld; and they therefore all have a real stake in how the others act. If a member fails to respect the common understanding, disapproval will be expressed by other members, first informally, and then, if necessary, by the group as a whole. Individuals are expected to respond to the expression of disapproval both by acknowledging, when appropriate, their lapse in behavior and by changing their behavior.

3. Being a member of kibbutz group involves not only respect for its normative expectations, but also a growing emotional attachment to the group, as the anchor of one's social identity. A member develops a real sense of care for and pride in the achievements and reputation of one's group. One wants to be known by others as a member of his or her group, and one becomes tied into the group's successes and failures. When the group in any of its activities does well, individual members feel personally enlarged, and when the group fails, one feels a corresponding sense of personal letdown. Members also grow emotionally attached to fellow members not only because they may have become one's friends, but also (even when they are not one's friends) because they share with one a common social identity. Meeting a fellow member outside the context of the group reminds one that "she is one of us."

4. Members are encouraged to develop a sense of common fate so that they come to perceive that what happens to one happens to all, and what happens to all happens to each one. Whether members are on a sports team together or are working on a group project or are being compared with some other class in school, they learn that the error of one member reflects on the whole, and therefore becomes the responsibility of the whole. A sense of collective responsibility develops, with members realizing that each is in a sense responsible for the actions of the others. One is therefore motivated to help the others to become

better members of the group and to share some of the negative consequences of the actions of others.

5. The discussion of values and value conflicts plays an important part in this model of group life, but not only as a means to the end of promoting individual development but also as a way of deciding how the group will function as a social unit. Individual members are encouraged if they find themselves in conflict with other members to bring the conflict to the group. The group will discuss the conflict in terms of the rights of the individuals and the norms of the group; but the discussions will be oriented to problem solving and not just the clarification of abstract issues. Members will work for fair decisions, for everyone realizes the precedent set may have implications for resolving future conflicts to which one may be a party. Members want there to be a fair and consistent standard for dealing with intragroup conflicts so each can be assured that if any other member violates his rights, he will have a fair hearing in the group.

6. As the nature of group experience prescribed by this model changes, so does the role of the educator as a group leader. Though the kibbutz model of the educator's role includes the leading of values discussions, there is a different sense in which the educator relates to the group. His concern is not only with the process of the discussion, but also with its outcome. As the group makes decisions about its members, the educator has a stake in whether the decisions are substantially fair to the members involved, consistent with the basic values of the larger society, and representative of a logical progression in the group's history of decision making. He is not only a facilitator, but also a representative of and an advocate for certain value positions that he sees as crucial to the group's development as a cohesive and morally concerned social body. Yet he has to take care that the youth see him as neither a self-interested party nor as the final word, but rather as a fair broker who can keep the interests of the whole in mind when the group is itself split by conflicting subgroup interests.

Kohlberg does not claim that this model of group practice is unique to the kibbutz, but that the kibbutz school has used it to particular advantage in morally educating their adolescents. That advantage shows up both in gains in the stage of the adolescents' moral judgment (referring especially to the working-class youth brought into the kibbutz from the city) and in their successful adaptation to the morally rigorous expectations of kibbutz society.

Yet problems do arise in trying to apply a kibbutz model to an American educational setting. Primary among these is the cultural divide between the kibbutz and American societies. A group-oriented moral education would seem to fit a socialist-collectivist society more than a capitalist-individualistic society such as our own. And it is even a bit simplistic to speak of this model representing contemporary kibbutz society. That society is itself moving away from its collectivist assumptions as its members are demanding more space for the development of personal interests. Second, a kibbutz is a multigenerational community in which the practices taught in school are modeled by adults in the community, while American high schools stand off as islands within teenage culture. Third, left-wing kibbutz high schools are boarding schools that can work their influence twenty-four hours a day, while American high schools occupy a far less central place in the adolescent's life and are forced to compete with other social institutions for influence over the students' minds and hearts.

For all these reasons Kohlberg could not make a wholesale adaptation of the kibbutz model, but had to learn from it what he could in constructing an approach that would fit the social realities of American schools. This he did by returning to Durkheim's work and trying to integrate it—in light of the kibbutz experience—more fully with the cognitive-developmental perspective.

RECONSIDERING DURKHEIM

To the reader familiar with Durkheim's (1925/1973) *Moral Education*, much of what Kohlberg presents as a model of kibbutz practice closely resembles Durkheim's model. In particular, there are these emphases in the kibbutz model that appear as if they could have been derived (though they were not) directly from Durkheim:

1. the primacy of the collective over the individual;
2. the stress on group discipline through respect for rules;
3. developing an attachment to the group as a social body greater than the self;

4. cultivating a sense of collective responsibility in the group for the actions of each member of the group;
5. the educator's representing the larger society to the group.

Given these similarities in conception, we are faced with a paradoxical situation: Kohlberg is attracted to a social-psychological model which has rich implications for moral education, but which he had earlier rejected on the grounds that "it leads to a definition of moral education as the promotion of collective national discipline which is consistent with neither rational ethics nor the American constitutional tradition" (Kohlberg 1971e:28). Has Kohlberg modified his initial conceptions, or has he found a way of incorporating Durkheim via the kibbutz into his initial position? Actually he has done both: modified some of his initial conceptions, but also democratized the Durkheim model so it would more easily complement his conceptions of how moral education ought to proceed.

What continually appeals to Kohlberg in the Durkheim model is the power of the collective that it evokes. As we commented in chapter 1, although Kohlberg authored a theory of individual moral development, he believes that "the unit of effectiveness of education is not the individual, but the group" (Kohlberg 1971e:82); and the theory of group life that is most convincing to him is that shared by Durkheim and the kibbutz. They, more than most other theorists, view the group—particularly the peer group in the school—as having a distinctive social reality and moral force. They, more than the progressives, stress the need for the educator to employ the social reality and moral force of the peer group to create a morally educative social climate in the class and the school. And they resist the seemingly pervasive tendency in American culture to focus on the individual as the measure of all value. For while Kohlberg's theory of moral development places respect for the rights of the individual at the pinnacle of moral concern, the theory is not—as some might think—a celebration of individuality per se, but one of the development of moral reasoning and action that is philosophically *autonomous.* Autonomy of judgment, as we noted in the last chapter, does not free the individual from his or her ties to society, but redefines those ties and places them on a more equilibrated plane.

To the frequently made objection that Durkheim devalues the individual psychologically, Kohlberg (1985) appeals to a tradition of "organic social theorists" from Rousseau to Dewey. This tradition elaborates an ideal of community that is compatible with our most developed sense of equality, autonomy, and personhood. For example, Dewey maintains that a concern for self and a concern for others are not mutually exclusive, but can and should be integrated into a larger concern for the community in which self and other are parts:

> Our discussion points to the conclusion that neither egoism nor altruism nor any combination of the two is a satisfactory principle. Selfhood is not something which exists apart from association and intercourse. The interests that are formed in the social environment are far more important than are the adjustments of isolated selves. We must realize the fact that regard for self and regard for others are both secondary phases of a more normal and complete interest, regard for the welfare and integrity of the social groups of which we form a part. (Dewey 1960:163–64)

For Dewey a vital community is not a threat to individuality but the only context in which the self can develop. Thus in his classic *Democracy and Education* he stresses the importance of democratic schooling for the development of a character with a strong sense of social responsibility.

While Kohlberg acknowledges Dewey's basic insight into the interdependence of self and other in community, he finds that Josiah Royce (1908/1982) provides a far more detailed and compelling psychological account of the process in which this occurs, particularly during adolescence. According to Royce, moral authority is originally experienced as something external to our wills, but as we reach adolescence and adulthood we seek moral autonomy. Royce sees a genuine paradox here, since our wills, which have previously been formed through the influence of others, are incapable of self-direction. In Royce's words, when we look within for guidance we find our hearts to be "a wayward and a blind guide" (p. 279). Nevertheless, we discover that conforming to the expectations of our social world and its authorities does not satisfy our desire to express our unique and free selves and will. Royce sees the conflict between self-will and social will as capable of being overcome in the "special passions" that express an exalted sense of self in loyal commitment to a cause shared by others.

Royce postulates that the cause to which one is loyal is not another person but a suprapersonal reality, which unites persons and members of the community with common ends. He warns that finding causes worthy of one's loyalty and giving of one's self to those causes is a difficult and perilous task.

Erikson describes a similar position in articulating his well-known theory of identity crisis:

The young person in order to experience wholeness, must feel a progressive continuity between that which he has come to be during the long years of childhood and that which he promises to become in the anticipated future; between that which he conceives himself to be and that which he perceives others to see in him and to expect of him. . . . Identity is a unique product, which now meets a crisis to be solved only in new identifications with age mates and with leader figures outside of the family. (1968:90, 91)

For Erikson loyalty or fidelity is *the* virtue of adolescence. It is the capacity for commitment, made in the breach between the experienced values of the self and the world: "Fidelity is the ability to sustain loyalties fully pledged in spite of the inevitable contradictions of value systems" (1968:125).

While Erikson places great emphasis on adolescents' struggle to find a suitable occupational role, as crucial to the resolution of their identity crisis, he is acutely aware of their more basic problem of "fitting into" social institutions that allow them to be true to themselves and to their ideals. Kohlberg thinks that the school is one institution to which adolescents could be loyal if the school community were capable of meeting simultaneously their growing demands for autonomy and self-expression and their need to be recognized, affirmed, and supported by their peers and elders.

Durkheim's theory of moral education provides the best elaborated approach for building such a school community, although a democratic element must be supplied. Kohlberg readily appropriated Durkheim because he felt confident he could integrate Durkheim's powerful sociological insights into a still larger theory of democratic communitarian education. Durkheim's social psychology offers Kohlberg a vehicle for redressing an imbalance that arises from his focusing on individual moral development. Yes, Kohlberg is saying that individuals do construct their own modes of moral judgment that are not simply reflections or internalizations of societal values or institutional arrangements. Yes, most programs for moral education (including Durkheim's) can be faulted for neither sufficiently respecting the autonomy of the individual's development nor actively promoting that development. But these observations do not imply that the best means of moral education is to concentrate solely on promoting their individual moral judgment or their sense of individuality apart from their ties to society. Rather adolescents need to be intimately involved in the inner workings of social institutions so they can learn from within how they work and why their roles and norms are usually deserving of respect. But these institutions—and particularly the urban American high school—do not often invite such participation and thereby contribute little, from a communal or a developmental perspective, to the moral development of their students.

The just community approach begins with the question of how American educational institutions can be restructured to allow—and even invite—the participation of its students so they can learn how to balance their self-interest with the interests of society and its institutions. Durkheim provides this approach with a social psychology that emphasizes that developing individuals become moral agents as they learn to take the perspective of the generalized other, to respect its rules and become emotionally attached to the achievement of its goals. The kibbutz contributes a model of both how to operationalize (in another cultural setting) a Durkheimian community that promotes adolescent moral development and how to democratize its authority structure.

THE PRISON PROJECT

When after returning from his kibbutz visit Kohlberg began looking for a setting in which to try out his new ideas about moral education, he found his first opportunity not in a school but in a correctional system. Shaken by the uprisings of the late 1960s, such as occurred at the Attica prison, correctional officers were open to new approaches to prison reform. Joined by two colleagues, Joseph Hickey and Peter Scharf, who were interested in prison work, Kohlberg received a two-year grant to study the applicability of moral development theory to the reform of prison inmates.

Their first efforts consisted of leading the types of moral discussions that Blatt had pioneered. They soon discovered in practice what Kohlberg was formulating in his writings: even if one could positively influence the ways inmates thought about moral issues, there was little way the inmates could translate that learning into practice as long as they remained in prison. The prison environment particularly shut out that possibility, making attempts by inmates to act on higher-level moral reasoning at best counterproductive and at worst self-destructive. Clearly in prison life moral education would have to involve working with the institution and changing its moral atmosphere if there were to be any hope of morally educating the inmates.

Addressing the development of the individual through changing the environment in which he lived fit well with what Kohlberg had learned from his kibbutz visit, and he, Hickey, and Scharf aimed "to create a prison community that might have the cohesiveness and moral charisma associated with a stage 4 community, but would operate according to stage 5 principles of an open social contract and a persistent concern with due process and fairness" (Kohlberg, Hickey, and Scharf 1972:62). That is, they would look for a prison setting in which they could set up a kibbutz-like community of inmates and staff, with an emphasis on group cohesion and group-enforced norms, but do so in an American way by equally emphasizing a constitutional process of law making within the community.

Negotiations with correction officials of the State of Connecticut led the three to the Niantic State Farm, a correctional facility for women. The Niantic Farm seemed a suitable site for their planned intervention. The farm was broken into small cottage units of twenty to thirty women and, as a minimum security facility, allowed the possibility of a cottage being granted a wide degree of autonomy to establish its own rules. In 1971 they secured permission for a model just community cottage.

Lessons from Prison

The story of the Niantic prison project goes well beyond the scope of this chapter and is told in fuller detail by Hickey and Scharf (1980). Our purpose here is to note how the prison project laid the groundwork for future just community programs.

1. Before Niantic the just community approach consisted of a set of ideas in Kohlberg's mind. At Niantic these ideas gave rise to institutions and observable operations that were both manageable and exportable. If prison inmates and guards could maintain a just community, there was hope for teachers and students as well. By starting with an inmate population, the intervention at Niantic made it seem more plausible that

the just community approach could work as a form of compensatory education within urban schools. The high percentage of minority women from inner-city areas at Niantic reinforced the sense that that population of youth also could benefit from this approach.

2. The Niantic experience established that this approach could work for the benefit of inmates and staff. Though not systematically tested until several years later, there was a commonly shared sense among most participants in Niantic that 1) this was a reasonably efficient and far more pleasant way to run a prison cottage, 2) the inmates and staff were learning skills of social discussion, decision making, counseling, and moral reasoning, and 3) inmates felt better prepared to return to "the real world" as productive citizens.

3. Developmental moral education—as embodied by the discussion of moral dilemmas and the enhanced opportunity for role taking and social participation—was at Niantic successfully combined with a communitarian emphasis on respect for rules and attachment to the group. Inmates and staff not only participated in the discussions about making rules, but also were willing to enforce those rules for the sake of preserving the integrity of the community. On a group level, a consistent "moral atmosphere" was created which usually promoted a translation of moral judgment into action.

Niantic gave Kohlberg the encouragement to move ahead with the just community approach and try it out in American schools. But it was becoming evident—though not yet articulated—that this direction in the practice of moral education would lead to revisions in Kohlberg's theory of education. Before describing the next steps in the practice of moral education, let us look at the specific revisions in theory this approach entails.

INTEGRATING THE JUST COMMUNITY APPROACH WITHIN THE DEVELOPMENTAL PARADIGM

The just community approach represents Kohlberg's effort to balance "justice" and "community"; to introduce the powerful appeal of the collective while both protecting the rights of individual students and promoting their moral growth. To maintain this balance, however, entails a reconsideration of some of the fundamental issues in moral education that Kohlberg had earlier discussed (see chapter 1). In particular, *these* five issues need to be reexamined:

1. the role of conventional vs. principled moral judgment;
2. the form vs. content distinction;
3. the cognitive and affective dimensions of moral education;
4. the relationship of judgment to action;
5. indoctrinative vs. nonindoctrinative approaches to moral education.

Conventional vs. Principled Moral Judgment

Of the three levels of moral judgment presented in Kohlberg's theory of moral development, the first and third levels have attracted more attention than has the middle, conventional level. It is in dealing with the first, preconventional level that readers are introduced to the moral worldviews of young children. As these are at times distinctly different from those of most adults, they have major significance for understanding child development (Damon 1977). Similarly, the third, postconventional level has drawn attention because of its challenging assumption that there are stages of principled morality which only a few people reach but which are judged to be more adequate than the modes of judgment generally employed in our society. But those middle conventional stages simply do not attract much attention. They are there; we know because we see and hear them every day. But what is interesting about the familiar, the conventional?

Kohlberg (1980) has increasingly come to value the significance of the conventional stages not only because his data show that the stage 5 adolescent is a rare find, but also because his experience with American adolescents indicates that with the weakening of the stability and moral authority of conventional institutions, the power of even conventional morality is waning. While in the 1960s Kohlberg could take for granted the claims of conventional morality and argue for the merits of a principled morality, after Vietnam and Watergate that commonly held belief in social conventions could no longer be taken for granted. The just community approach was fashioned in the 1970s to initiate adolescents into creating a conventional moral system which they could believe in because it embodied on a conventional level the values of fairness, equality, and community.

R. S. Peters (1973), the British philosopher, is helpful in trying to understand the implications of this shift in emphasis. He has long maintained that the significance of the conventional stages for moral education has been underestimated, especially by progressive educators, and that there is no contradiction between having as an immediate goal the initiating of students into conventional morality while maintaining as a more ultimate goal the students' eventual attainment of principled moral reasoning. For if the later stages are thought of as developing as a result of the individual's gradual realization of the limits of conventional reasoning and the need to devise a prior-to-society perspective on moral issues, it makes good sense to want to introduce students at an earlier age to the inner workings of conventional institutions so that they can eventually work through that developmental sequence on their own. As Piaget warns educators not to rush children through concrete cognitive operations, for a firm grounding in that logic sets the stage for a balanced development toward formal operations, so Peters warns that to rush students toward moral autonomy before they "understand from the inside the inviolability of rules" (p. 46) is to risk building autonomy on an unstable developmental foundation.

Peters' line of argument can be joined with the Durkheimian notion that learning respect for rules is one of the two basic elements of moral education. Kohlberg learned from his kibbutz visit that respect for rules need not be viewed as an allegiance to an arbitrary set of rules handed down from an authority on high, but can be seen as respect for the agreements that a group of students make among themselves and with their educators. Thus, as we will see, the developmental goal of generating rules can be integrated with the Durkheiman ideal of learning respect for the rules.

The Form vs. Content Distinction

To speak seriously of educating for the conventional levels of morality leads to reconsidering the delineation between the form and the content of morality that Kohlberg had emphasized in his earlier writings. Kohlberg had maintained that developmental education focuses on the form or structure rather on the content of morality; that "the experiences by which children naturally move from stage to stage are . . . not experiences of being taught and internalizing content . . . [but] those involving moral conflict (in the cognitive-conflict sense) and exposure to other, higher modes of thinking than one's own" (1971e:72). While this emphasis on the form or structure of moral reasoning will always remain a hallmark of developmental moral education, it no longer seems necessary or advisable to embrace that emphasis at the cost of dismissing any teaching of moral content. For, as Peters (1973, 1981) has argued interpreting Kohlberg's work, there is no way of initiating youth into conventional morality without introducing specific rules, norms, or values that they may adopt as the content of their moral code.

In a sense this balancing of emphasis becomes inevitable once developmental moral education moves beyond the discussion of moral dilemmas. In such discussions teachers can more singularly focus on students' forms of reasoning, for the content—the specific values espoused—is not immediately relevant to the outcome of the discussion. But once dealing with the real life of classrooms and schools, teachers can no longer afford that distance from moral content; for *what* is decided is important as well as *why* it is decided upon. Peters has wryly commented that "if I was robbed in the street, my interest in whether the thief is at stage 1, 2 or 3 in the way he views the operation is a trifle academic" (1973:152). Similarly, if students decide—even democratically—that they can leave class whenever they feel bored, the teacher is not as likely to focus on the reasoning behind their decision as on how to impress upon them the virtues of patience and consideration for others.

Cognitive and Affective Dimensions

To stress the structure of morality is to place a premium on the cognitive bases of moral reasoning. To balance the stress between structure and content is to raise anew the question of the affective bases of moral motivation.

As a Piagetian, Kohlberg has long assumed the inseparability and the parallel development of cognition and affect (Kohlberg 1969). Moral dilemmas "work" to promote moral development because they arouse in people not only cognitive conflict but also affective disequilibrium. When a person is faced with a moral conflict that she cannot easily resolve but that she cares about deeply, she is likely to be strongly motivated to think through new possible solutions to the conflict. The affective dimensions of the crisis may prove growth producing when they do "motivate" the construction of new modes of moral judgment (Gilligan and Belenky 1980).

There is, however, a second issue of motivation which is less directly addressed by developmental theory: the motivation to act on one's moral judgment. In schools it is clearly not sufficient, as we have discussed earlier, to have as an educational goal the elaboration of new modes of judgment. Also needed is the goal of having students try to act on higher-stage judgment. But, as the Blatt study showed, that is where the developmental paradigm is at its weakest and where it needs bolstering from a more communally oriented approach.

Kohlberg (1980) at this point introduces the power of the collective—the moral authority of the group—to provide a support system for adolescents to act on their higher-stage modes of reasoning. If students who operate at a stage 2 or stage 3 level lack the consistent internal motivation to act on what they judge to be right, then the group or community can provide the external motivation for such action. That motivation comes in the form of what Durkheim calls "attachment to the group"—an affective bond between the individual and his peers which leads the individual to want to live up to the normative expectations of the group.

An illustration of this motivation at work may make this point clear. In his research on kibbutz adolescents, Reimer interviewed a kibbutz-born adolescent who explained why he would not (in his group) make a sexual pass at an unsuspecting girl. "Let's say that some of us were going on an overnight hike and I wanted to neck with one of the girls. I could not do that because afterwards I could not live with my friends. Maybe in another group, but here I'd be violating the norms or angering my friends or both. In their opinion it is immoral to do that to a girl if she isn't interested or willing. It would be awful" (1977:328).

As he tells it, this adolescent does not seem sure of how, were he on his own, he would handle his sexual desire. But in the context of the group, he knows there is no way he would act on impulse. Belonging to the group, being accepted as one who lives by group standards, is too important to risk even when impulse is hot. The group's norms and his emotional attachment to the group function to keep his action in line with the group's commonly shared moral judgment that "it is immoral to do that to a girl." In Kohlberg's current view it is the extra support provided by attachment to the group that adolescents need at the conventional stages to learn how to act consistently on their moral judgment.

The Relationship of Judgment to Action

Prior to 1980 Kohlberg approached the judgment-action issue with the Socratic, cognitivist assumption that if one knew what was right, one was very likely to do it. The most relevant question was, did one *really* know what was right? According to his developmental account, genuine moral knowledge is not possessed until stage 6. At earlier stages one may have true opinions but not real knowledge. For example, almost all children and adolescents will acknowledge that cheating is wrong, but few if any will give philosophically adequate (stage 5 or 6) reasons for why it is wrong. Kohlberg, like Hartshorne and May (1928–30), found that simply agreeing that cheating was wrong did not predict to whether one cheated or not. What did predict to cheating behavior was the moral stage: the higher their moral stage the less likely children would cheat. Thus the better reasons children had to support their belief that cheating was wrong, the better able they were to resist the temptation to cheat.

What does reasoning add to one's belief that a given behavior is right or wrong? Kohlberg originally argued that there was a difference between espousing a "bag of virtues" in the abstract and applying values in a specific situation, especially when they come into conflict with each other. For example, it is one thing to rate the value of honesty highly on a questionnaire and something else to be honest in an examination that one is in danger of flunking. For a student reasoning in the second stage of morality, "honesty is the best policy," that is, honesty is usually the best way to keep out of trouble and impress the teachers. However, when taking a test, that student may conclude that honesty is not the best policy if it is possible to cheat for a good grade and get away with it. A similar scenario may be constructed for the student reasoning at stage 3. It is important to be honest in order to live up to the teacher's trust; but what should you do if your friend asks for "help" during an exam, or if by getting a low grade you will let your parents down?

While the preconventional and conventional stages do not adequately resolve the cheating dilemma, they do, according to Kohlberg's early interpretation, progressively eliminate certain factors as morally relevant to the decision of whether or not to cheat. For example, at stage 3, students no longer think that pragmatic self-interest is in and of itself a morally justifiable reason to cheat. However, an unselfish reason may be acceptable, such as not to disappoint one's parents. While we may find that some students argue at stages 2 and 3 that they should cheat, most students at all stages believe cheating is wrong. Perhaps many cheat anyhow because they do not feel responsible for acting on their moral judgment. Competing considerations may excuse them from feeling responsible for acting as they think they should, if those excuses are "good enough" from their moral point of view.

A powerful example of the discrepancy between judgments of moral rightness and judgments of responsibility comes from Kohlberg and Candee's (1984) reanalysis of the Milgram data. They show that while the higher (stage 4B) subjects were the ones least likely to administer shocks under orders from the psychologist-authority, almost all of the subjects recognized that administering the shocks was wrong. The psychologist-authority did not influence their determination of what was right as much as excuse them from taking responsibility for the consequence of their actions.

In Kohlberg's revised account of the judgment-action problematic, he distinguishes two judgments, a deontic judgment of what is right to do and a responsibility judgment of what *I* should do. While Kohlberg claims the two are related, he speculates that stages of deontic judgment may be necessary but not sufficient for parallel stages of responsibility judgment. Here we can make a connection between loyalty and responsibility. Adolescents may be tempted to be mere moral spectators and avoid moral commitments. Indeed, this is the role their society seems to have assigned to them in denying them opportunities for responsible action in the workplace or the civic society. In the typical high school, they are responsible only for themselves—to get their work done and to stay out of trouble. When there are problems in the school, for example when a fight starts or when cheating gets out of hand, it is not up to them to do anything—it is the teachers' and administrators' job. Within the just community approach adolescents have the responsibility to be "their brothers' and sisters' keeper," as members of a community. While their sense of moral responsibility may originally be limited to their particular community, it was Kohlberg's hope that it would develop and generalize to humankind, leading to Royce's "loyalty to loyalty" or Erikson's "virtue of fidelity."

Indoctrinative vs. Nonindoctrinative Approaches

In his earlier writings Kohlberg (1967, 1970a, 1971c) took a strong stand on the issue of moral indoctrination. He criticized both deliberate and nondeliberate approaches to values education that seek to instill in children particular values that are defined as "right" or as "the American way of life." Upon reflection most of these values turned out to be those of the middle class, which had no inherently rational justification (for example, "Cleanliness is next to godliness"). Thus to instill them systematically was to impose them arbitrarily on children and to violate their rights and the rights of their parents. In contrast, Kohlberg maintained that a program designed to stimulate a natural sequence of moral development "defines an educational process respecting the autonomy of the child," for "the experiences by which children naturally move from stage to stage are nonindoctrinative; that is, they are not experiences of being taught specific content" (1971e:72). But the just community approach does involve the teaching of specific content. Does it thereby violate Kohlberg's own standards for nonindoctrinative moral education?

Kohlberg's (1980, 1985) response is complex and, we believe, somewhat confusing unless it is made clear that he has broadened his own criteria for what constitutes nonindoctrinative moral education. For while his earlier writings suggest that the systematic teaching of any moral content could be considered indoctrinative, his more recent thinking comes closer to Peters, who considers an indoctrinative approach to be "a special type of instruction . . . [that] consists of getting children to accept a fixed body of rules in such a way that they are incapacitated from adopting a critical attitude towards them" (1973:155). Thus, the main distinction is based not on whether a specific content is taught, but on how it is taught. Blatt's program was nonindoctrinative not primarily because it did not teach moral content, but because its participants were encouraged to think critically, discuss assumptions, and, when they felt necessary, challenge the teacher's suggestions. Indoctrinative programs allow none of that, but rather posit that the teacher owns the moral knowledge that the students should accept without question.

The just community approach, with its Durkheimian stress on respect for rules and attachment to the group, would run the risk of becoming indoctrinative were its rules preestablished by the educators and were conformity to the rules enforced by a monolithic group structure. But in setting up this model, Kohlberg has attempted to insure that it would not become indoctrinative by stressing both its developmental and democratic bases.

From a developmental perspective, the approach recognizes the necessity that students operating between stages 2 and 3 learn to maintain a consistent, conventional moral order in which classes are attended, school work is done, commitments are kept, property is not stolen, and fairness is not violated. Nevertheless, students are not taught that a particular social order or authority defines the right and the just. They are taught that the right and just require social order and authority. They are taught to use their own moral reasoning capacities to think through what shape that order and authority should take and how they, as a group, will take responsibility for contributing to the maintenance of a sensible order and authority. Since the program moves from reason to order rather than vice versa, it is meant simultaneously to promote the exercise of moral reasoning and give the students a real voice in shaping the authority to which they will be bound.

This developmental perspective leads to a democratic governance procedure; for, as discussed in chapter 1, democracy provides the best social arrangement for promoting the free exercise of participants' moral reasoning. Democratic governance, however, becomes even more crucial in the just community approach, for it is needed to insure both that the educators will have to base their appeal for authority on reasons that the students can understand and accept and that the individual student will retain the right to freely dissent from the opinions of the educators and the group without incurring a negative sanction for doing so.

What Kohlberg envisions is a group consisting of students and educators that would evolve through moral discussion their own value positions and translate through democratic decision making those positions into rules and norms for group behavior. The educators would not only facilitate discussion among students, but also lead the way toward decision making by advocating certain value positions which they see as being in the best interest of the group. However, they would be conscious of the difference between advocating and indoctrinating; that is, they would present positions that could be criticized, encourage students to formulate their own perceptions on issues, and accept as binding the democratic judgment of the majority of the group. The educators obviously would have special authority by virtue of their positions, but would try to operate as formally equal members of a democratic group and exercise authority by virtue of their wisdom and by means of consent rather than by virtue of their position and by means of coercion.

CONCLUSION

The aim of this and the previous chapter has been to spell out as clearly as is currently possible the just community approach to moral education. What we have tried to share is a sense of the evolving nature of this approach. Since Kohlberg's return from his kibbutz visit in 1969, aspects of this approach had been germinating in his mind. In some of his articles he gave voice to these ideas, but primarily they have been communicated not in writing but in application. Through application, experimentation, and dialogue with teachers, students, and other theorists, these ideas have changed, and as they have changed so in turn have the applications. An oral tradition of the just community approach has arisen, and it is this tradition that we have tried here and will try in the chapters that follow to describe in writing.

3

A Week in the Life
of Cluster

with Joseph Reimer

The Cluster School in Cambridge, Massachusetts, had the distinction of being the site for the first application of the just community approach to a school setting. An alternative school-within-a-school, Cluster was founded in 1974 and pioneered this approach for five years before being reorganized as K-100, a leadership program within the regular Cambridge high school (Cambridge Rindge and Latin School). It received much publicity from the Boston newspapers, *Newsweek,* and *Psychology Today.* In this chapter we will present a description of the Cluster School as it embodied a developing just community approach. First we will focus briefly on the beginnings of the school and the evolution of its institutions and then concentrate primarily on the weekly functioning of the major institutions of the school. This portrait should convey how the theory of the just community was translated into daily practice.

THE BEGINNING OF CLUSTER

The Cluster School was born of the coincidence of two originally unrelated events. In the spring of 1974 Kohlberg received grants from the Danforth and Kennedy foundations to undertake the training of high school teachers in developmental moral education and the just community approach. The grant application called for two programs in the Cambridge schools: one would train teachers in a variety of moral, discussion-based curricula, and another would create a just community school-within-a-school in one of the Cambridge high schools. The Cambridge schools were a particularly attractive setting because of the racial and social diversity in the student population. Kohlberg intended to have the first program precede the second by a year's time: but developments within the Cambridge schools led to a change in his schedule.

At the suggestion of the superintendent of the Cambridge schools, a group of parents invited Kohlberg to join them as a consultant in planning for a new alternative high school. The existing alternative school, the Pilot School, had grown from 60 to 180 students and had a waiting list of 55 applicants for the incoming freshmen class. A group of parents with children on that list had made the proposal to the school committee and won funding to plan for the new school, which would open that September. When Kohlberg joined the planning group of parents, teachers, and students, he took the opportunity to present his ideas on the just community, and they were interested enough to invite him to join a committee on governance. That committee came up with the following principles for governing the new school:

1. The school would be governed by direct democracy. All major issues would be discussed and decided at a weekly community meeting at which all members (students and teachers) would have one vote.
2. There would be additionally a number of standing committees to be filled by students, teachers, and parents.
3. A social contract would be drawn between members which would define everyone's responsibilities and rights.
4. Students and teachers would have the same basic rights, including freedom of expression, respect from others, and freedom from physical or verbal harm.

This plan was incorporated in a report which called for a new alternative school housed in three classrooms, with a half-day schedule and a curriculum based around a double-period, required core course, integrating English and social studies. The report was presented to the school committee, which approved opening the new alternative school in September. It would be called the Cluster School.

THE CLUSTER STAFF

Of the eight teachers from the Cambridge high school who applied for the eight half-time positions in Cluster, all were accepted. They were all veteran teachers; most were under the age of thirty. There were four men and four women, and all were white. As a group, they were articulate and self-assured and saw themselves as experienced teachers who had now been given the opportunity to put their beliefs to practice by establishing a new school-within-a-school. But, significantly, none had previous experience teaching in an alternative school, and they had very little lead time to learn the ropes before Cluster opened. They, as the students, would have to do much of their learning in the course of running the school.

Most of the training occurred in evening meetings which the staff took turns hosting. While the major item of business was looking ahead to the community meeting, a significant amount of time was spent discussing problem students. As we will note in our section on adviser groups, each staff member had a responsibility to monitor the overall progress of the students in their group. Since quite a few students came to Cluster with significant learning and adjustment problems, this was a very demanding role.

Cluster was different from the other alternative schools we studied in that there was no coordinator or principal. The Cluster faculty took turns representing the school at meetings within the parent high school and within the school system. Needless to say, this system of rotating representatives and of sharing responsibility for administrative chores proved to be somewhat inefficient. While all of the staff recognized this, a significant number of them consistently and passionately rejected Kohlberg's and others' suggestions of having a part-time administrator. They feared that if such a step were taken, their democratic character as a staff and as a school would be seriously compromised.

THE ROLE OF CONSULTANTS

Most of the Cluster faculty had not previously known Kohlberg or much about his educational writings, but intuitively agreed that democratic governance was the way to go at Cluster. They wanted Kohlberg as a consultant with the assurance he would not use the school as a research laboratory. He agreed to consult as long as the school was a participatory democracy and left the issue of research to be settled by student and faculty vote after the school had been established.

He wished not to come as the expert with the ready-made model to be applied, but to present a set of ideas, to see if there was interest in them, and then work *with* the participants to develop the model that would make most sense for Cluster. He expected that the governance structure would emerge and his previous experience with just community would be a helpful resource. As it turned out, he underestimated the extent to which he as consultant would initially be called upon to supply "hands-on" knowledge about how to run a democratic school.

From the beginning, several consultant researchers worked in Cluster with the approval of the staff. One of these, Elsa Wasserman, a former guidance counselor at Pilot School and one of the coordinators of the summer planning group, joined the staff in the second year. The coauthors, Power and Higgins, who joined Kohlberg during Cluster's third year, were less involved participants than Wasserman, although Higgins eventually became a voting member.

THE OPENING OF CLUSTER: FROM CHAOS TO PARTIAL ORDER

Cluster opened in confusion. Classrooms were promised, but had to be located. Students (who, as planned, came mainly from Pilot's waiting list) had to be scheduled so they would take social studies, English, and physical education in Cluster and their other courses in the regular school. In spite of the chaos, all seemed to be going relatively smoothly until about a week into school, when the first community meeting was held. The community meeting, as we will see in detail later in the chapter, was the one time during the week when the whole school convened to discuss and decide democratically upon school policy. From the first week Kohlberg insisted that every member—student, teacher, and consultant, who would have one vote—should be required to attend. The meeting was scheduled as a regular part of the school's activities. This policy differed from that of other alternative schools, in which attendance at these meetings was not mandatory. Kohlberg argued at the time, "If you do not get the tough white and black kids coming to the community meetings, the intellectual kids will come and dialogue on boring issues with the staff and drive away the very kids who most need this experience."

At the first community meeting the main issue was the curriculum. The staff had listed a number of possible electives that could be offered during the last periods of the school day and wanted the students to choose among them. Toward the end of the meeting a student made the radical proposal that "everyone could leave before the close of school if they did not like the courses offered" (Wasserman 1977:36). A vote was taken and that proposal passed. The staff was stunned. This was democracy, but it also violated the rules of the Cambridge high school, which were operative for Cluster as well. At the last moment Kohlberg called out that that was only a straw vote and a real vote would have to be taken at the next meeting.

This tragicomic situation showed the staff that democracy was not going to be born of itself; it needed to be carefully nurtured. The students, or at least the majority, who had not been through the summer workshop, were coming to Cluster because they wanted an alternative school and could not get into Pilot. They understood little about and had even less commitment to the democratic process. It was natural for them to view democratic governance as an opportunity to push the limits. The staff would have to structure democracy carefully if it were not to break down into anarchy.

THE CURRICULUM

As the community was learning to deal with the emerging democratic process, the faculty had to make curricular decisions about the core course. There was initial discussion about whether students should be grouped homogeneously or heterogeneously by level within core courses. The question would arise several times for faculty and community discussion during the next three years, but what made it hard to resolve was the conflict of values: on the one hand, homogeneous groupings might better facilitate a matching of teaching and learning styles, but on the other hand, heterogeneous groupings allowed for both more self-regulation in learning and more social integration in classes. The solution that came closest to satisfying both sides of the conflict emerged during Cluster's third year: the students would choose the level and style of instruction best suited to their learning needs, but would do so with an eye to maximizing the possibility of students from different backgrounds participating in the same classes.

As to philosophy of teaching, though the faculty were never formally requested to train in the philosophy and methods of developmental education, most tended in that direction. The core classes served to reinforce, complement, and expand upon the socio-cognitive learning that took place during small group and community meetings. Focusing on developing these capacities is in line with the idea of "development as the aim of education," which is opposed to a view of education that separates the "academic" learning of classes from the "experiential" learning of participatory governance (Kohlberg 1972). Kohlberg saw a need for school experience that as a whole represents real-life experience to the students and, in so doing, stimulates development. Class time should be an occasion to reflect upon real life and to expand one's view of real life by considering other perspectives and options. In turn, experiential learning should be challenging and thought provoking and have students wanting to know more about the concepts they have been employing. Thus "democracy," "community," "law," and "authority" were the subjects of both classes and meetings; and if in one context students thought *about* these concepts and in the other thought *through* these concepts, the net result was meant to be an integrated learning experience that promoted the students' cognitive, social, and moral development.

THE EMERGING JUST COMMUNITY APPROACH

As the complexities of starting a new school, planning a curriculum, and getting into place a system of governance became apparent, the faculty came to rely more heavily on Kohlberg's consultation and his previous experience with democratic governance. The teachers were learning under fire how to lead small groups, participate as *Madrichim* (moral leaders) in the community meetings, and integrate a developmental-democratic orientation into their classroom teaching. They met with

Kohlberg in semiweekly consultations (after school hours) and at other odd hours during the school week, as circumstances dictated. One of the first opportunities for ad hoc consultation arose when several teachers arranged for their students to see a film shown at Harvard. The students agreed previous to going that they would not smoke cigarettes in the viewing room. But as soon as the lights went off, out came the butts. The teachers present did not react. Kohlberg, who was also present, had the film stopped and took the teachers out of the room. He told them that in a democracy it was crucial that the rules or agreements that the community makes be taken seriously. To sit by and watch the students violate the rules without reacting is to undercut the democratic authority of the community. The teachers agreed and upon reentering the room led a short discussion about smoking and upholding agreements. The film was then continued without interruption.

The staff were impressed by Kohlberg's serious attitude toward upholding the rules of the school. Some alternative schools allow such "expressive behaviors" as smoking to go by without much fuss. The "fuss" Kohlberg made had little to do with smoking per se, but had everything to do with what Durkheim calls respect for rules. The teachers learned quickly that without strengthening respect for rules, democratic governance will fail. For when adults cease to enforce the rules unilaterally, other means of social control have to come into play. In the just community mode, "the other means of social control" is the group that expects its members to live up to its agreements.

This incident also illustrates the relation between advocacy and the role of the consultant. Kohlberg, as consultant, advocated to the faculty a position based on the just community approach. They, agreeing with his point, in turn advocated a position to the students about the importance of upholding social agreements. The consultant by this model of intervention does not wait to be consulted; he or she takes an active, interventionist stance in relation to the staff. Similarly, the faculty intervened to raise the question about broken agreements. The objective in both interventions is for the second party to become more aware of their thinking and acting in the context of their effect on the community. The faculty were expected to learn "to take the perspective of the community" and ask, as Kohlberg did here, how the behavior of smoking is affecting the life of the community. Similarly, at least some of the students would learn to advocate to their peers a concern for how their behavior affects the community. The final decision, as to whether a given behavior should be changed in light of its effect on the community, is made democratically by the group as a whole; as in this case, when they had agreed by vote to see the film and not smoke while viewing it.

Perhaps the most severe test of whether the Cluster community could learn to make and stand by its own rules centered around the issue of drug use. The regular Cambridge high school had rules prohibiting the use of drugs, and as part of the larger school, Cluster students were subject to these rules and knew that if caught, they would have to pay the price. For most students that seemed a fair arrangement: the headmaster and the cops had to "do their thing," and students could do theirs as long as they were not caught. What upset this arrangement was the just community's call for self-governance. Students who were willing to accept rules in Cluster about curbing disturbances in classes and limiting the cutting of classes because they saw them as necessary for running the school were not willing to accept a self-imposed agreement that would impinge upon that great adolescent freedom: the right to get high when you want.

Drug use would probably not even have been raised as an issue that first semester had not a student come sauntering into a community meeting in November "reeking of weed" (Wasserman 1977:75). Confronted with an undeniable breach of school rules, the community had to react, but found it had no common voice. Some students felt that people coming in high ruined the whole atmosphere of the school; they were joined by some faculty who argued that no matter what the marijuana smokers claimed, they could not participate as well under the influence as they could when "straight." But the smokers were equally insistent that it did not hurt anyone else when one smoked, and it therefore was not really a community issue and did not require a community rule.

Unlike previous conflicts at meetings, this one challenged peer group loyalty and threatened the little bit of communal solidarity that had developed over the first months. After the meeting ended, one teacher invited those who wanted to meet after school. A group of fifteen stayed and decided that what the school needed was an overnight trip as a way of easing tensions and talking out problems. Their solution was adopted enthusiastically at the next community meeting and set a precedent for the annual retreat—a weekend away from school in which the community could be built on the basis of improved interpersonal relations.

For the staff, however, this solution, though welcome, only intensified the original problem. They knew that "fun away from school" meant for many students "getting high as a kite." They decided, with Kohlberg's support, to insist upon a prior agreement of no alcohol or drugs as a condition for those who chose to go on the retreat. Their decision was greeted with some student anger, but seeming acquiescence.

On the first evening of the retreat a staff member happened upon a group of students smoking marijuana. A community meeting had been planned for that evening, and it was monopolized by the discussion of drugs. The accused students were irritated at this teacher for having spied on them, but the teacher defended himself as upholding a prior agreement. Being an English teacher, he went on to deliver an impassioned statement that epitomized the just community ethic:

There is a statement that no man is an island. The man who was writing that statement on his deathbed had some very serious thoughts. He said when one man dies, a piece of the continent drops off. It is not just like some little island that drifts away, it is a piece of the continent. We are in this thing together. You can't just say well, most of us are okay and there are a few people doing their own thing and they are not harming anybody; that is not what this school is about. This is not a "do your own thing" school. The whole concept here is community. Just community. Those are the words we heard from the beginning. Just means fair and community means together; we are not talking about letting certain individuals do their own thing.

The speech sparked a discussion among students and staff about the ways people in Cluster talked to and treated one another. Their words were often rough and unpleasant, but paradoxically, the meeting itself was well run. For the first time, a staff member did not chair the meeting, as had been done since September in Cambridge. When the evening was drawing to a close, one of the students who had been involved in the drug episode stood up and said: "One thing I would like to say—all the other community meetings I went to were the lousiest ones, and I never wanted to go to another one again. I came to this one and I think it is the best one that the school has had since I have been here."

Although no agreement about drugs had been reached, Cluster had arrived at a turning point. The group had openly argued and vented some strong, angry sentiments but had emerged feeling more than ever before like a community. There had been some ardent expressions of concern about the community made by both staff and students that had made an impression.

THE ENFORCEMENT OF RULES

In the spring of the first year enforcement became a central goal of the emerging just community approach. It was not difficult for students to learn to vote democratically for establishing rules, but as long as they expected that it would be the teachers who would enforce these rules, the basic authority structure of the school would remain unchanged and there would be no just community. What had to happen was for the community as a whole to own these rules and to insist upon everyone's upholding them.

Standing most directly in the way of achieving this goal was a well-established norm among students against "ratting": if someone breaks a rule that does not personally harm or affect you, leave its detection to the authorities. Do not rat on anyone lest that person rat on you. Seen in this light, almost any student enforcement of a rule is ratting. The only way that perception could be undone was for the majority of students to reinterpret student enforcement as involving a group of people protecting their community by collectively upholding their agreements and helping the person breaking the rule to become a better community member. Community meeting participation was meant to be an education in reinterpretation by learning to see behavioral problems from the perspective of their effect on the community and not simply as an act of one individual which may or may not affect you as a second individual.

As central as was the goal of rule enforcement, its implementation proved tricky, even for the staff, as the following incident from the first year illustrated. In February 1975 one of the teachers came before the Discipline Committee (D.C.) to testify that two students had come to squash class high from smoking marijuana. He had not seen them smoking, but when he asked them, one boy had admitted he was slightly high. That boy, Bob, now contended that he had only been pulling the teacher's leg, and a second Cluster teacher, who was his faculty adviser, expressed his misgivings about using Bob's admission of guilt as evidence against him. The D.C. debated whether Bob was liable for punishment and voted 4 to 1 that he be expelled from the squash class and warned that a second violation could lead to expulsion from the school.

This was an unusually decisive stance for the D.C. to take, and was quite controversial given the circumstances. First was the problem of evidence. Without Bob's admission, the only evidence against him was circumstantial. Second, Bob had a reputation for being a drug user and was an unpopular kid. Neither was true about the other boy, Peter, who was also suspected of being high but denied it. The D.C. never even took up Peter's case, raising the question of whether the severity of Bob's judgment may have been related to his status in the school.

The procedure in Cluster was for cases judged by the Discipline Committee to go before the community meeting for communal review. At the faculty meeting held before the community meeting, the staff questioned the D.C. decision. This gave the staff an opportunity to clarify their thinking about the just community approach to the juridical process. Were the same principles of due process and admissibility of evidence that existed in an American court of law to define justice here, or were other principles at play? Kohlberg came out strongly for the position that a school like Cluster should not be run as a court of law, but as a community with a different set of concerns. He thought that concerns about due process and self-recrimination "were faculty issues and not issues for the kids." In his view what was at stake was not the violation of Bob's rights, but whether students would perceive Bob as being punished for having admitted a violation of the rules. He thus made a strong plea in the staff meeting that students be encouraged to be honest in admitting to wrongdoing.

> In a fair community there is an expectation that people will admit when they have done something wrong. In such a community the punishment must be mild and fair enough so that they are not getting screwed by it. Obviously, there has to be some commitment to telling the truth, whether it be confessing or ratting, if you are going to make the democratic system work. But it is not easy, because it depends on establishing a climate of fairness and trust. People have a reflex of denying anything.

From this perspective, the problem in Bob's case was to get the community to enforce its rules without discouraging its members from truthfully admitting when they had violated a rule. Kohlberg and the staff agreed that judging Bob without Peter was procedurally wrong, and the D.C. should meet again to hear the case of the two of them. The hope was that Bob and Peter would be more honest in their testimony this time.

At the second D.C. meeting Bob again denied being high on drugs and Peter backed up his story. The committee, though, ruled against the boys, and Bob, as was his right, decided to appeal that judgment to the community meeting. At the next meeting he challenged the community's right to judge him because many of those doing the judging had broken the drug rule themselves: "I don't know how to put this . . . don't try to say that since that rule was made, half of you have not come in high or stoned at least once. Maybe you didn't get caught, but maybe you are more sneaky and sleazy and you are going against the rules, anyway."

This is the kind of argument that had been making enforcement so difficult. If everyone is breaking the rules, how can anyone fairly judge another on his actions? But the students rejected it in this instance because those who may have been using drugs had neither been caught nor admitted to being high as Bob had. He was to be punished, for he was an uncautious user of drugs who had admitted more than he should have.

This communal judgment placed Kohlberg in an uneasy position. On the one hand, the community had for the first time voted to enforce one of its rules. But the vote also implicitly communicated the message that if you don't want to be punished, don't admit your having done anything wrong. Kohlberg and one student appealed to the community to clarify their stance by allowing that if someone honestly admitted to misbehavior, the punishment would be lessened. The motion, however, was narrowly rejected.

The pursuit of justice at Cluster was slow. Yet the process of rule enforcement did progress over the course of years (see chapter 5). Although it never reached the point it did in the Scarsdale A School, where students regularly admitted to their own wrongdoings (see chapter 6), they at least learned to accept the community's right to vote them a punishment and agreed, in most cases, to make amends for breaking the rules. More important, they came to expect in most cases that a rule passed would be a rule enforced and that without respect for rules there could be no communal life.

We will return to the history of the Cluster School in Chapter 5. Our attention turns now to the institutions of the just community as they were established during Cluster's first year. We have already alluded to the three main institutions to be described: the small or adviser group, the community meeting, and the Discipline Committee. Each of these convened once weekly, and together constituted the democratic governance structure of the Cluster School.

The aim of the remainder of this chapter is to describe the working of these institutions as part of Cluster's weekly order. We will present selections from the transcript of one meeting of each of the major institutions, explicate the movement within the meetings, show how the meeting was representative of the operation of the institution, and comment on the relative quality of the meeting in terms of its realizing the goals of the just community approach. The resulting view of a week in the life of Cluster will, we hope, give the reader a sense of both the Cluster experience and the thinking that went into translating the theory of just community into a working educational intervention.

ADVISER GROUPS

Adviser group meetings were held on Thursdays, sandwiched between the faculty meeting the night before and a community meeting the next day. The purpose of this scheduling was to prepare students and staff for the community meeting through a preliminary discussion of the proposal(s) on the agenda. Although adviser group meetings set the stage for the community meeting, this was not their only function. Adviser group meetings provided an opportunity for a small group of students and a teacher to socialize and share more personal concerns than those typically discussed in the community meeting. During the summer after Cluster's first year, Elsa Wasserman, a consultant, gave a workshop to the Cluster staff that focused on developing their group leadership skills in order to make adviser groups more effective as a context for counseling and guidance. The staff assigned students to adviser groups by juggling two criteria: their choices and the diversity of each group. Some racial imbalance was tolerated in order to accommodate to student preferences as generously as possible. The staff believed that successful counseling depended upon the students' feeling comfortable with their teacher-advisers and peers.

THE MISSING DOCK

The adviser group and community meetings we will present took place on June 9 and 10, 1977, at the end of Cluster's third year. They dealt with a dock that had been lost by a number of Cluster students on a school retreat several weeks earlier. The question to be resolved was who should be responsible for paying for the missing dock. We chose these meetings for three reasons: their central issue, communal responsibility, is vital to the just community approach; their central question, who should pay for the dock, raised a division of opinion among members which in the meetings generated a substantive moral discussion; and their procedure, though flawed in places, illustrates how the democratic process operated at Cluster.

The dock was lost on the annual spring retreat over a weekend during the third week of May at a camping site outside the city. The retreat's official purpose was to enhance the sense of community in the school, which meant it was an opportunity for students and staff to mix more freely and get to know one another better as people. In planning the retreat, one staff member suggested that it be held at a summer camp that had beautiful facilities and was owned by a relative of hers. She contacted the owner, who was a bit nervous about the arrangement, but he agreed to let them use the camp facilities, emphasizing that they would have to be careful not to damage camp property and not to use the lake, which would be off-limits to them. The community agreed.

Before each retreat a community meeting would be held at which the staff and students would try to come to a clear agreement on the rules of behavior for the retreat. The third-year meeting did not go smoothly. The issue of contention was drug use, which, while having been a constant problem during Cluster's first year, had subsided during most of the second and third year. Yet when the staff confronted the students with explicitly agreeing not to bring any drugs with them on the retreat, it took some extended negotiations to get the agreement the staff sought.

The retreat was judged by all who went to have been a success. The planned activities came off well, the students and faculty enjoyed one another's company, and there were no reported violations of the agreements that had been made. There was a shared sense, expressed in meetings after the retreat, of the third year's ending on a high note. However, in the week preceding the June 10 meeting, the camp owner reported to his relative on the staff that during the retreat three docks tied to the shore of the camp's lake and been untied and allowed to float away. Subsequently two had been found, but one was still missing. It would cost $350 to replace, and the owner felt that the Cluster School was responsible for the loss.

When an issue of this urgency arose, it would move to the head of the school's agenda. First to deal with it were the staff who learned of the problem from the owner's relative at their weekly Wednesday evening meeting. To our knowledge none of the staff had previously known that the docks had been unfastened; but when they found out, they had to formulate a response. With the consultant's help they had to decide how best to raise this issue for discussion in the small adviser groups and the larger community meeting. As we will see from the transcript of the community meeting, they agreed to focus the discussion on the issue of moral responsibility: who should take responsibility for replacing the missing dock?

The Central Issue: Who Is Responsible?

Although no recording was made of the staff meeting that week, it nevertheless would be helpful to reconstruct the theoretical rationale for focusing the discussion on the issue of moral responsibility.

Consider the situation the staff faced that night. For two and a half weeks they had been under the impression that this retreat had gone especially well and the agreements made previous to going had been upheld. Now they discovered that the agreement with the camp owner had been broken, presumably by a few students, and these students had kept that information to themselves. The staff may have experienced a sense of disappointed expectations, of a breach in trust and responsibility on the part of the students involved. They may have wanted to find out who was involved and why they did what they did.

Imagine the staff's following up on those feelings: where would it lead? Obviously the individual students who were involved would feel under a lot of pressure. They might react by guiltily making confessions;

but more likely, given that a bill of $350 could be seen as the price tag for confessing, they may have decided to deny responsibility and to let it be known among their peers that they did not want anyone telling on them. Faced with no admissions of guilt, the staff could post a reward for any information leading to the guilty party, talk privately to students to get privileged information, or even hold everyone responsible and punishable until someone talked. In following any of these scenarios, they would be setting themselves against the students as cops in pursuit of robbers.

The just community approach suggests a different direction. First, it does not see the question of "who did this" and "why did they do it" as primary. Rather, it focuses on the event as an incident which occurred within the community. The primary questions are "Given who we are as a community, how did this occur in our midst?" and "What are *we* going to do about it?" The emphasis is on the collective "we," and those who committed the act are not "others" whom we accuse, but part of the "we" that is collectively constituted as a community. Part of us did this, and therefore we are all involved in assuming responsibility for the act.

For the staff that means that whatever they are personally feeling about the individuals who untied the docks, their first educational task is not to press for the conviction of individuals, but to raise as an open question "who should take responsibility for the dock." Raising this as a question may lead the students to consider whether it is just to place blame on only the few. The staff can then probe for the extent to which they see the whole community as having a responsibility for what occurred. Finally, they can present the argument that the community ought to make amends. When there is in the group a healthy sense of "being in this together," the majority of students are likely to agree to assuming partial responsibility for what occurred.

Assuming responsibility as a community does *not* mean exculpating those who were actually involved in untying the docks. Rather, the purpose of this approach is (a) to separate moral responsibility from financial liability and (b) to demonstrate that in breaking the rules or agreements, individuals are not only hurting other individuals (like the camp owner), but also are affecting the community as a whole. The community takes responsibility because its word, its agreement, was involved; but in doing so, it sets up the expectation that the individuals who were actually involved will follow suit and take individual responsibility for what they did. Once the community is willing to share the financial burden of recouping the lost dock, the price of confession is no longer primarily financial, but moral. What is at stake is making amends to one's peers for breaking agreements and not the ability to pay $350 back to the camp owner. Thus the moral expectation for confession is heightened because others are willing to share in the moral and financial burden.

The call for assuming communal responsibility needs to be distinguished from the use of collective punishment in which a group is *involuntarily* held responsible for the act of one of its members. Yet even collective responsibility remains an undoubtedly controversial educational strategy. It raised questions of normative ethics ("Is it fair to ask those who were not involved to share moral and financial responsibility for the loss of the dock?") as well as of educational efficacy ("Does this approach accomplish its ends?"). These are the questions, among others, that we will be dealing with in reviewing the adviser and community meetings.

The Adviser Group Meeting

Two staff members, Dora and Rob, decided to combine their adviser groups for this particular discussion. Since Rob was a new faculty member, his group frequently met with Dora's, as was the practice with all new faculty members. The meeting began at 10:50 A.M., after students had formed a sloppy circle. Dora began by breaking the news that the owner of the camp had assessed Cluster $350 for the loss of a dock during the retreat. She then asked the students what they knew about it. We pick the meeting up with Dora clarifying a student's statement that she and others saw a dock float away.

DORA (T): * You are saying that some of you went out on the dock, and you did see one float away and you didn't go get it.
SANDY: No, no, a bunch of kids took a raft and they jumped on it and were trying to get it out in the water, and then one fell off and they all fell off and so they just let it float away.

* (T)-staff member. In Cluster school, the A School, and S.W.S. students address staff by their given names.

ROB (T): It seems pretty clear, then, that their charge, $350, is for the raft you saw float away.

BEV: $350 for one raft?

BEV and other students: That's hard to believe!

ROB (T): *What do we do with that situation, that is, the dilemma that is presented to us?*

SANDY: We can say we want to see the bill, what it actually costs, exactly how come this cost $350.

DORA (T): Sandy, try to make a comparison. Say you ask me to let you go into my house and you ask me to let you use something of mine, like maybe my record player. What if I said no, I would really prefer that you not use it, and what if I stepped out for a little while and you would say, well, she is not really using it, and she doesn't care, and then you used it and then you broke it.

Commentary

As the students make the connection between the $350 bill and the dock escapade some of them witnessed, they are incredulous at the price of restitution. Sandy's suggestion that the owner of the campsite let them see the bill shifts the burden of responsibility from the Cluster students to the owner. Instead of expressing moral indignation at those who disobeyed the owner's rule and went out on the dock, she is indignant at the owner for trying to gyp them! Dora intervenes with an analogy which helps the students focus on their responsibility. Unfortunately, she is unprepared to defend the justice of the $350 charge. She will make sure that she can the next day when the whole community meets. One of the benefits of the advisory group meeting is that it can serve as a dry run for the community meeting and give the staff an opportunity to attend to such loose ends.

DORA (T): For purposes of discussion, say that we went as a community on a retreat, and a dock was lost and replacing it will cost $250, never mind the insurance, we don't know about that. *Who should replace it?* Elena, who did not go out on the dock, should she have to pay? Is it only those people who went out who should pay?

SIMON: That's like getting back to the hotel. If I rip off towels and she, Sandy, stays there the next night and pays more money, she's paying for the towels I ripped off. I look at that as . . . unfair. . . . I think we are all in it together. It's just the fact that we went out and did it.

DORA (T): Remember Monica's purse. If we have to pay, and we agree on the amount, then everyone should pay.

BEV: Everybody who's in there now [in the school] should be required to have some fund-raising thing.

SANDY: What about the kids who lost the dock?

BEV: But maybe they'll admit it. Then we'll have one big fund-raiser. Because I know there are some people who just can't pay the money.

KARA: We all went on the retreat. It doesn't matter if it cost a dime. The point is we all went on the retreat. . . . It is like saying everyone went on the retreat and therefore that is like saying something might happen and we will all be responsible.

SIMON: We are responsible, we are a community. We are all together. What one does, we all have to take fault for, we have got to realize that.

KARA: That's what I'm saying.

BEV: OK. I am not sure. I really don't think it is fair that all the people pay for what some people did, but I think if we just say those who did it should pay, a lot of people won't admit it, and three or four people will end up paying and that is not fair at all either. I don't think it is fair for some people, say seven people, that is too much, even if it was their fault. No one wants to pay $50 for a dock.

SIMON: That should have been thought of before it happened.

DORA (T): Do you think the people who were responsible should have to do it all alone?

BEV: I was on a dock, but the dock I was on I brought back so I shouldn't have to pay anything in that case.

SIMON: Who was there when the thing floated out? Whoever was there should have said; Do you realize if something happens, we are going to have to pay a lot of money for that if we lose it?

SANDY: In fact, I was on the beach, and I just sat and watched, and it just sat out there in the middle of the lake.

Commentary

For the sake of moral discussion, Dora lowers the cost of replacing the dock from $350 to $250 and then asks who should have to pay (assuming the owner has not deceived them). Simon's response is a bit difficult to interpret. He apparently wants to make a fairness distinction between penalizing one individual for the behavior of another and penalizing a community for the behavior of some of its members. Presumably it is unfair to penalize an innocent individual but fair to penalize the community because "we are all in it together." Dora builds upon Simon's plea for collective responsibility with an appeal to the precedent set over a year ago, when the community agreed to collectively chip in to restitute the victim of a theft (see chapter 4). Yet this issue seems more complicated, as Sandy and Bev note in asking about the responsibility of those who actually lost the dock.

In terms of building a sense of community and commitment to shared norms, this meeting has been moderately successful. A number of students accepted collective responsibility in spite of its cost to them. On the other hand, although students uphold a norm of collective responsibility when asked to choose between that and individual responsibility, it is clear from the beginning of the meeting that they would prefer to avoid the responsibility issue altogether.

THE COMMUNITY MEETING

Participatory democratic governance was most clearly practiced at the community meeting. Each Friday at 10:50 A.M., the membership of the Cluster School would gather in the large double-classroom for the community meeting. Everyone—teachers, students, consultants, and researchers—was expected to be there; and almost everyone came. It was the only regular time during the week when the whole school was assembled, when everyone could see and hear each other. The meeting *was* community incarnate.

The meetings had a definite rhythm. They began slowly, almost incoherently, as people would gradually file into the large room and take seats along the walls. (It was an unwritten rule that no one sat in the middle of the room.) The rotating chairpersons, sitting on a desk in the front, would call for order, usually several times, before the proceedings could begin over the dull roar of the crowd. If there were any visitors present, they would stand, announce their names and reasons for coming, and receive by vote the community's welcome. Business would open with smaller agenda items that could be dealt with quickly so that the central issue of the day could be raised. Early in the discussion a proposal would be made suggesting a way to deal with the issue, and a straw vote would be taken to gauge how the members stood—for or against the proposal. Those in the minority on the straw vote would be first to present their views and reasons, followed by the majority. The stage was set for debating the merits of alternative options, raising questions, and trying to sway undecided voters to one's side. At their best the discussions would simmer with drama and even continue during the lunch break. But they were always goal-oriented. By 12:50 P.M. a final vote would be taken, and the community would have arrived by democratic process at a majority decision that would hopefully work in the community's best interest.

The community meeting functioned, in a sense, as Cluster's major ritual event. It "celebrated" Cluster as a community, and the proceedings were infused with references to "working together as a community." Participation in the meetings bound the members together as a group, and although there were suggestions from time to time that the meetings be held less often, the ritual quality of the meetings kept them anchored in their weekly spot. It was as if Cluster would not be Cluster without the community meetings.

The meetings also functioned, as did the adviser group meetings, as a context for moral discussion. Issues that arose were to be dealt with as "moral issues" and were to be discussed in rough accordance with the procedures of good moral discussion. Finally, the meetings were the occasions for communal decision making. All the other institutions led up to the community meeting. There the whole community would establish the rules and policy of the school, which were to be implemented by the staff and students. The success of Cluster as a democratically governed, just community school depended on how well the community meeting functioned. It depended on the ability of the community, as led by its staff members, to arrive at decisions that would be judged as fair, motivate the actions of the members, and be enforceable in cases when deviation would occur. It was a tall order, but a lot of thought and planning went into making these meetings as effective a means as possible for democratically governing the school.

Plan of Presentation and Background to the Meeting

The selections from the transcript of this community meeting generally follow, with one exception, the normal Cluster School meeting procedure. This procedure can be summarized as follows:

1. meeting called to order by the chair;
2. visitors introduced;
3. report of the Discipline Committee given;
4. discussion held and vote taken on D.C. report;
5. adviser groups report on their previous discussion of central issue;
6. floor opened to discussion on central issue;
7. member makes a proposal for dealing with the issue;
8. straw vote taken;
9. minority present their positions and reasoning;
10. majority respond in kind;
11. real vote taken;
12. meeting adjourned.

This procedure had evolved over time to allow for a maximum of direct give and take over the issues while minimizing the need for complicated discussions of the procedure itself. To facilitate its presentation, we will divide its twelve steps into three parts: the adviser group reports; the discussion of the dock issue; and the real vote and aftermath. The opening (steps #1–4) and the closing (step #12) will be deleted, and the transcript will open with the adviser group reports (#5) and close with the real vote (#11).

Adviser Group Reports on the Dock Issue

BEN (T): They feel that they don't want to pay, that was the feeling that generally came out of my adviser group.

KARL: We don't want to make too much of a thing out of this, but we just feel that it was an accident that happened and the community should share the responsibility for replacing it. We should try to make up the money among the lot of us.

WILLIAM (T): Our group said that yes, they were indirectly responsible, but not directly responsible for the loss of the dock, but they are members of Cluster School and they are responsible for overall things that happen in Cluster School. They did feel, however, that there were members of the community that were directly involved in the loss of the dock, and they should take major responsibility for the fundraising.

BEV: Our group said a couple of things. First of all, we said that none of us thought that the dock cost $350 and we definitely should check that before we pay anything. People said this is our community—we went on this trip together and we should pay for it as a community.

But the people who lost it should start a fund to repay it. Then some people said that the people who did it should repay it. Then they said it would be like $50 a person, and who is going to admit they did it if it costs that much?

STUART: Some people felt that the whole community should be responsible, while others felt that others should pay for the dock.

Commentary

The first adviser group representative to report is Ben, a black teacher whose adviser group is made up primarily of black students. He tersely reports that "they don't want to pay"—meaning they are opposed to taking communal responsibility for paying for the dock. He does not explain their reasoning, though that may have been helpful for others' understanding of their position.

Second is Karl, a long-haired, "freaky" white student reporting for two adviser groups that met together. Though they "don't want to make too much of a thing" out of this issue, because the loss "was an accident," they think "the community should share the responsibility for replacing it." Again, no reasoning is offered. William, a teacher, speaking for his group, proposes a more complex scheme: let the whole community be "indirectly responsible" for "overall things that happen in Cluster School"; but the "members of the community that were directly involved in the loss of the dock . . . should take major responsibility for the fund-raising." Instead of favoring collective *over* individual responsibility, this group favors collective *with* individual responsibility. But we are still short on any reasoning for justifying these positions.

Bev, summarizing the recommendations of the adviser group meeting that we reviewed, supplies some of that reasoning. "This is our community—we went on this trip together and we should pay for it as a community." To be part of a community means to be in it together even when the going gets rough. Yet "the people who lost it should start a fund to repay it." They are responsible, as William's group suggested, to take the first step; but they cannot be held wholly responsible because "who is going to admit they did it if it costs that much?" There is a mix of pragmatism in this moral argument; taking moral responsibility as a community is supported by a pragmatic assessment of the infeasible alternative. A majority of adviser groups—all but Ben's—support the idea of collective restitution. Yet they also believe that the individuals who were involved in losing the docks should demonstrate their individual responsibility by playing a leading role in raising the money to repay the camp owner.

General Discussion of the Dock Issue

CHAIR: Open for discussion.

ELLEN (T): Maybe I could give some information. I called the owner and he has already engaged people to build the dock. They are opening the camp on Sunday. . . .

And the reason that the dock cost so much was it was made of a special kind of wood and constructed in a special way. It is not his desire to be punitive or to be hard on people unnecessarily. He told us the true figure for the dock, and he is willing to listen to whatever possibilities and is agreeable to whatever negotiations we have.

SEAN (T): There was discussion in all the groups about who is really responsible in this case. And that has to be determined yet. Who really is responsible? Is the community, are all members of the community responsible for this loss? If we say yes to the community, then how do we make restitution, and if we say yes to the individuals, how do they make restitution? So let's talk about that; let's get some ideas about that. Perhaps I should make a motion about that, to get things started. I propose that the community cough up the $350 and pay him back. Now let's hear some feedback about that, your ideas about it.

LEE: First of all, kids don't have money to just put in. Second, it is the end of the year and kids are going away. Kids aren't coming any more. Half the seniors who went on the trip aren't here.

SEAN (T): First of all, who would you think is responsible?

LEE: I think the whole community.

SEAN (T): Why do you think that?

LEE: Because the community is a community, and they are responsible for each other, and a small group can't do it.

SEAN (T): Yeah, but a small group of people went out there and ruined it.

LEE: Lost it.

SEAN (T): I'm not saying I disagree. I just want to understand why I should have to pay. If they went and burned down one of those little houses there, does that mean I have to pay?

LEE: No. I am just saying that as a community we should do it. It shouldn't be put on the people who did it.

FRED: The people won't admit it. You won't be able to find the people.
SEAN (T): How do you know?
FRED: We already know that, but I have a good idea who did it.

Commentary

A common concern among the students present was how the camp owner arrived at a figure of $350 and whether that was a reasonable price for a lost dock. Ellen, the staff member related to the camp owner, responds with some information. She explains the cost and tries to show, sensing a general mistrust of the camp owner, why the claim against Cluster is reasonable.

Sean (T), after summarizing the discussion to that point, moves the meeting ahead by making a concrete proposal: "I propose that the community cough up the $350 and pay him back." That is helpful in pinpointing for everyone what the focus of the discussion is and what one will be voting for or against. Normally a proposal would be followed shortly by a straw vote, but in this meeting the chair never calls for that preliminary vote.

Lee speaks to the difficulties, given the lateness in the year, of raising this kind of money. Sean (T) properly engages her in some moral discussion, asking Lee to clarify where she stands and why. She does so well, separating out—as Bev had before her—both a moral ("the community is a community, and they are responsible for each other") and a pragmatic ("a small group can't do it") reason for supporting collective restitution. Sean presses again, making sure, as he should, that Lee is not simply mouthing the expected clichés, but is herself convinced of this solution. She seems to be—more so than Fred, who simply argues that anyway "you won't be able to find the people."

TOM: I have a good idea. If we split the money between the whole community, everybody would give a certain amount. If everybody who is willing to give something right now would give it, we could see how much we have.
BEV: Two things. One, the reason I think the whole community is in it together is that we all went on a trip together and sort of agreed to be liable for everyone else, and we agreed to be part of the community. But obviously a lot of kids can't pay it, so maybe we'll have to do something, have a fund-raiser, I don't know. Not many people can pay $7.50 or whatever it is.

SIMON: I think maybe we should all do something. And I want to make a motion now that nobody on the staff ask us to go on a retreat to some relative's place, because we have to think about who is responsible and who it belonged to.

KOHLBERG: I just wanted to clarify the proposal that Sean was making, just to make it concrete for discussion. I guess each member of the school, staff and students, would have to chip in about six dollars apiece to repay for the dock. I assume that if that motion is going to be discussed that what it means is that those who can pay now, would pay now, and otherwise every student would be charged for it, and by some date like in the fall, they would have to pay up. In the meantime we would try to borrow the money or something.

RACHEL: Some kids won't be here in the fall.

Commentary

Some students—like Tom—have a tendency to focus on the practical, and here he is suggesting how they could proceed to collect money from the community. The suggestion is, though, a bit premature as they have yet to vote on the proposal, and Tom is not arguing why vote for the arrangement he is already implementing. Bev, though, does make that argument, and though she is repeating what she said earlier, this time she is more explicit: "The reason ... the whole community is in it together is that we all went on a trip together and sort of agreed to be liable for everyone else." She spells out what she sees as the implicit social contract involved in going on a retreat together.

Simon thinks familial obligation requires them "to think about who is responsible," and he moves that they never again go to a relative's camp for retreat. The discussion is beginning to drift and Kohlberg, speaking as a consultant, tries to refocus it on the particulars of Sean's earlier proposal. He attempts to make the implications of the proposal as clear as possible, but unfortunately he misses the opportunity to call for a straw vote and get, at this point, a reading of communal sentiment.

ROB (T): In response to Sean's proposal, I would sort of like to go back to William's [T] group proposal, and that is, I don't want to totally dismiss the idea that it happened; that those people who were immediately involved, the ones who were actually on that raft and let it float away—there were a lot of people, it wasn't just one person, there were probably a half dozen—are the ones who were actually responsible. For those people, in terms of fairness issues, they might think it was fair to the rest of the community that after being told not to use those docks and not to go on them and not to go in the water, at the very least they could make some kind of statement about that and maybe some kind of contribution, as William said, of more money. I don't want to dismiss it completely and say that it was a community-wide issue and everyone should take part because this is a Cluster community, which may seem convenient for everyone, not convenient for everyone, but convenient for most people, but unfair to those people who chose not to go down to the docks. I would like to hear what people have to say to that.

MIKE: It is ridiculous for people who weren't involved to have to pay for it. Why should I have to pay for something that I had nothing to do with—the sinking of the dock?

LEE: You weren't on the retreat. So you won't have to pay.

SEAN (T): But he is saying what if he were?

JOHN: This proposal doesn't make sense. Even you people who didn't go are responsible. The whole school should be responsible. You kids who didn't go could have been there to prevent something like this. Everybody is responsible.

KOHLBERG: I guess people are saying that the whole community ought to pay for it, that everybody ought to chip in; some people are saying that. What I would like to ask is last year, a year ago, there was a case where Monica's purse was stolen and the community decided that everybody ought to be responsible when the person who stole the money did not return it. So then everybody was going to be assessed a certain amount of money to pay Monica back. Now I wonder if people think that this is the same case as it was then.

Commentary

Rob makes a straightforward argument for the fairness of upholding agreements and holding individuals responsible for their actions. There were a number of students "who were actually on that raft and let it float away." Rob is both making clear the rationale for balancing communal with individual responsibility and wondering out loud if some of the support for communal responsibility is not more a matter of convenience than principle. It would be convenient, he suggests, for those who actually broke the agreement if their actions were covered over by everyone's taking responsibility for the loss. That, however, would be unfair, and Rob wants to be sure that their individual responsibility will not be lost in implementing this proposal.

Rob's statement is followed by a classic moral discussion interchange among four members. Mike, interpreting Rob at a lower-stage level, agrees that "it is ridiculous for people who weren't involved to have to pay for it." Lee points out that he was not on the retreat anyway, but Sean reminds him that the question of fairness stands in any case. John, though, responds directly to Mike and to Rob, stating more fully the rationale behind communal responsibility: everyone is responsible because as a member of a community everyone has the responsibility to prevent such deviations from occurring.

Kohlberg joins in not by directly addressing the issues raised by Rob, but by raising as Dora did in the adviser group the historical precedent for this case. Acting as group historian, he wonders "if people think that this is the same case as it was then." In the deleted portion of the transcript that follows, a student and a teacher, Rob, answer no. The student simply does not see a relationship between the two cases. Rob does, but worries that collective responsibility may be understood as incompatible with a sense of individual responsibility.

DORA (T): I agree with Rob [T]. Go back in history a bit. Last year, as soon as the group decided that in fact they were all going to cough up the money, people thought that was not fair, and someone volunteered to help the person who took the money to step forward and admit it. I think we are kind of treating this like a game and sweeping a few things under the rug. It isn't just that a few people decided to go on the water. There was more to it than that. There were a few rules broken.

RACHEL: Like what?

DORA (T): Here is my impression of what happened. I think that people went out and probably decided that it would be nice to get a little high [Many students boo.]. . . . And, in fact, I think kids have already admitted it; and then beyond that, it would be nice to be stoned on the raft. All I am saying is that we went on the retreat with an agreement, the idea of everybody, the whole community, including staff, paying equally for this; I agreed to buy, I am happy to help, but I think that some people are more responsible than other people.

SIMON: I don't want to drop that, getting high. There were a couple of teachers, and you can't tell me, because there were a couple of teachers who did know that there were students who were getting high. We were there to have a good time, and some people had too much of a good time. They went out on the raft, floated around on the raft, and lost it. All right, let them pay for it.

SEAN (T): How do you go about that? That is what we are doing.

SIMON: Think about it. Everybody is talking about the whole community paying for it, right? Is that going to have to be figured [where it's coming from]?

SEAN (T): We have to come up with a solution; we have to decide who is the one responsible here.

SIMON: A lot of people were getting high and a lot of people knew they were getting high. So I think that should just go by.

ELLEN (T): I did not know that kids were getting high. When I heard it yesterday, I was surprised. But I think that is another issue. I think we should take it up, but let's not mess it up with the issue right now of how we are going to pay.

EVAN: You shouldn't be disappointed that people got high. They conducted themselves in an orderly fashion, and you should not have been disappointed.

DORA (T): I brought the drugs up to support what Rob said and what William's groups proposed. I think some people are more responsible than others. The community should discuss it [drugs] after the retreat.

Commentary

Dora raises the issue of smoking marijuana to explain why those individuals should assume a primary responsibility; but as soon as she mentions getting "a little high," the meeting erupts in a roar of boos. It is as if it were an improper fact to mention—though no one denies its having taken place. The two students to respond—Simon and Evan—both confirm the smoking, but believe it should not be of grave concern. Simon thinks that retreats are for having a good time, and if the staff did not make a fuss on the retreat, why start now? Evan believes that as long as those who smoked "conducted themselves in an orderly fashion," teacher expectations (the lost dock notwithstanding) were not disappointed. Ellen believes that the drug violation will have to be dealt with, but urges that within the confines of this meeting, the discussion continue to focus on the main issue of who is responsible for paying for the lost dock.

Real Vote

CHAIR: Real vote.

SEAN (T): We have a two-part proposal. First, that the community cough up the $350 to pay him back for the dock. Second, that those who were on the docks take more responsibility and organize the effort to raise the money.

CHAIR: All in favor? All opposed? In favor carry it.

Commentary and Overview:

The meeting ends with a majority (we do not have the exact count) voting in favor of the community taking responsibility for paying for the docks and the individuals who were on the dock taking special responsibility to organize the effort to raise the money involved.

In making sense of and evaluating the whole of this community meeting, we need to consider the following:

1. the procedural flow of the meeting,
2. the quality of moral discussion, and
3. the effectiveness of the just community stress on communal responsibility.

Procedure: There are two procedural flaws in this meeting: a proposal is made but not followed by a call for a straw vote, and Sean is a bit overzealous in helping the chair, who is his advisee, run the meeting. Yet, on the whole, we would judge this meeting to have flowed smoothly and the procedure to have facilitated raising the issue of responsibility, discussing the issue, and coming to a communal decision about it.

Quality of moral discussion: There are, we would judge, ways in which the discussion of the dock issue meets the criteria of a "good moral discussion" and ways in which it does not. On the positive side: there is a genuinely moral issue (responsibility) for discussion; there are voices on both sides of the issue; there are reasons offered in favor of both sides; there is an active interchange or give and take between sides; there is probing, mostly by Sean, of the reasoning on both sides; and there is a final resolution which integrated concerns from both sides (those favoring communal and those favoring individual responsibility).

On the negative side, although there is at points, substantive moral discussion between students, too much of the substantive discussion takes place between the staff.

Effectiveness: On the positive side, the staff's planning for the meeting, the adviser group meetings which preceded this meeting, and the moral discussion with staff advocacy at this meeting did lead to a final resolution that reflected not only a strong communal consciousness, but also a fairness concern that the individuals involved in losing the dock not get away without taking some responsibility for their actions. At the heart of the just community approach is the concern that the group view itself as a collective moral agent. Kohlberg and others were successful as advocates in raising that awareness. On the negative side, the emphasis on collective responsibility threatened to become in the eyes of many a collective "coverup." Fortunately, from our perspective, Rob picked up on that negative side effect. Without undoing the positive aspects of the communal responsibility proposal, he was adamant that the individuals involved not get away without making concrete amends to the community. Thus we view the final proposal adopted as being more evenly balanced than was the initial proposal made by Sean.

Aftermath

On the following Monday another short community meeting was held. It was decided that the individuals involved in losing the dock should identify themselves to the community. A roll call was taken and twelve students admitted to having been involved. They were assigned the responsibility of planning a fund-raising event to gather the money for the dock.

THE DISCIPLINE COMMITTEE

The D.C. had three functions: adjudicating fair punishments, mediating disputes between individuals in the community, and counseling students with disciplinary problems. The first of these functions was the primary one, as the name Discipline Committee suggests. The process of adjudicating fair punishments involved settling on the facts of the case, relating the case to a particular Cluster rule and stipulated punishment, and deciding on a particular punishment once all arguments had been heard.

As we noted, each Cluster community meeting began with a report from the Discipline Committee. The D.C. was made up of six students, one from each advisory group, and two faculty members. Membership on the D.C. was voluntary and rotated every quarter. Meetings were held on Wednesdays during the sixth period and could extend into the seventh period. Because class schedules often created conflicts when meetings ran for two periods, one alternate was chosen in each adviser group and faculty members frequently substituted for each other.

While most of the cases that came before the D.C. concerned rule violations, occasionally students and faculty members brought cases of interpersonal conflicts to the D.C. for mediation and sometimes arbitration. In this role, the D.C. members acted more as facilitators than jurors as they attempted to help the disputing parties reach some fair and satisfying agreement. If the conflicting parties were unable to reach such an agreement, then the D.C. would, as a last resort, arbitrate. The counseling function of the D.C. was most salient in those cases in which a student was perilously close to being expelled. Although the D.C. members had a responsibility to enforce the rules of the school, they also had a responsibility to help rule breakers live up to those rules. In this sense the D.C. assumed direct responsibility for the rehabilitation of the rule breakers, a responsibility that in our legal system belongs to the penal authorities, not to the court.

The D.C. is a somewhat more controversial institution than the community meeting because it violates our conventional ways of thinking about issues of student privacy, peer group loyalties, and responsibility. Generally, high school administrators and adjustment counselors handle disciplinary cases behind closed doors to avoid embarrassing the students. To understand why in Cluster School disciplinary decisions were made in public and with student participation we must return to Durkheim. As we have seen, he would have us think of discipline as "the morality of the classroom as a small society." Morality for Durkheim is by definition a public, social institution. The rules of the classroom are analogous to the laws of society. When the students break the rules, the morality of the school society is threatened. The restoration of the public morality requires a public event or ritual which expresses disapproval and renewed respect for the community's rules.

The public expression of disapproval should be seen not as subjecting students to a verbal "stoning" but as a means of showing them that members of the community care for them. D.C. members were rotated in part to prevent it from becoming a group of self-righteous students who never broke the rules themselves and who scolded those who did. Since many students on the Cluster D.C. had broken the very same rules they were asked to enforce, more often than not they identified with the students before them and expressed their interest in helping them out. Helping out meant two things: supporting students so that they could better acknowledge and live up to the expectations of the community, and letting students know that they were not alone, that they belonged to a caring community.

Background to the Discipline Committee Meeting

This meeting took place in April during Cluster's first year. Margie's adviser reported her to the D.C. for having missed school (hooked) for eleven consecutive days. After considerable prodding from her Cluster adviser, she consented to come to school in order to go to the D.C. meeting. According to Cluster rules, she was liable for expulsion, although, since this was her first appearance before the D.C., no one expected this to happen.

The ideal D.C. meeting has seven parts. First, there is a presentation of the facts about the case. Second, the accused student is asked to explain why he or she broke the rule(s). Third, some expression of a desire to remain in Cluster is sought. Fourth, admonishment is given to abide by the school rules in the future. Fifth, help for the students to live up to these expectations is offered. Sixth, a probation or a specific penalty is discussed and voted upon. Finally, if the D.C. does decide to punish a student, that student is given an opportunity to discuss the fairness of the punishment and to appeal it at the community meeting.

Discipline Committee Meeting

(After a summary of the facts of the case)
CHAIR: Margie, did you come to the community meeting when we made the hook rule?
MARGIE: No.

CHAIR: Well, this is the rule. [Reads the rule and punishments.] We called you to come yesterday and you didn't come. Why not? You didn't feel like it?

MARGIE: I was afraid. The more days I missed, the harder it was to come in.

DON: I can see how you feel and I don't think it's unreasonable. First of all, you should have some impression of what we are. We have set rules, but they are not set, no excuses or no leeway.

JANE: In other words, we can make compromises, we don't go strictly by the book.

HARRY: Margie, why haven't you been coming to school?

MARGIE: I don't know.

DON: If you didn't come here you would be pretty much of a mess at Latin [Cambridge Rindge and Latin School, the parent high school], because first of all, they are not going to try to understand you like we are here. You are just another hook to throw around.

JULIE: If you are absent one day, come back the next. . . . I don't think that anyone is going to ask any questions. If you come back in two weeks they might ask questions.

HARRY: I know how you must have felt when you stayed out all this time. It's like when you miss a train and you miss your stop, and you want to go around again, but every time you miss it, you are a step further away. So to get off it as fast as you can is the best thing.

JULIE: I think we should give you another chance: two more hooks and you are up for expulsion.

(There are nods of approval.)

CHAIR: Let's vote. All in favor? Opposed? Margie, you get two hooks. Does this seem fair to you?

MARGIE: Yes, I'm going to get in here.

Commentary

These excerpts from the D.C. transcript illustrate most of the parts of an ideal meeting. Unfortunately, Margie remained virtually silent throughout the meeting and never really offered any excuse for her behavior or gave any verbal indication that she was sorry or was really intent upon amending her ways. The students on the D.C. seemed to understand why she felt uncomfortable and went out of their way to reassure her that they would be understanding. They wanted her to know that Cluster was not like the regular high school and that she need not fear Cluster. Unfortunately, the D.C. members were so intent upon alleviating her fears that they did not clearly state their disapproval or press her to say anything to indicate her own willingness to abide by the rules in the future.

The purpose of the D.C. is to bring students who break rules into a conversation so that they can understand more adequately why their behavior presents a problem for the community and can feel the support of members of the community who genuinely want them to remain a part of the group. Margie was an isolated, lonely adolescent, who told her faculty adviser she found it hard to believe that anyone in school *really* knew her, let alone cared for her. Perhaps the most the D.C. could do for her was to convince her that she was not alone with her problems.

The meeting concluded with a vote in Margie's presence. Kohlberg strongly opposed secret ballots or closed sessions for two reasons. First, he felt that students should learn to stand up for their opinions in public and not be intimidated by others. Second, he thought it was important for the sense of openness and honesty in the Cluster community that everyone be able to understand the relationship between the outcome of a meeting and the discussion that had taken place. Although public voting may confront the students with a dilemma between following their consciences and maintaining their relationships, facing and resolving this dilemma can help them as individuals and as members of a community. After all, true relationships require honesty and moral conviction.

No one volunteered in the context of this meeting to help Margie catch up with the classes she missed or to accompany her to school for the rest of the year. Such offers became more frequent by the end of the first year, particularly when students were much closer to being expelled. This willingness to take responsibility for a member of the community is an extension of the principle of collective responsibility we discussed earlier. The decision in this case, to allow Margie two more cuts seemed adequate to the members of the D.C., who were satisfied that Margie had come to appreciate Cluster better and was determined not to hook in the future.

CONCLUSION

Our introduction to the just community approach is now complete. We have sketched the evolution of the approach from Kohlberg's developmental research through the first year of Cluster School. In this chapter we have described Cluster's major institutions: the community meeting, the adviser group, and the D.C. They provided the organizational framework for all the just community programs that followed. In presenting these institutions we have tried to convey something of their "feel" by excerpting from actual meeting transcripts. In a sense, the just community approach "lives" in meetings like the ones we selected. The meetings do not provide textbook-perfect exemplars of an approach derived from theory and applied to a specific setting. Rather, the theory of the intervention is derived in part by reflecting on the meetings themselves and learning from them how just communities are formed and developed.

4

Assessing the
Moral Culture of Schools

In the first three chapters of this book we have discussed the theoretical principles, the institutions, and the practices that make up the just community approach. We explained that the major goal of this approach may best be conceptualized as promoting a highly developed moral culture. Until now we have not defined the term "moral culture" in any rigorous way, but we have used it to refer to the quality of community life in the schools we have studied. Here we will investigate the concept of moral culture more closely to clarify how it figured into the just community intervention as well as to articulate the way in which we evaluate the development of moral culture in the schools.

MORAL ATMOSPHERE RESEARCH

In the 1970s Scharf (1973), Reimer (1977), Wasserman (1977), and Jennings (1979) postulated a relationship between institutional climate or moral atmosphere and individual moral development. In their view, moral atmosphere influenced moral development insofar as it provided certain conditions for moral growth. While the number and description of conditions varied somewhat according to the author, they all agreed that the conditions included those present in good moral discussions and others specifically related to democracy and community.

The Moral Atmosphere of the Prison

Scharf's (1973) research on the creation of a just community in a prison was the first effort to study the social atmosphere of an institution from the perspective of Kohlberg's moral developmental theory. He postulated that prisons operated according to justice structures and treatment ideologies which could be classified according to Kohlberg's stages of moral judgment.

Scharf focused on the ways in which the institutional framework determined how decisions were made and conflicts resolved. He showed that although inmates tended to perceive the prison culture according to their own stage of socio-moral reasoning, their judgments of the fairness of various aspects of their institution indicated an interaction between individual stage and institutional justice type: the lower the justice type, the greater the likelihood of inmate dissatisfaction, especially if the inmate's stage of moral reasoning is high, relative to the parallel type of the institution.

Scharf hypothesized that there would be an interaction between inmates' stages of moral judgment and how they would judge a particular justice structure and treatment ideology. He found this was the case. Inmates with a stage of moral judgment higher than the "stage" of an institution's justice structure or treatment ideology tended to reject it as unjust; while inmates with a lower or parallel stage of moral judgment tended to accept it as just.

Scharf's research helps to explain why little moral development occurs in most prisons. Because most inmates, reasoning between stages 2 and 2–3, generally do not find life in the stage 1 and 2 traditional, custodial prison to be particularly fair or morally uplifting, they experience no impetus for moral development. For example, Scharf documents that these inmates were systematically excluded from making moral decisions or even discussing matters that affected their common lives and that their treatment by guards was often harsh and demeaning. The inmate culture was no better—as inmates often abused each other and formed relationships more for mutual protection and instrumental gain than for friendship.

The Moral Atmosphere of the Kibbutz

The second major study of the moral atmosphere of an institution was undertaken by Reimer (1977), who analyzed the effect of kibbutz living on the moral judgments of adolescents. Reimer found that city-born adolescents upon entering the kibbutz displayed less developed reasoning than their counterparts born on the kibbutz. After two years on the kibbutz the city-born youths developed such that there were no statistically significant differences between the two groups.

Reimer attempted to explain the moral development he found in terms of the stimulating effect of the kibbutz environment. His account of the impact of the environment stressed the influence that a concentration of students at a given moral stage can have in determining a moral atmosphere. He did not differentiate the stage characteristics of the population from the stage of the moral culture, as we will do. Reimer's research complemented Scharf's in that while Scharf demonstrated how a relatively low stage environment could stunt development, he showed how a relatively high stage environment could foster it.

The Conditions for Moral Growth in the School and the Youth Home

A somewhat different approach to moral atmosphere was taken by Wasserman (1977) and Jennings (Jennings and Kohlberg 1983) in evaluating the effects of just community programs. In her dissertation research, which focused on the first two years of Cluster School, Wasserman analyzed community meeting transcripts to determine the extent to which these meetings provided conditions for moral growth. The conditions which Wasserman thought relevant were (a) a focus of meeting agenda and meeting discussion on moral concerns, (b) the existence of moral conflict (defined in terms of a relative balance of pro and con statements on a particular proposal), (c) the presence of relatively high stage reasoning (defined in terms of the incidence of statements expressing stage 3 and 4 moral concerns), (d) the opportunity for role taking (defined in terms of the variety of points of view offered in a meeting), and (e) the "student centeredness" of the discussion (defined in terms of the ratio of staff to student statements in the meeting). Wasserman assumed that if the conditions for moral growth increased from Cluster's first to second year, greater individual moral development would occur. Unfortunately, she could not test this assumption because no stage change data was collected during Cluster's first year. However, she did find evidence for moral atmosphere development by noting that the conditions for moral growth improved.

In his study, Jennings compared a group home for delinquents that operated on the just community approach with group homes operating on the behavior modification and transactional analysis approaches. He assessed the conditions for moral growth in each program by rating resident responses to an ethnographic moral interview about the following: the amount of moral discussion and dialogue, the amount of resident power and responsibility for making rules and policies, the degree to which rules and decisions were perceived as being fair, and the perception of self-change. As predicted, there were clear differences among these programs, with the just community home being the highest on all conditions, the transactional analysis home the next highest, and the behavior modification home the lowest.

A CLASSIFICATION SCHEME FOR MORAL ATMOSPHERE ANALYSES

This review of moral atmosphere studies indicates a common concern for identifying conditions for moral growth. Taken together, the following conditions were presumed to have the most influence on moral judgment and behavior:

1. open discussion with a focus on fairness and morality;
2. cognitive conflict stimulated by exposure to different points of view and higher-stage reasoning;
3. participation in rule making and the exercise of power and responsibility;
4. the development of community at a high stage.

These conditions make up the moral atmosphere of a school. The term "moral atmosphere" is a global one that involves a number of distinctive aspects of the school environment. We can begin to sort out these aspects by applying Taguiri's (1968) taxonomy of climate dimensions. Taguiri defines climate as "the broadest term for describing the environment of an institution." He divides climate into four dimensions—ecology, milieu, social system, and culture. Anderson (1982) demonstrates that these dimensions can be effectively utilized in classifying an extensive and variegated body of school climate literature. Within the ecological dimension, she groups variables having to do with the physical and material resources of the school, such as size, appearance, and facilities. The milieu of the school encompasses variables having to do with the aggregate characteristics of the staff, for example their salaries, stability, and educational levels, and the student body, for example their family backgrounds and achievement levels. The school's social system is made up of variables pertaining to its organizational structure and operating procedures, particularly the instructional program. The dimension of school culture includes variables relating to the norms, values, and meaning systems which members of the school share.

If we apply Taguiri's taxonomy to the previously cited research on the conditions for moral growth that make up the moral atmosphere of the school, we find that the conditions cut across several of these dimensions. For instance, all of the conditions for moral growth presuppose certain ecological factors, such as small size and frequent opportunities for face-to-face interaction. They also directly involve the social systems dimension. As social systems variables, they refer to the roles, rules, and procedures that define the practices of moral discussion, democratic governance, and community building.

The research methdology that we will outline in this chapter focuses on the cultural dimension of the moral atmosphere. This dimension may be thought of as embodying the conditions insofar as the conditions are valued as part of the normative structure of the environment. For example, we knew that democratic participation in rule making (a social systems variable) had become a cultural norm when students spontaneously groaned at a new staff member's suggestion to bypass the democratic process in order to resolve a sensitive issue and then explained how important democracy was to the identity of the school. Although all of the conditions may be related to the culture in this way, our analysis of culture will for the most part be limited to the fourth of the conditions, the development of a community at a high stage.

Moral Culture

Sociologists of education from Durkheim onward have pointed out that the school's culture tends to be a "hidden" or "unstudied" curriculum in the school. Because school staff focus on the formal curriculum of classroom instruction, the hidden cultural curriculum is not perceived or appears beyond staff direction or control. In spite of its elusiveness, sociologists such as Parsons (1968) and Jackson (1968) tell us the hidden curriculum is quite effective in shaping student attitudes and values.

In the just community approach there is the assumption that a positive school culture or, more specifically, a positive moral culture can over time develop. The word "culture" is derived from the Latin *cultura,* meaning to cultivate or to till the soil. Culture thus expresses a process of development or acculturation which takes into account both natural growth and conscious efforts to promote or enhance that growth by the one(s) doing the cultivating or tilling. It is useful to recover the root metaphorical meaning of culture in order to emphasize its dynamic and purposive nature. To promote culture we must understand how school societies grow or develop. Our approach to group development has much in common with the cognitive, structural approach to individual development in that we are focusing on an aspect of group life which has a cognitive basis, plays a crucial role in determining the functioning of the group as a coherent whole, and progresses through a sequence of hierarchically ordered stages and phases.

Given these considerations, we base our understanding of culture on Levine's definition: "Culture is a shared organization of ideas that includes the intellectual, moral, and aesthetic standards prevalent in a community and the meaning of communicative action" (1981:67).

A recurrent experience of ethnographers is that culture is a shared, supra-individual phenomenon and that it represents a consensus on a variety of meanings among members of an interacting community. Generally the concept of culture is used to refer to large social systems, such as societies or ethnic groups. Our use of this concept to refer to a specific social institution—the school—obviously is not meant to be as inclusive or as self-contained as a societal culture. As Minuchin and Shapiro (1981) noted, our attempts to create a specific kind of moral culture are limited by the influence of the wider societal culture. Although we readily acknowledge that the building of a school culture does not occur in a vacuum, we have based much of our intervention and research efforts on the hypothesis that school cultures have a powerful impact on adolescent development.

Before we develop our notion of the moral as distinguished from the nonmoral characteristics of a school culture, we must first relate the notion of culture to the proximate goal of our approach to schooling: the creation of just communities. By just community we mean a school culture, based on a particular conception of both community and justice. In the sociological literature "community" is often used to refer to a territorial unit. However, Tönnies, Weber, and their followers have used the term more specifically in making a contrast between two basic types of societal organizations: community and association. So well known has this contrast become that Tönnies' German terms *Gemeinschaft* and *Gesellschaft* are generally left untranslated when referring to these contrasting types. Unfortunately, when the *Gemeinschaft-Gesellschaft* polarity is introduced, it is often done in the context of comparing traditional, folk societies with modern, urban societies. In this comparison community is often viewed as somewhat of an anachronism. While the transition from *Gemeinschaft* to *Gesellschaft* society is of great historical significance, we will focus on the types as ways of classifying contemporary social organizations in terms of the nature of the interpersonal relationships supported by the organization of the group.

According to Tönnies, *Gemeinschaft* is made up of relationships valued as ends in themselves. In such a group the actions of individuals proceed from and express an underlying communal identification. On the other hand, *Gesellschaft* is made up of impersonal, atomistic, and mechanistic relationships, valued as a means to ends outside the relationships. In this type of group, individuals act on their own, as it were, without referring to a group's norms or values. Tönnies described the individualism of *Gesellschaft* as follows: "There are no actions . . . which manifest the will and the spirit of the unity even if performed by the individual; no actions, which, insofar as they are performed by the individual, take place on behalf of those united with them" (1957:65).

Since *Gemeinschaft* and *Gesellschaft* are ideal types, it is not possible to categorize unambiguously a society or an organization as one or the other. Secondary schools generally seem to be closer to *Gesellschaft* than *Gemeinschaft* insofar as students go to school willingly or with some coercion from family or the state in order to acquire those competencies believed to facilitate their future participation in work, familial, and political roles. Formal classroom relationships among students are often competitive, and teacher-student relationships are largely based on a system of exchanges (for example, grades and promotions are exchanged for class work and discipline). Nevertheless, schools do provide opportunities for *Gemeinschaft* to develop generally outside of the formal school curriculum, for example through extracurricular activities, lunch hall, and between-class breaks.

The just community approach goes further than the typical public school, which simply lets *Gemeinschaft* happen; the just community approach purposely fosters *Gemeinschaft* as the principal project of the school. We define community as a *Gemeinschaft* culture in which interpersonal and collective relationships are valued in themselves and given such priority that members are willing to make personal sacrifices for the sake of their common life. This definition of community stands in contrast to what we will call a pragmatic association in which the relationships linking members to each other and to the school are valued instrumentally in relation to individual goals and pursuits.

We can further specify what we mean by community by viewing the approach taken in Cluster. There the consultants and staff constantly called students' attention to the kind of school they wished to have. Typically they would ask students to decide whether Cluster should be "like a family," in which everybody cares for everybody else, or "like the street," in which everybody has to look out for himself or herself. Belonging to a community demands living up to norms of sharing, self-sacrifice, and collective responsibility. This was a radically new way of life for many students inclined to operate according to different norms, based on individual responsibility and self-protectiveness.

In the following pages we will present a method of assessing the extent to which schools like Cluster achieve a sense of community, by examining in some detail these related aspects of a school culture: the way the school is valued as an institution and the nature of its shared norms, specifically their content, strength, and moral adequacy. The conception of community provides the basis for our articulation of the structure of an ideal moral culture of the school. The focus of communal life is essentially moral insofar as members of a community make the quality of their relationships and common life a conscious preoccupation. On the other hand, in a pragmatic association socio-moral considerations are at the periphery of concern, as members of such organizations pursue personal goals and desires, cooperating with others for mutual advantage. Although pragmatic organizations are primarily oriented toward nonmoral ends, even the Hobbesean state has laws that protect members from each other's egoism and form the basis for a limited moral culture.

The Moral and Nonmoral Features of School Culture

In making a distinction between the moral and nonmoral we are following in the formalist tradition of moral philosophy from Kant to Rawls. Within that tradition the moral is defined in terms of categorical principles that regulate social interactions. These principles are universalizable prescriptions, supported by reasoned argument. This understanding of the moral domain makes it possible to distinguish the moral from other domains; for example, the prudential. Prudential concerns such as preparing for a job or college are important in any school culture. Later we will discuss another nonmoral feature of school culture —social conventions. Conventions regulate social interactions but lack the prescriptivity and universality of moral norms and values.

The distinction between the moral and the nonmoral domains of school culture is one not commonly made in the research literature on school climate (Anderson 1982; Epstein 1981). For example, Anderson lists the following as "culture variables": teacher commitment, peer norms for advancement and seeking help with studies, cooperative emphases, expectations for high achievement, emphasis on academics, rewards and praise, consensus on norms and values, and clear goals. Those variables having to do with academic achievement reflect a nonmoral, pragmatic cultural concern. A variable such as cooperative emphasis may be viewed as moral or nonmoral depending on whether cooperation is valued instrumentally, as a means to a particular learning objective, or intrinsically, as a reflection of mutual respect among persons. Similarly, a variable such as consensus on norms and values may be moral or nonmoral, depending on the nature of the norms and values being studied.

One reason why Kohlberg has been successful in his psychological research on moral judgment is that he has been able to define morality as a specific cognitive domain. Basing his definition of moral judgment on formalist criteria, he has limited the moral domain to universal, prescriptive judgments that resolve conflicts of claims among individuals. This understanding of morality is operationalized through the use of moral dilemmas that are relatively free of contextual peculiarities and probe questions directed specifically to elicit prescriptive reasoning. In the moral culture research we include obligations arising from group membership within our definition of morality. The question raised in moral atmosphere research is not "What should any moral agent do?" but "What should and would a member of this school do?" We are interested in shared expectations, how they were formed, how they are understood, and how they relate to real-life problems and behavior. In shifting our focus from the universal to the context-bound and from purely prescriptive reasoning to descriptive reasoning, as well, we have opened the purview of the moral domain to include norms and values vital to community life, such as care, responsibility, trust, participation.

The Data

We began research on the school's moral culture by collecting transcripts of community meetings and by administering an ethnographic interview. The primary question for the community meeting analysis was this: Did the moral culture of Cluster School develop over its first four years? In order to assess this, we first grouped the topics of meetings from Cluster's first four years according to a common issue or problem. We then selected four issues that were discussed each year and that involved moral concerns: stealing and property damage, class cutting, racial tensions, and alcohol and marijuana use. With guidance from the just community approach, students and staff attempted to deal with these issues by developing shared norms and values that reflected a sense of community. For example, they tried to respond to the problems of stealing and property loss by developing norms of trust and collective responsibility, to the attendance problem by developing a norm of participation, to racial tensions by developing a norm of integration, and to alcohol and marijuana use during school activities by developing norms of participation and respect for democratic authority. All meetings, used in this analysis, were audiotaped, transcribed, and reviewed by a participant-observer who kept notes during the meeting.

The focus of the community meeting analysis is on the group as a whole, on Cluster School as a social entity. But we can only learn about the collective expectations, norms, values, and community spirit that characterize the group through the perceptions of individuals. Therefore, it is necessary to carefully examine the statements made by individuals in a community meeting to determine what they may reveal about the group, or more specifically about the moral culture of the school.

Admittedly, generalizing from statements of individuals about a particular issue of group concern to a shared or collective moral culture is a formidable task. Individual perceptions are likely to offer only pieces of the whole, colored by individual differences of various kinds, especially by the moral stage, length of experience in the school, and role within the school (e.g., leader, rule follower, isolate). Given individual differences among group members' statements, we have to look for what they have in common. As all ethnographers in search of a shared cultural reality do, we listen to individual reports, factor out the individuality of the report, and come up with a description of what exists across subjects.

While community meetings are an important source for perceptions of a moral culture, they are limited. First of all, not everyone speaks in a community meeting: generally we found no more than one-half of those present spoke. Second, many of the statements are elliptic, making interpretation difficult. Third, there is no guarantee that the students who speak represent the population. It is conceivable, for instance, that they are a vocal minority. In order to respond to these limitations, we supplemented our community meeting analysis by reviewing transcripts of other meetings (adviser group, D.C., and faculty meetings) and by interviewing a representative sample of approximately twenty students each spring with the ethnographic moral atmosphere interview. The ethnographic interview allowed us to "fill out" the community meeting analysis and to compare data from two different sources to check on the validity of our assessment.

The ethnographic interview was modeled after those developed by Scharf and Reimer and had students report on their perceptions of disciplinary practices, peer and student-teacher relationships, and the sense of community and democracy in the school. During the first year of our research project the interview provided much needed positive feedback that showed that Cluster students understood how their democratic institutions functioned and judged them to be fair. The interview also served to supplement our analysis of community meeting transcripts as we had hoped it would. Finally, while structured primarily to gather data about the culture of the school, it also revealed a great deal about the ideals of the interviewee with regard to fairness, democracy, community, and social order in the school. In chapter 9 we will discuss how Cluster students' reasoning about these ideals (or, as we call them, "political values") developed after being in the school a year.

After we developed our taxonomy for categorizing the various dimensions of moral culture from the community meeting analysis, we applied this analysis to the ethnographic interviews with mixed results. The ethnographic interviews were designed to be as open-ended as possible and obviously were not structured to probe into the specific categories we later developed out of the community meeting analysis. Because of the open-ended nature of the interviews, it was difficult to make comparisons among schools, which was an important part of our research design. Our answer to the limitations of the ethnographic interview was to devise a more standardized school dilemmas interview. This interview built on the ethnographic interview and community meeting analysis in that the dilemmas we constructed were based on actual dilemmas students in different schools were experiencing. We will describe this interview and the results we obtained from it in chapter 9, but now let us return to our original research on the community meeting data.

AN ILLUSTRATION OF
THE MORAL CULTURE CATEGORIES

In order to provide examples for the categories we employ in our analysis of moral culture and to illustrate the empirical method through which we developed them, we will describe the series of community meeting discussions on the issue of stealing and property damage. During these meetings shared norms and values concerning respect for property, trust, and collective responsibility were established and upheld.

The Third-Year Collective Restitution Discussions

Recall that the community meeting discussed in the previous chapter was held at the end of Cluster's third year and focused on the loss of a dock during a Cluster retreat. The students generally agreed with a proposal that all should contribute to some extent toward the cost of restoring the dock. Let us consider three student statements. The first two report adviser group support for the proposal:

BEV: People said this is our community—we went on this trip together and we should pay for it as a community.

KARL: We felt it was just an accident that happened, and the community should share responsibility for replacing it.

LEE: I think the whole community is responsible because the community is a community and they are responsible for each other, and a small group can't do it.

All of these statements indicate that these students accept responsibility for helping to defray the cost of the dock. They speak not just as individuals willing to pitch in to resolve a problem, but also as members of a community which obliges its members to care for one another. Their statements imply the existence of a norm of collective restitution that is somewhat shared and established in Cluster. They feel this norm should be applied in this case. Furthermore, the obligation to accept collective *responsibility* for restitution follows from a shared understanding of the communal nature of the group; as Lee put it, "because the community is a community."

The status of this norm of collective restitution and of the valuing of community underlying it can best be understood in the context of their developmental history and the developmental history of related norms and values. We will trace this developmental history by selecting one meeting from Cluster's first and second years.

The First Year: Stealing Rule

During the first semester of Cluster there were several incidents of students stealing from each other and from a volunteer teacher.[1] Stealing was a frequent occurrence in the larger school, and the Cluster students at that time were not particularly perturbed by these incidents. As one student, Terry, said in a D.C. discussion about stealing: "School isn't a

---

1. This discussion is a revised and substantially elaborated version of an earlier article by Power and Reimer (1978).

place for trusting stuff, even at Cluster. Community or not, if you want something, you'll take it. It goes to show you can't be too friendly."

When the staff raised the problem of stealing at the weekly community meeting, the students realized something had to be done and proposed the school adopt a rule that those caught stealing should be punished. The staff objected. Such a rule would address only the individuals involved in stealing and would ignore why the stealing had been occurring. At the meeting Kohlberg said: "Maybe someone can explain why the stealing has been going on. Don't people think it is wrong and a violation of the community?" Student reaction was subdued. One responded to his concern by saying, "I don't think you should worry about that. The fact is that it happened. To worry about why it happened isn't worth it." Yet Kohlberg persisted: "I think ripping off is not an individual business; it is a community business. It is not a discipline issue as much as some feeling by the community that people have to have some level of trust which is inconsistent with anybody ripping off from anybody else in the community."

Most of the students wanted to have a practical deterrent against stealing but felt that the staff was overreacting. "Just because a few things are stolen, you don't have to cry about it." It seemed unreasonable to expect trust in school. "There are people you can't trust; you can't do that [trust] at home let alone in the Cluster School." Even though students felt that trusting others was unrealistic, they knew that stealing was wrong: "I know lots of people who steal . . . you really feel cautious and I feel really bad about that." But they only appealed to individual conscience. What was lacking in their remarks was a concern that everyone in the school should reach a common agreement on the obligations which they should have as members of a community. Only one student saw the point: "We are not just a group of individuals. . . . If this is supposed to be a community I think that we have to work together." The others believed making a rule against stealing was the best that could be done. They voted for the rule that students caught stealing would be reported to their parents and that they would have to make restitution and offer a public apology. This vote ended the meeting; but the problem of stealing persisted. Discussions about the necessity for building trust and mutual care continued through the first year.

The Second Year: Origins of Collective Restitution

Cluster began its second year optimistically. However, in October nine dollars were taken during a Cluster class from the purse of a student, Monica, when she went to the blackboard. It became clear to all that Cluster's rule about stealing was of little help in this case, since no one came forward to admit to it or to report the thief. This time student reaction to theft was mixed. Some students, particularly a few who had just joined the school, reacted the way most students had the year before —that stealing was inevitable and Monica was paying the price of carelessness. Second-year students were clearly surprised and disappointed that stealing had occurred in their "community." They felt that this incident precipitated a crisis of trust in the school and were frustrated that they could not identify the thief. The community meeting convened to discuss this incident began with some students reporting that their adviser group meetings had been discouraging. "We said it really wasn't a community, that there were people in it we could not really trust." Other students, in spite of their frustration, expressed the determination to "really make a community out of this school." One group of students came to the meeting with the proposal advocated in the staff meeting by Kohlberg and in their adviser group meeting by their adviser, Elsa Wasserman, that each member of the school should chip in fifteen cents to make up for the nine dollars stolen from Monica's purse. Phyllis, a member of this adviser group, offered an elaborated rationale for reimbursing the stolen money. "It's everyone's fault that she don't have no money. It was stolen because people just don't care about the community. [They think] they are all individuals and don't have to be included in the community. [However], everybody should care that she got her money stolen [and therefore] we decided to give her money back to her."

Not everyone agreed with the proposal. Simon was worried that if they adopted the proposal "then anyone can say I lost ten dollars." Jill wanted to know "how do you know whether to believe someone who says their money has been stolen?" Simon and Jill both thought the fault lay not with the community, but with the victim for having left her pocketbook unattended. As Jill put it, "She gives you a chance to steal it; if you had it in your arms, wouldn't you be thinking about stealing it?" In response, Phyllis reiterated her point. She picked up on the claims of lack of trust, asserting that "this school is supposed to be a community and we are supposed to be able to trust everyone else in the community." She did not deny that mistrust existed, but refused to take it as a sign that Cluster could not be a community. Rather, she began with the assumption that Cluster ought to be a community and its members ought to trust one another. If people could not be trusted, it was the group's failure and they would have to assume responsibility for it.

Simon continued to object to the collective restitution proposal by offering an analogy of Cluster School to a bank. He said: "That someone stole the money is pretty bad, but to me, that I have to pay because she lost her money is like someone robbing a bank and the bank owner comes to my door and asks me to pay a couple of bucks because they lost their money. That's crazy!"

Several students rejected this analogy by arguing that Cluster was a community, not a bank. One, Albert, asked Simon to define what he thought community meant. Simon replied, "My definition of community is that people can help one another right there. But I didn't say nothing about giving money out." This notion of community and helping brought him into further conflict. Albert responded with a very different conception of community. "The money was lost or stolen or whatever and it's not really to return the money, it is to help someone in the community, altogether. I think that would be the first real community thing that we have ever done, really. It doesn't concern the money, it concerns community action."

Peggy followed up Albert's remarks with a direct rebuke. "I think if Simon feels so strongly about [giving] his fifteen cents to Monica that he shouldn't belong in this community. I am sure if it was his money that he would feel the other way around. He wouldn't want nine dollars taken from him, he would be crying."

Having agreed that Monica should not be held responsible for the theft because she was careless and that the community should show some responsibility for getting Monica's money back, Cluster members shifted to the question of whether taking collective responsibility for restituting the money meant letting the thief off the hook. As one student put it, "That person who is ripping her money off is getting away clean. We ought to find out who did it; instead of paying fifty cents or twenty-five cents or fifteen cents, find out who did it." That argument, while it led to faculty and student exhortations that those who knew the thief ought to put pressure on him or her to return the money, did not convince members to give up on the idea of collective restitution. Thus they adopted a compromise: "If the money is not returned anonymously by a certain date, everyone will be assessed fifteen cents." The combined proposal was accepted in the voting.

When the dock incident occurred in Cluster's third year, Phyllis and others had already graduated, but the norms they had advocated, trust, care, and collective responsibility, survived. In that year students' statements revealed a sense of belonging to a community of care and shared responsibility. The problem before the community was not whether the norms of care and collective responsibility ought to be adopted by the community but how to apply these norms to the particular problem at hand, which also required the taking into account of individual responsibility. By contrast, in the first year there were no shared norms or shared valuing of community.

THE METHOD FOR ANALYZING COMMUNITY MEETINGS

The basic units of the moral culture analysis, the collective norm and institutional value, were derived from the moral judgment, the unit of analysis in the Standard Moral Judgment Scoring Manual (Colby, Kohlberg et al, 1987). The moral judgment is a discrete moral argument composed of two parts: the norm, which prescribes a particular value (e.g., trust, care, and respect for property), and an element, which supplies a terminal value justifying upholding the norm (e.g., group harmony or individual welfare). Sociologists (e.g., Blake and Davis 1964) distinguish norms and values. They define a norm as the expectation for a concrete action in a specified set of circumstances. They use the term "value" to refer to the intentional or motivational aspect of the expectation. In the standard manual and in the moral culture analysis this distinction between norm and value is not made; the norm refers to a complex of specific behavioral expectations that share a common value. For example, the norm of trust may behaviorally be broken down to mean: one should be able to share one's private possessions with others; one should not violate private possessions which have been left unguarded; and one should safeguard the possessions that others have left unguarded. Taken separately or together, these behavioral norms lack an important motivational or valuing component that gives them meaning. Trust entails a concern for a relatedness to others that is manifested in but goes beyond these specific behavioral norms.

The element completes a moral judgment by providing it with a rationale that both justifies the norm and grounds its significance. Colby, Kohlberg et al. (1987) group the elements into categories, called orientations, which relate to the basic types of arguments used in moral philosophy: normative order, ethical egoism, utilitarianism, perfectionism, and fairness. The specific elements further elaborate differences found within an orientation. For example, within the fairness orientation one element relates to merit and another to equality. In the analysis of moral culture we are particularly interested to see if certain elements, particularly those related to a concern for community, become more prevalent in community meeting statements and interviews as a result of the just community experience. As a result, we focused on the group related elements in the standard scoring manual and elaborated a scoring system specifically for them.

The two major units in this analysis, the collective norm and the element of institutional value, correspond to two of Durkheim's goals of moral education: discipline and attachment to the group. For Durkheim, moral education involves practices designed to foster respect for group norms and to build a strong sense of belonging to the group. In the language of moral philosophy, Durkheim attempts to join the "right" and "the good" in a conception of collective life in which the limitations imposed on one's choices by the demands of morality could be willingly accepted as necessary for participating in a desirable and fulfilling social existence: "Morality appears to us under a double aspect: on the one hand, as imperative law, which demands complete obedience of us; on the other hand, as a splendid ideal, to which we spontaneously aspire" (1925/1973:96).

Durkheim's third goal of moral education, autonomy, corresponds most closely to our analysis of the stage of norms and elements. For him, autonomy entails the willingness to do one's moral duty, not out of any external constraint but because reason commands it. Fostering the element of rational autonomy in children requires a moral education that explains the reasons behind social obligations, not a moral education that preaches or indoctrinates. Without attention to this third goal of

Table 4.1.
Levels of Institutional Valuing

---

0. *Rejection:* The school is not valued.
1. *Instrumental Extrinsic:* The school is valued as an institution that helps individuals to meet their own needs.
2. *Enthusiastic Identification:* The school is valued intrinsically at special moments when members feel an intense sense of identification with the school, for example when a team wins an important game.
3. *Spontaneous Community:* The school is valued as the kind of place in which members feel a sense of closeness to others and an inner motivation to help them and to serve the community as a whole.
4. *Normative Community:* The school as a community is valued for its own sake. Community can obligate its members in special ways, and members can expect others to uphold group norms and responsibilities.

---

moral education, the collectivist model with its stress on discipline and solidarity with the group would be nothing more than a powerful means of inducing conformity and heteronomy. Numerous cases of the immoral use of the collectivist model by various sects and totalitarian governments make the inclusion of an index which assesses group norms and values according to explicit criteria for moral rationality crucial. Within our methodology Durkheim's element of moral rationality is evaluated by applying Kohlberg's scheme of moral stages to the collective norm and institutional value.

The Valuing of the School as an Institution

In assessing the way students value the school we ask two questions: first, to what extent do students value the school intrinsically, as a community (the level of institutional valuing); and second, at what stage are meanings that students give to the community in considering it as a terminal value (the stage community)?

The Levels of Institutional Valuing

We describe levels of institutional valuing in table 4.1. The lowest level on this scale, level 0, represents a failure to value the school either instrumentally or intrinsically. At the next level the school is valued instrumentally for what it can contribute to students' education in the limited sense of preparing them for a desirable college or job or in a more full sense of promoting their intellectual, moral, and personal development. At level 2 the school is valued intrinsically but only for a short time, during which there is usually an intense sense of unity and school spirit. Often this second level is achieved at high points in a football or basketball season. The next two levels refer to a more intrinsic and lasting sense of community valuing. At level 3, the community is valued for the friendships and group spirit that develop spontaneously through common activities and everyday interactions. At level 4 the building of community is regarded as an obligation that is made more specific through particular norms, supportive and expressive of community. The Cluster staff appealed to this level in the first stealing meeting when they asked the students to consider the impact that stealing has on the sense of community in school. The students valued the school at level 1 and did not pick up on the faculty's suggestion. By the second year their valuing had developed to level 4.

The Stage of Community

The second dimension of institutional valuing that we assess is the stage of the shared understanding of community. We describe the stages of community in table 4.2. In the first-year stealing meeting, insofar as there was any concern for community, it was a stage 2 concern that members "get along." In the second year there was a concern for maintaining a relationship of trust and care. We see this preliminary valuing of the community as a caring, trusting group as stage 3. In the third year of the school there was a further development in the way in which community was valued with the emergence of the conflict between individual and collective responsibility. In the dock meeting students and staff worked out a stage 4 understanding of the contractual nature of community, which achieved a new balance between individual and collective responsibility.

The Relationship Between Institutional Valuing and the Norms

Although we distinguish between norms and elements of institutional valuing, they are interrelated. This may be seen in the stealing meetings

Table 4.2.
Stages of the Sense of Community Valuing

STAGE 2

There is no clear sense of community apart from exchanges among group members. Community denotes a collection of individuals who do favors for each other and rely on each other for protection. Community is valued insofar as it meets the concrete needs of its members.

EXAMPLE: The community is like a "bank." Members meet to exchange favors, but you cannot take more than you give.

STAGE 3

The sense of community refers to a set of relationships and sharings among group members. The group is valued for the friendliness of its members. The value of the group is equated with the value of its collective normative expectations.

EXAMPLES: 1) The community is a family in which members care for each other; 2) The community is honorable because it helps others.

STAGE 4

The community is explicitly valued as an entity distinct from the relationships among its members. Membership in the community is understood in terms of entering into a social contract to respect the norms and ideals of the group. The community is perceived as an organic whole composed of interrelated systems that carry on the functioning of the group.

EXAMPLE: Stealing affects "the community more than the individual because that is what we are. We are not just a group of individuals."

by considering the norm of trust. As the faculty stated in the first meeting, trust was necessary in an instrumental sense if any progress were to be made toward community. By the second meeting trust clearly had more than an instrumental meaning: it had become a sign of real community. The lack of trust that some students felt after the stealing incident indicated a breakdown of community and required some further symbolic act, such as collective restitution, to restore it. The very fact that students took the norm of trust so seriously in the second year is in itself revealing. In the first year they approached the problem of theft by making a rule that would protect their individual property rights. This is a response consistent with an extrinsic level of institutional valuing, typical of a *Gesellschaft* type of organization in which individual interests are paramount. In the second year students dealt with stealing very differently by referring to shared norms of trust, care, and collective responsibility, which specify the relations of a *Gemeinschaft* organization.

Later in this chapter we shall elaborate these points in far greater detail by describing four different types of norms—norms of community, fairness, procedural justice, and social order—which relate in an important way to the way in which the institution is valued. Because there is a close correspondence between norms and the sense of institutional valuing, we have chosen to focus on the norms. This focus provides a finely tuned picture of group development that includes at least implicitly the dimension of institutional valuing. As a consequence of this focus on norms, we will not report scores for institutional valuing in this chapter or the next unless there is some discrepancy between those scores and the ones we would give for the norms.

The Collective Norm

The collective norm as norm defines what is expected from group members *qua* group members, in their attitudes (e.g., caring about others) and in their actions (e.g., not stealing from others). We assess four dimensions of collective norms: their *degree* of collectiveness, their *content,* their *phase* of commitment, and their *stage.* These dimensions correspond to the following questions: To what extent is a group regulated by shared norms? What is the content of these expectations? How committed are members of a group to seeing that the norms are upheld? What shared meaning do the norms have?

The Degree of Collectivness

The degrees of collectiveness are listed in table 4.3. Each one is followed by a brief definition and evaluation according to three criteria, used for the assessment of the degree of collectiveness: affiliative constituency, speaker perspective, and prescriptivity. In the original moral culture scoring system, norms were classified as either individual or collective. Later the more elaborated scale was developed with individual and collective norms at each pole.

In this chapter we will focus on the distinction between individual and collective norms, and in chapter 9 we will describe the intermediate

Table 4.3.
The Degrees of the Collectiveness of Norms

Individual-Based Norms or Descriptions of Lack of Collective Norm

1. I—Rejection:	No one can make a rule or agreement in this school which would be followed or taken seriously. No group constituency. I as an individual. Descriptive.
2. I—Conscience:	An action in accordance with the norm should not be expected or demanded by the group because it should be left to each individual's free choice. No group constituency. I as an individual. Prescriptive or possibly descriptive.
3. I—No awareness:	Does not perceive the existence of a shared norm concerning this issue and does not take a position pro or con about the group's developing such a norm. Also does not have an individual norm concerning this issue. No group constituency. I as an individual. Descriptive.
4. I—Individual:	An action should be performed which is in accordance with the norm where this action is not defined or implied by membership in the group. There is no suggestion that the task of the group is or should be to develop or promote the norm. Universal constituency applied to people in the group as much as to people outside the group. I as an individual. Prescriptive.
5. I—Individual ambiguous:	An action should be performed which is in accordance with the norm where this action is implied by membership in the group. Ambiguous constituency but seems to apply to people in the group more than to those outside. I as an individual. Prescriptive.

Authority Norms

6. Authority:	An action should be performed because it is expressed or demanded by the teacher or administrator whose authority derives from his/her status or the law which makes the teacher a superior member of the group. Group constituency. Teacher as authority. Prescriptive or descriptive.

Table 4.3. (continued)

Authority Norms (continued)

7. Authority—
   acceptance:

   An action should be performed because it is expected by authority or law with the clear implication that the group accepts this authority and thinks promoting and upholding the norm is in the interest of the group's welfare. Group constituency. Teacher as authority. Prescriptive.

Aggregate Norms

8. They—aggregate
   (I disagree):

   They, the group or a substantial subgroup, have a tendency to act in accordance with a norm in a way that the individual speaker does not share or disagrees with. Group constituency. I as a member of the group. Prescriptive or descriptive.

9. I and they—
   aggregate:

   They and I have a tendency to act in the same way in accordance with a norm. Group constituency. I and they as members of the group. Prescriptive or descriptive.

Collective Norms

10. Limiting or
    proposing I:

    The speaker thinks the group or all members of the group should follow or uphold this norm better or should have this new norm. (This category overlaps with phase I.) Group constituency. I as a member of the group. Prescriptive.

11. Spontaneous—
    collective:

    They or they and I think that group members should act in accordance with the norm *because* they feel naturally motivated to do so as a result of the sense of belonging to the group. Group constituency. They and I as members of the group. Descriptive.

12. They—limited
    collective:

    They think that group members should act in accordance with the norm without the speaker identifying her/himself with that normative expectation. The speaker differentiates her/his own normative perspective. Group constituency. They as members of the group. Prescriptive.

13. I and they—
    limited
    collective:

    Both I and they, as members of the group, think that group members should act in accordance with the norm. Group constituency. I and they as members of the group. Prescriptive.

Table 4.3. (continued)

Collective Norms (continued)

14. Implicit—we collective:	The members of this group think that all of us should act in accordance with the norm. Group constituency. We (implicit) as members of the group. Prescriptive.
15. We explicit— collective:	We, the members of this group, think that we should act in accordance with the norm. Group constituency. We (explicit) as members of the group. Prescriptive.

degrees. The most obvious distinction between individual and collective norms is the affiliative constituency explicitly bound by the norms. A collective norm has as its affiliative constituency the members of a specific group. For example, Phyllis' statements in the second stealing meeting indicate that she feels that her fellow students are obligated as members of Cluster to be trusting and caring. Individual norms obligate individuals, as persons, but not as members of a particular group. Note that some individual norms, like the norm prohibiting stealing, may be thought of as having a universal affiliative constituency (e.g., humankind). Such a constituency should be distinguished from the particularized affiliative constituency of the collective norm. For example, during Cluster's first stealing meeting Cluster students felt stealing was wrong for everyone whether or not they were members of Cluster. This was clear in the first meeting when one student, Sam, said, "I think that most people think it [stealing] is wrong, and probably the only person who does not think it is wrong is the person who stole. I don't think we have to talk about why it is wrong anymore, because we all have our own reasons why it is wrong. I think it is what we should do about it that is more important."

Sam's observation that students all had their own reasons for knowing that stealing was wrong indicates that they had no conscious sense that their affiliation with the Cluster community bound them not to steal.

Why was it important to build a collective norm against stealing when most students already felt bound by an individual norm? The answer lies in the students' apathetic response to incidents of stealing in the school. Not only were they resigned to stealing, they readily excused it, blaming the victims themselves for their carelessness. The following statement made in a D.C. discussion of stealing was typical: "John is to blame because he was stupid to bring valuable stuff to school, you don't bring valuable stuff to school without expecting to get it ripped off." In order to encourage a sense of social responsibility and caring, Cluster staff proposed that stealing should have special significance for a school that was trying to become a community.

In addition to the affiliative constituency, a collective norm is also characterized by its speaker representation. Speaker representation refers to the *subject* expecting others to follow the norm. The subject of a collective norm is the collective itself. For example, in the second-year stealing discussion, when Phyllis says, "We are supposed to trust each other," she speaks for the community; she does not appeal to her personal expectations. *"I think that one ought to trust," but to the group's — "We are supposed to . . ."* We analyze speaker representation in two ways. First, we look at each statement made by an individual and ask, who does the speaker represent or, in other words, who is doing the expecting? Second, we compare statements made by different individuals which purport to speak for the group in order to ascertain if they are, in fact, in agreement.

In our illustrations affiliative constituency and speaker representation overlapped; but this is not always the case. Let us take an example of a norm for which these criteria do not overlap, the norm that students address teachers by title and last name. The affiliative constituency of this norm is students in a particular school. The speaker representation is broader; it includes teachers as well as students. Sometimes the affiliative constituency may be broader than the speaker representation. For instance, a principal may decree that there is to be no smoking in the school. The affiliative constituency would include all members of the school, but if the decree only reflects the arbitary will of the principal, the speaker representation would include only him or her.

The third criterion used to assess the degree of collectiveness of a norm is the prescriptivity of statements of the norm. Not all norms obligate in the same way or to the same extent. Some norms obligate through external compulsion and are classified as descriptive. For example, the sense of obligation to observe a norm may arise out of a fear of adult authority, backed by sanctions, or a fear of peer disapproval and ostracism. Other norms obligate internally through duty or desire or both. If a norm obligates through desire, that is, if the sense of obligation depends upon whether individuals feel they want to uphold the norm, then the norm is judged to be descriptive. If a norm obligates through duty, that is, if the sense of obligation is unconditional, then it is judged to be prescriptive. Ideally, from our Durkheimian perspective, a collective norm should be both prescriptive and descriptive. Students should feel a duty to uphold the norm because they accept the authority of the group and a desire to uphold it because they value their membership in the group.

While we believe that the way in which normative agreements are reached is important for the establishment of collective norms, we distinguish between the form of that agreement and the collectiveness of the norm. Collective norms may in principle be established in a number of ways, for example through explicitly democratic procedures, through the decree of an authority, or through less formal modes of interaction. One issue for our research, which we take up in chapter 8, is whether the democratic schools promoted a higher degree of collectiveness than did their parent comparison schools with a bureaucratic authority structure.

The Content of the Norm

In addition to assessing norms according to their collectiveness, we may also classify them according to their value content. Four general kinds of norms emerged from the community meeting analysis: norms of community, substantive fairness, procedural fairness, and order.

Norms of Community

The collective norms of community are caring, trust, integration, participation, publicity, collective responsibility, and attachment to community. These norms uphold the intrinsic value of community; that is, they are directed toward building the harmony of the group as a community. Collective norms of community value relationships of individual to individual, individual to group, and group to individual for their own sake. The essential quality of these norms is that they prescribe sharing among members: *caring* implies sharing concerns and affection; *trust*, sharing one's confidence and property; *integration*, sharing of communication between subgroups; *participation,* sharing time, energy, and interest; *open communication,* sharing knowledge about matters which affect the group; and *collective responsibility,* sharing obligations, praise, and blame. It is through this sharing that community is maintained and developed. All of the values intended in these collection norms of community are related to and have as their justification the element of community.

Norms of Substantive Fairness

The collective norms of fairness entail a respect for the equal rights and liberties of individuals. They directly proscribe actions that infringe upon the dignity of others and indirectly provide standards of evaluation to determine whether the application of norms, rules, governance procedures, and discipline has been just. Such norms include respect for individual physical and mental integrity, respect for property and possessions, and respect for privacy and freedom. Any social organization must see to it that these norms are observed and enact protective legislation when necessary, for example through rules and a bill of rights.

Norms of Procedural Fairness

The collective norms of procedural fairness relate to the processes through which rules of the group are made and enforced. In a democracy such as Cluster School, they include the norms of freedom of expression, equality of power, rational dialogue, respect for individuals, due process, and respect for the majority will. These norms may apply to a pragmatic association or to a community. They are based on considerations of individual rights and fairness and may be viewed as a subclassification under norms of fairness. We treat them separately because they relate to procedural as distinguished from substantive justice.

Norms of Order

Collective norms of order are those norms that protect the survival and orderly functioning of the organization. For example, an attendance rule was made in Cluster because, as one student put it, "if people don't come to class then we can't have no school." We include as norms of order the norms of regulating drug use, attendance, and disruption of classes. Generally norms of order focus negatively on those actions which must be avoided so that the existence of the organization is not threatened and the task-related goals of the organization are achieved. Thus rules are made to protect the organization's property (e.g., rules prohibiting stealing the library books or defacing the desks) and to promote the organization's productivity (e.g., rules prohibiting disruptive behavior in the classroom, etc.).

One major content shift which occurred in Cluster's moral culture development was from norms of substantive fairness and order to norms of community. We viewed this as a positive development because the purpose of the just community approach was to go beyond the establishment of a just social system to a just *community*. In the case of stealing, concern first focused on a norm of fairness embodied in the rule to respect property rights. In the second through the fourth years of the school concern focused on the community norms of trust and collective responsibility. Similarly, when the problems of attendance and drug use arose in the first year of the school, rules reflecting norms of order were instituted. Later these norms of order were superseded by the communal norm of participation. A third example of this phenemonon may be seen in the response to the problem of racial division. Initially fairness in the sense of nonprejudice was emphasized. In the third and fourth years a communal norm of integration was formed, prescribing civic friendship and communication across racially segregated cliques.

THE CONVENTIONAL AND THE MORAL

By classifying norms by their content we can say more precisely what we mean by a "moral" culture. Turiel (1983) and Nucci (1982) make a compelling case both theoretically and empirically for distinguishing between two broad domains of social judgment: the conventional and the moral. They define social conventions as arbitrary norms that coordinate the actions of individuals in a social system and thus serve the social organizational ends of the system. In contrast, they define moral prescriptions as nonarbitrary judgments that are determined by considerations pertaining to individual rights, welfare, and fairness. According to their distinction, the norms of substantive and procedural fairness would clearly be included within the moral domain, while the norms of order would be included within the conventional domain.

Although we accept a distinction between the moral and the conventional, we are not convinced that the moral domain can be delimited as neatly as Turiel and Nucci suggest, nor are we convinced that moral and conventional issues need to be approached differently in practice. First, let us examine some of the norms that Turiel and Nucci commonly cite as conventional: not calling teachers by their first names, not chewing gum, and dressing properly for school. Violations of these norms are judged wrong because of custom and authority and not because they involve actions which are inherently evil. Typically, children feel that the violation of these norms is much less serious than the violation of norms that Turiel and Nucci cite as moral, such as hitting another child or stealing. Nevertheless the lines between conventional and moral blur when norms typically taken to be conventional are interpreted within a cultural context in a way that entails psychological hurt. For example, Arab schoolchildren consider calling teachers by their first names to be highly disrespectful and a serious moral offense (Nisan, 1984). Turiel (1983) admits the conventional and the moral overlap in such cases, but he sees this as a "'second order phenomenon" that does not invalidate the basic distinction. In his view social events have a structure of their own that will predispose them to being interpreted as either conventional or moral across different social contexts. We are more inclined to believe that meanings of events vary more significantly from culture to culture and that maintaining the conventional-moral distinction requires great sensitivity to the symbolic value of social actions within a particular social context.

A second and more important objection to Turiel's and Nucci's distinction is that it does not include communal norms. These norms focus neither on individual rights and welfare nor on the functioning of a social organization but on the personal relations that individuals have to each other and the group. We think that Nucci (1982) confused the communal with the conventional when he criticized our handling of marijuana and alcohol use in Cluster. In most schools use of these substances is typically viewed as a personal choice or a convention because their use does not directly result in injury or unfairness to another. However, in the just community schools an effort was made to think about drugs as having a significant impact on students' participation in the community. The development of communal norms to take the place of conventional norms entails a "moralizing" which we feel is appropriate, given the new context. Had we decided to treat drugs as a strictly conventional issue, we may have argued as follows: "We cannot tell you what your obligations are in these matters; however, if you care about the school you will not jeopardize it with your behavior." This, of course, is a paraphrase of the advice A. S. Neill (1960) gave to his students in attempting to dissuade them from having sexual relations at Summerhill (quoted in chapter 1). The advice we gave was to argue that no drug use was a moral obligation *in a community,* since it affected participation and hence the fabric of relatedness in the school.

Having indicated that conventional norms can be "moralized" by making them communal, we will now see how typically moral norms may be further developed by making them communal. First, it is important to recall from our discussion of the community value that communal justifications presuppose but go beyond justifications involving concerns for individual rights and welfare. This means that the members of a community commit themselves to supererogatory acts, such as care and collective responsibility, which do not violate but go beyond the minimal dictates of a morality, based either on utility or fairness. An illustration of the difference between a communal justification and one Turiel would define as moral may be found in the way Kohlberg and the staff dealt with the problem of stealing in Cluster. When the students first discussed how they should handle the rash of stealing incidents, they responded as would *any* moral agent in any social context by objecting that stealing represented a violation of individual property rights. However, when the moral culture developed, they viewed stealing as a violation of trust and a threat to their sense of solidarity.

The Phase of the Norm

We derived the phase dimension of this analysis as we began to describe the process of norms taking root or becoming institutionalized in a community. The scheme of phases from 0 to 7 traces a sequence in which group members commit themselves to upholding shared norms (table 4.4). It begins with a phase 0 when there is no collective norm for a particular problem. Each individual is left to act according to his/her own norms. Phases 1, 2, and 3 are the proposing and accepting phases.

Table 4.4.
Phases of the Collective Norm

Phase 0:   No collective norm exists or is proposed.

Collective Norm Proposal
Phase 1:   Individuals propose collective norms for group acceptance.

Collective Norm Acceptance
Phase 2:   Collective norm is accepted as a group ideal but not agreed to. It is not an expectation for behavior.
Phase 3:   Collective norm is accepted and agreed to, but it is not (yet) an expectation for behavior.

Collective Norm Expectation
Phase 4:   Collective norm is accepted and expected (naive expectation).
Phase 5:   Collective norm is expected but not followed (disappointed expectation).

Collective Norm Enforcement
Phase 6:   Collective norm is expected and upheld through persuasion.
Phase 7:   Collective norm is expected and upheld through reporting.

At this point the norm is not yet collective because members of the group do not expect it to be upheld. At phase 1 individuals propose norms for acceptance by the group. They try to collectivize that which they feel should be normative for the group. In Cluster this usually entailed an intense process of persuasion in the community meeting as well as in smaller, formal and informal meetings. At phase 2 members recognize a shared ideal for behavior. However, there is not yet a specific agreement on a definite norm or rule. Often norms remain at this phase because members believe them to be impossible to live up to. At phase 3 agreements and rules are made for realizing normative ideals; however, there is not an expectation for these agreements to be upheld in action. These agreements and rules, although they may be flagrantly violated, remain at phase 3 instead of sliding back to phase 0, because members of the group do not want to revoke them. It is important to make a theoretical distinction between norm acceptance at phases 2 and 3 and norm expectation at the higher phases. Acceptance implies that members agree that they should have a particular collective norm. Expectation means they not only agree on a collective norm but also experience it as binding on their behavior.

Phases 4 and 5 are expecting phases. At phase 4 there is a general expectation that members of the community live up to the collective norm. This may be a terminal phase if there are no known violations of the collective norm. At phase 5 real disappointment is expressed when the collective norm is violated. The fifth phase does not represent a progressive evolution of the collective norm but rather a state of crisis created by deviance from the collective norm. At this point members of the group may choose from a variety of responses. They may: propose a new collective norm to replace the existing one; simply cease to expect behavior according to the norm, in which case the phase of the norm would regress to a lower phase; or decide to reassert the collective norm through exhortation and various forms of enforcement. If group members reassert the collective norm in response to deviation, the phase of the norm advances.

Phases 6 and 7 define actions that group members feel are obligatory in order to uphold a collective norm. At the sixth phase members are committed to persuading each other to live up to the norm. At the seventh phase members of the group recognize a duty to report norm violators to the group. Persuading and reporting may be treated as second-order collective norms of enforcement. As norms in their own right, they may be assessed as having their own phases.

In the first meeting the norms of trust and collective responsibility are scored as phase 0, indicating that students had not yet even established common ideals or agreements about such norms, let alone committed themselves to expecting or enforcing them. Kohlberg and the staff made phase 1 proposals for trust and expressed their dismay at the students' apathetic response to stealing. The students with one exception failed to pick up on the staff's proposals. Some went so far as to suggest that a norm of trust was impossible to have in a school. Note that while the students failed to respond to the problem of creating trust in the school, they did wish to make a rule against stealing. A rule simply states that a given action is proscribed and that the perpetrators of these acts will be punished. The students' wish to have a rule about stealing indicated a concern for upholding a norm of respect for individual property rights. The phase of this norm is 3: the students made an agreement not to steal, but they did not really expect each other to uphold it. In fact, their preoccupation with finding a suitable deterrent for stealing indicated the opposite—that they thought their peers would steal.

In the second- and third-year meetings we have evidence that the norms of trust and responsibility had developed to higher phases. For example, at the beginning of the second-year stealing meeting students expressed their shock and frustration that stealing had occurred. While these statements are negative in their assessment of the Cluster community, they clearly arose out of disappointed expectations for trust and care and, therefore, are scored as phase 5. Phyllis was a spokesperson for a higher phase (phase 6) of the shared norms of the community. She stressed to members of the community that "we are supposed to be able to trust each other," "we are supposed to care about each other." As a response to the breakdown of trust and care, Phyllis proposed a new norm of collective restitution at phase 1. Later in the meeting other students supported her argument in a way that implied that collective restitution was at least a phase 2 ideal for their community. This was not the only response to the stealing; indeed, attention was given to finding a way for the anonymous return of the money and, failing that, to the importance of identifying the thief. All of these responses reflect a departure from the casual acceptance of stealing in the first year. While they indicate that development to "expecting" phases 4 and 5 on the norm of trust had occurred, few students as yet felt a personal responsibility for persuading the thief to return the money or for reporting the thief, should persuasion fail (phases 6 and 7).

In the third-year meeting about the dock, the phase of the norm of collective responsibility, which in the second year was no higher than phase 3, had developed to a phase 4 expectation, although there remained a number of dissenters at phase 3. Bev's and Karl's adviser group reports ("People said this is our community . . . and we should pay for it as a community" and "We felt . . . the community should share responsibility for paying for it") are coded as phase 4 because they imply an expectation for collective restitution. The problem before the community was not whether all should share responsibility (this most students took for granted) but to what extent those directly involved with the loss of the docks should be held especially accountable. We should note that faculty opposition to the proposal was based not on a rejection of the norm of collective responsibility but on a belief that responsibility should be intensified for those Cluster members who actually lost the dock. As one teacher (Rob) expressed it, "I think individual and community responsibility are not mutually exclusive concepts. Individuals still have some responsibility whether they exist in democratic communities or not." While there were few arguments in direct opposition to collective responsibility, one adviser group at the beginning of the meeting reported simply that they did not want to pay. This lack of willingness to collectively restitute and the failure to demand it of others indicate that for a subgroup, the norm of collective responsibility was no higher than phase 3—an agreement without an expectation for action.

The Stage of the Norm

The most conceptually difficult problem in our methodology concerns the sense in which it is possible to speak about a stage structure of shared expectations and values that is distinct from an individual stage structure. The cognitive developmental psychology of Piaget, Kohlberg, and colleagues maintains that individuals construct their own social reality through interacting with the social environment. Thus every social experience involves assimilation to some extent. How, then, is it possible to differentiate collective stages from individual stages when analyzing individual statments in an interview or in a community meeting? In the context of our study of the Cluster School, the question becomes whether students reasoning at stages 2, 3, and 4 have a shared perception of the school's collective norms and values that can be scored according to a structural stage scheme.

To clarify what a stage of the collective norm is we must distinguish between assessing stages according to an individual's prescriptive socio-moral reasoning about hypothetical dilemmas, an individual's prescriptive socio-moral reasoning about real-life dilemmas or problems, and the shared prescriptive socio-moral reasoning characteristic of a group. Cognitive developmentalists following Kohlberg's approach typically study prescriptive socio-moral reasoning. Posing hypothetical dilemmas is a methodological strategy for eliciting a subject's best prescriptive thinking about a moral problem by standardizing the stimuli given to each subject and eliminating extraneous factors which may confound an interpretation of the subject's reasoning. Reasoning on such dilemmas is interpreted to be "context-free," that is, it could be elicited by another set of dilemmas posing similar problems. As such, this kind of reasoning has been considered to be generally representative of an individual's competence.

To know about an individual's performance, we cannot rely on hypothetical dilemmas or even real-life dilemmas divorced from real-life decisions and consequences, but must study individual reasoning in real-life situations. This requires the investigation of reasoning in action, as Jacquette (1978) has done, and reasoning affected by a particular social context, as we are attempting to do. In this regard, we understand the social environment as having two possible kinds of influence. First, it can promote or hinder one's natural socio-moral reasoning such that one can either be encouraged to reason at the height of one's capacities, as in the kibbutz environment studied by Reimer (1977), or discouraged from optimal reasoning, as in the prison environment studied by Scharf (1973).

Second, in addition to promoting moral development, which we regard as a universal cognitive function, the environment can also lead to the development of social values that may not develop universally but depend upon particular social contents and ideologies. Vygotsky (1934/1962) referred to these as "scientific concepts" in his attempt to define a middle ground between the individual's spontaneously constructed knowledge and the individual's internalization of culture. In chapter 9 we will discuss how Cluster students developed their reasoning about two core elements of the Cluster School ideology: community and democracy. That analysis confirms Vygotsky's claim that certain concepts are developed through the influence of particular social environments but not through an internalization of the social input.

Those conducting research on prescriptive socio-moral reasoning in an actual social context assume that there is an important interaction between the stage of the individual and the environment (Jacquette 1978; Reimer 1977; Scharf 1973). They explore the influence which the environment has on the structure of reasoning of the individual. Our research leads in another direction, to a study of the cultural dimension of the environment as having its own stagelike character. The same data are relevent for our research as for theirs. The difference between the two kinds of research is the perspective taken on the material. In investigating collective stages of the moral culture, we examine the data from the perspective of a social psychologist, looking for characteristics of the group as a whole. In this respect we differ from those taking an individual-psychological perspective, who focus solely on individual psychological processes.

Phyllis' statements in the second meeting nicely illustrate the relevance of taking this group-oriented perspective. She argued that members of the community should assume collective responsibility for the theft— "It's everyone's fault that she don't have no money"—and then exhorted, "Everyone should care that she got her money stolen." Phyllis' statement in this meeting cannot be adequately interpreted without reference to the group. She does not intend merely to express her personal opinion on this matter, nor does she intend to speak generally about the responsibilities a member of any group has. No, Phyllis wishes to speak for a particular group, Cluster School, and as a representative of that group she speaks differently from the way she would as a member of another group, like her family or neighborhood peer group. Although Phyllis may *intend* to speak for the group, we may wonder to what extent she assumes that her own point of view is shared by the group. In other words, is there any reason to claim that because Phyllis represents the group's norms at a stage 3–4 level the group really is at a stage 3–4 level? If Phyllis reasoned at the stage 2–3 level (as measured by Kohlberg's standard dilemmas), would she not also represent the group's norms at that stage?

Clearly any claim we wish to make for a collective stage must go beyond the intentions of the speaker to represent a collective norm and take into account reactions from other members of the group that might indicate whether or not the speaker's viewpoint is shared. We think it is significant that Phyllis' stage 3–4 line of argument was accepted by most students in the second year, while a similar attempt by Kohlberg, several staff members, and one student in the first year was rejected by the students. This lends some credibility to the claim that there was some group development in terms of the stage of the norm.

Further support for this claim comes in considering how students in the second-year meeting rejected arguments at the stage 2 and stage 2–3 level, arguments that they accepted in the first-year meeting. For example, during the second year at the community meeting about stealing, several students disagreed with Phyllis' restitution proposal, saying that the theft was the victim's fault because she was careless. This led one student, representing the group, to respond that such an uncaring and individualistic position was not in keeping with the community: "They are individuals and don't have to be in the community. Everybody should care that she got her money stolen." Simon, one of the students most adamantly opposed to collective restitution, continued to object, saying that he could not understand what being in a community had to do with his position. Someone finally asked him what *he* meant by "community." He answered, "People can help one another, but I didn't say nothing about giving money out." From this statement and others it became apparent that Simon thought of "helping" in stage 2 terms, that is, helping should be contingent upon the desires of the helper. He went on to make an analogy to Cluster as a bank—"If the bank gets robbed, does that mean that you can knock on my door and tell me I have to pay for it?" Simon, then, agreed that the community had a collective norm of helping; but he misinterpreted the meaning of the norm. It was his stage 2 mininterpretation that brought him into conflict with other community members who thought that his *reasoning* was inconsistent with the true meaning of the collective norm, which was seen by most students as being at least stage 3.

This example indicates that students have some interest in clarifying the shared meanings of norms in their group. It also indicates that the stage of the norm may depend upon but not be reducible to the moral reasoning competence of individual students. Further evidence in support of the notion of a collective stage comes from the relationship between a norm's meaning and its implications for action. As we will show in this and the following chapter, many community meeting decisions on specific courses of action seem to depend upon development to a requisite collective stage. For example, it is unlikely that Phyllis' proposal for collective restitution would have passed in the first year because, as we have seen, students' responses to incidents of stealing focused on issuing stage 2 warnings for greater vigilance and stronger deterrents. The proposal had a better chance the next year, when stage 3 concerns for trust and care had developed.

THE CONCEPT OF COLLECTIVE STAGE

Although we refer to collective norms and elements as having a stage, we do not wish to imply that collective stages are the same as Kohlberg's stages of moral reasoning. For example, Kohlberg (1984) maintains that moral reasoning competence develops through an invariant sequence of increasingly differentiated and integrated structures. The process of collective stage development is rather different. First of all, only individuals think. We do not believe in a "group mind," even though we do maintain that individuals interacting in groups construct common norms, which in turn influence their thinking in the group. The construction of such common norms reflects moral reasoning performance, not moral reasoning competence. Collective stages are not derived immediately from the moral reasoning of individual group members, but through their actual interactions or performances in a group context.

This understanding of collective stages as collective performances leads us to modify two key assumptions of the invariant sequence claim. First, the collective norms of a group need not originate at stage 0 or stage 1 but might begin at any stage. The starting point for collective stage development will, in our view, partly depend upon the stages of the individual members of the group. Their stages may set an upper limit but not a lower limit for the collective stage. For example, in a school with students reasoning at stages 3 and 4, the collective norms may initially be as high but not higher than stage 4 or as low as stages 1 or 2. Second collective stages may regress because unlike cognitive competencies, performances may fluctuate, and because each year graduates are replaced with a younger and generally less developed freshman class.

Although the invariant sequence expectation is not integral to a theory of collective stage development, as it is to a theory of individual cognitive development, we nevertheless entertain as a hypothesis that collective stage development will ordinarily proceed without skips or reversals from whatever its starting point may be. We adopt this weaker hypothesis because we think that ongoing groups, as individuals, tend to conserve existing normative structures, and that group change, like individual change, is cognitively based. Thus while we acknowledge the possibilities of regression and stage skipping, we maintain that these possibilities are highly unlikely under the normal conditions of an ongoing educational group. Our hypothesis of collective stage development even in this modest form is, of course, quite controversial. While sociologists are likely to agree that there is some "environmental press" for normative stability, many are likely to object to the notion that normative structures and their evolution have a cognitive foundation. Of course, our hypothesis of collective stage development relates to a particular type of social organization, the school, in which a high value is placed on cognitive development. Other kinds of groups may not be as amenable to normative development. One further qualification is that our test of the hypothesis will be a weak one, since we will investigate Cluster School, which was established to promote group development.

Collective stages present us with further difficulties when we consider their structural wholeness. Kohlberg operationally defines the structural wholeness of the individual moral stages as a consistency in the stage of responses across a number of different dilemmas, which put various norms in conflict. A parallel definition for the structured wholeness of a collective stage would be consistency in stages across various school problems and collective norms. We hypothesize that some consistency will be found, but we do not believe that it necessarily or invariably will occur. We expect more intra-individual consistency than intragroup consistency for reasons, cited earlier, having to do with distinctions between individual intelligence and collective consciousness and between reasoning competence and performance. According to Kohlberg and Piaget, the structural wholeness of individual reasoning arises from a logical demand for consistency in problem solving. However, the structural wholeness of group norms clearly depends less on logical demands than on demands for group stability and coherence, which may admit quite a bit of logical inconsistency.

Perhaps the most significant problem raised by the notion of structural wholeness is whether collective stages are really logical structures at all or whether they are contents that change in a sequence analogous to the structural development of the individual stages. One way of looking at this is to ask to what extent shared reasoning develops with sufficient clarity and logical coherence that it can be structurally assessed utilizing the scoring method for staging individual moral reasoning (Colby, Kohlberg et al. 1987). We may rightly be skeptical that such shared reasoning, in fact, develops, since in any group it is more important that members agree on *how* they should act than *why*. For example, in the second stealing meeting the students are most interested in deciding whether they should restitute or not. In attempting to resolve the issue they do, of course, argue about what norms they do and should share, and they even find themselves clarifying what they mean by a particular norm, such as caring. Nevertheless, what predominates in their discussion is a concern for "content," the behavioral decision and the norms and values related to it, over "structure," the reasoning that gives the decision and the norms and values a moral meaning.

Because of this predominance of content over structure we have adopted a more content-oriented scoring approach, similar in that respect to the one Loevinger (1976) uses to assess ego development. Loevinger treats responses on her protocols as probabilistic "signs" of an underlying stage without requiring logical face validity for each response. In some cases it is relatively easy to stage-score individual student statements representing collective norms in a community meeting with more strict criteria. For example, consider Lee's statement from the third-year dock meeting, that "the whole community is responsible because the community is a community and they are responsible for each other, and a small group can't do it." We scored this as a mixed stage 3–4 concern because Lee appeals to the stage 3 notion that members of a community should care about other members' misfortune and to the stage 4 notion that responsibility is also based on the group's institutional definition of itself as a community. The statements we quoted earlier by Bev and Karl from that meeting are not sufficiently elaborated to be scored according to stage. However, later in the meeting Bev offers a stage 4 elaboration of the argument for collective responsibility: "The reason the whole community is in it together is that we all went on a trip together, and we sort of agreed to be liable for everyone else and we agreed to be a part of the community." Her statement, like Lee's, links the obligation of collective responsibility to the nature of the group—its being a community. She goes beyond Lee's statement, however, in offering a further social contract explanation for why all members of the community should be responsible.

Often there are few statements which may be straightforwardly staged using purely logical criteria. This is particularly the case in meetings in which the major arguments on each side of the issue have been presented and minor points are being resolved. On that occasion a more content-oriented assessment becomes necessary. For example, in the second-year stealing meeting, when those who supported the collective restitution proposal gave scorable reasons, they were generally between stage 3 and 4. There is a good reason for this: the collective restitution norm has a content that ordinarily seems to require at least a transitional stage 3–4 structure for its justification. This is not to say that it is impossible to argue for collective restitution at a lower stage. Indeed, in the third year, some of the students directly responsible for losing the dock argued in stage 2 terms that collective restitution was a good idea because it would relieve them of a heavy financial burden. Thus, while there seems to be a relationship between content and structure, that relationship is only a probabilistic one.

This last example suggests that a good way to determine the "stage" of a norm under discussion in a meeting is to focus those statements in which that norm is first proposed. Proposing a new norm is a production task in which content is likely to follow directly from an underlying structure. Agreeing or disagreeing with a proposal that is already "on the floor" does not require that one understand correctly and then react to the original intent behind the proposal. Later arguments may be made in support of or against the proposal that fail to comprehend or misinterpret its original meaning. Because norms can change their meaning in the course of a discussion, it is important to ascertain whether they retain their original meaning. The stage given to the group norm must reflect the understanding that members of the group finally reach through discussion.

Often the best we can do in assessing the collective stage of a norm is to consider to what extent the proposal for a concrete action in a meeting has a generally shared symbolic significance, scorable through probabilistic criteria at one stage or two adjacent stages. For example, although some students in the third-year dock meeting may have voted in favor of collective restitution for stage 2, self-interested reasons, it appears to us from the content of the meeting that support for collective restitution generally symbolized a commitment to collective responsibility at stages 3 and 4. This does not mean that most students who supported the motion could have produced stage 3 and 4 reasons for it. However, it does mean that most students would identify stage 3 and 4 reasons as better expressions of the shared significance of the motion than stage 2 reasons. The claim that individuals recognize and prefer higher-stage arguments than those they can produce is a well-substantiated one (Rest 1979; Walker 1982). It allows us to define the stage of a collective norm as the stage most individuals would identify as the best expression of the norm's meaning for the group. Without such a claim it would be difficult to understand how a group could develop norms at a higher stage than the moral reasoning competence of most of the members.

A final problem with the collective stage concept concerns the hierarchical integration of its stage sequence, such that each stage is transformed and displaced by the next highest one. In our discussion of the stealing meetings, we have described collective norm development from stage 2 to stage 3–4 in a way that implied that stage transformations and displacements did, in fact, occur. However, this depiction of stage change oversimplifies what is in reality a far more complex picture, since we derive a collective stage score for a group norm from individual representatives of that norm. Rather than reporting the collective norm at a single stage or adjacent stages, we could just as easily present distributions of the stages of individual representations. By noting changes in the distributions of stage scores over time, we could back away from the strong claim for stage transformation and adopt a weaker position that increased numbers of students would represent the collective norms at a higher stage over time. This weaker position is somewhat similar to Rest's (1979) "layer cake model," in which higher and lower stages coexist, and development entails an increased preference and use of higher stages over lower ones.

While we do not wish to press the strong claim for our collective stages, we have decided to fit our data as best we can within the hierarchical integration model and thus present single or adjacent stage scores for the collective norm each time it is assessed. In our community meeting analysis we found that the modal stage of the individual representative of the collective norms matched our more clinical impressions of the collective stage, and so we used it as our collective score. In addition, we discovered that the distributions of scores in the meetings were skewed such that the modal scores were generally the higher scores in the meetings. This was also the case in the ethnographic interview analysis.

Our decision to adopt the hierarchical integration model was also influenced by the usefulness such a model has in interpreting and guiding an intervention, such as the one at Cluster School. As in the discussion approach, the staff goal is to promote development to the next highest stage. The difference between approaches is that the just community focus is on the collective stage, not the individual stage. In the first-year meeting, then, the faculty task was to attempt to move the collective norm from stage 2 to stage 3. In the second-year meeting they hoped to consolidate the group at stage 3 and to push toward stage 3–4, and so on into the third year.

To summarize, this rather flexible method of collective stage assessment takes into account statements that can be structurally scored, statements that are structurally ambiguous but with contents that can be probabilistically related to structure, and statements that can confirm or disconfirm whether a particular stage best characterizes the shared understanding of the norm. Underlying this method is a weaker appropriation of the criteria of stage structure than we find in either Piaget or Kohlberg.

Without an analysis of the moral stage of collective norms, our assessment of school climate would lack any essentially "moral" character. Norms that are widely shared and strongly enforced may be unfair or woefully lacking in their moral significance. Examples of repressive totalitarian states, fanatical cults, violent gangs, and organized crime come to mind when we think of groups with strong but morally defective collective norms. These negative examples lead to a certain caution or wariness about collectivities in general. In our view, this caution may be exaggerated if one fails to differentiate the collective stage from the other two dimensions of norms (degrees of collectiveness and phase). Understanding these dimensions is especially relevant when considering adolescent moral education. Peer pressure should not be viewed as a problem per se but only as a problem if the pressure supports low-stage norms or norms that would be regarded as immoral from the perspective of a highest stage of morality. The point of the just community approach is, of course, to direct peer pressure toward higher-stage, more moral norms. Thus we have portrayed the stealing meetings as an effort to shift stage 2 peer-supported norms of self-protective concern for one's own property and apathy toward others to stage 3 and 4 collective norms of trust, care, and collective responsibility.

The Stage Development of Collective Norms in the Property Meetings

We summarize the stage development of Cluster's collective norms relating to property from years one through three in table 4.5. Note that

Table 4.5.
Collective Stage Development on the Stealing and Property Issue

	Year 1	Year 2	Year 3
Property	Stage 2	—	—
Trust	—	Stage 3	—
Collective responsibility	—	—	Stage 3–4
Issue score	2	3	3–4

the issue score, which we calculate by averaging scores for each year across norms, progresses from stage 2 in year one to stage 3 in year two to stage 3–4 in year three. Let us now explain how we arrived at those scores. In the first-year meeting the only collective norm is a substantive-fairness norm of property, which we scored stage 2 because of the general pragmatic, self-interested concern expressed for protecting individual possessions through establishing concrete deterrents. That norm was not discussed in the second and third years, as the students shifted their attention to the communal norms of collective restitution and trust.

In the second year trust is a stage 3 norm directed at the building of relationships among individuals in the community. As we have seen, it is a norm which has become a shared expectation, scored at phase 5. In the first year no such trust norm was present, except as a proposal by the faculty and one student.

During the second-year meeting students discussed a proposal for collective restitution in stage 3 and 4 ways. The stage 3 rationale focuses on the need for collective responsibility as an empathic response to another member's misfortune. The stage 4 rationale is based on a conception of collective guilt: "It isn't just one person's fault . . . we all share the guilt because we are a collective all together." The motion for collective restitution reflects the stage of the reasoning of the students advocating it rather than a shared rationale. By the third year collective restitution has become a collective expectation at stage 3–4.

THE PROPERTY ISSUE: A SUMMARY

In introducing the categories we use in our analysis of moral culture we have shown how Cluster's moral culture developed from the first to the third year. We have seen that the concerns present in the third-year meeting on the loss of the dock grew out of earlier discussions and resolutions of cases involving stealing. The most dramatic shift in moral culture occurred between the first- and second-year meetings. In the first-year meeting we found almost no student statements that referred to community or to any shared norms or values. In the second-year meeting students appealed to a shared sense of community and to shared norms of trust and care. We captured this development in our scoring system by assessing the collective norms of trust and caring as phase 0 in the first year and phase 4 in the second. The only exceptions to the phase 0 statements in the first year were proposals by several faculty members and one student. In the second-year meeting the norm of collective responsibility was proposed and agreed upon (phase 3). By the third year that norm had become a phase 4 expectation for the majority of students, although a subgroup dissented. The phase of the norm signifies the strength of commitment to uphold a shared norm. The stage of the norm signifies the moral adequacy of a shared norm. We noted that there were no truly collective norms in the first year, except for the norm of respect for individual property rights, which provided a basis for the stealing rule. We assessed that norm as stage 2 because of the concrete view of property rights and pragmatic assumption underlying the way in which those rights ought to be protected. In the second year stage 3 norms of trust and care developed, while in the third year a stage 3–4 norm of collective responsibility had taken root.

In the next chapter we will continue this analysis of the development of Cluster's moral culture by first returning to the property issue for a summary of how that issue was dealt with in Cluster's fourth year and then by proceeding to a series of new issues: attendance, integration, and drugs (alcohol and marijuana). We will add to our assessment of community meetings the results of our scoring of the ethnographic interviews from each year.

The hypotheses that we will investigate in the next chapter are as follows:

1. Cluster's norms will become progressively collectivized.
2. The content of the collective norms will shift over time from norms of substantive fairness and order to norms of community.
3. Collective norms will develop over time from phase 0 to the higher

phases without phase skipping. Phase regression will be possible, although it too will follow in a sequential pattern.

4. The collective stage development of norms within an issue, like property, will occur in an invariant sequence without skips or regressions.

5. There will be some consistency in development of phase and stage from norm to norm or from issue to issue, although neither collective stages nor phases will be expected to develop with the same consistency as individual moral judgment stages across different content areas.

5

The Development of Cluster's Moral Culture

with Marvin Berkowitz

In chapter 4 we described our method of assessing moral culture through the analysis of community meetings. We illustrated our method by discussing a three-year sequence of meetings that dealt with a common problem: property loss. In this chapter we will present community meetings dealing with property during Cluster's fourth year, and then we proceed to examine three other problem areas: class attendance, racial integration, and alcohol and marijuana use. We will focus on the development over four years of collective norms in each of these areas by summarizing key community meeting discussions in each year. Since we discussed a number of meetings from the first year in chapter 3, we will devote our attention in this chapter to the next three years.

STEALING AND PROPERTY LOSS

The Fourth Year

Our discussion of the property issue in the last chapter ended with an analysis of the dock meetings. The resolution adapted in those meetings was that the whole community should share responsibility for restitution but that those directly involved in losing the dock should assume primary responsibility for raising the money.

School closed for summer vacation before any restitution had been made. The following September the dock issue was back on the agenda with a new twist—should the incoming students have to contribute toward repayment? While a number of students and a new staff member argued "no, that was last year's problem," the majority felt differently. One of the new students summed up the majority view: "If your group [who had been in the school the previous year] would have made a lot of money last year, the new students would have had it. The new kids have to take the bad with the good." The meeting concluded with a resolution to sell Cluster T-shirts to raise the money.

In May Dan, Cluster's guidance counselor, reported that stamps had been stolen from his office. He had no reason to believe a Cluster student was the culprit, since other students had access to his office. Cluster students firmly believed that an outsider had stolen the stamps. Some questioned whether all should assume responsibility for his loss. Several senior students of the school adamantly urged that the community come to Dan's side. One put it this way: "We know that Dan is going to end up paying for them himself, and he said earlier today how he felt a part of the community. I mean he feels a part of the community and then the community says, "Go buy your own damn stamps.' I mean the community is supposed to help each other out." A majority voted to assess each Cluster member a quarter, and a collection was immediately taken.

Analysis

The statements made in favor of collective restitution decisions indicate that this norm was a relatively well-established expectation (phase 4). The stage of this norm appears to be 3–4, combining a stage 3 sympathetic concern for others with a stage 4 sense of responsibility, deriving from membership in the community.

Summary

In Cluster's first year faculty proposed a community norm of trust which all but one student rejected as "unrealistic" in a school setting.

Students were willing, however, to make a no-stealing rule with significant penalties which they hoped would deter further theft. By the fall of
the second year the students not only supported a norm of trust but they
also accepted a norm of collective responsibility for dealing with a
violation of trust. During the third and fourth years of the school the
issue of trust within the community was mute, since there were no
incidents of one member stealing from another. Ethnographic interview
analysis showed that Cluster members continued to feel strongly about
the importance of trust in the community during this time. The trust
norm then developed in phase from 0 in the first year to 4 in the second
and remained at 4 in the years that followed. Similarly, it developed in
stage from 2–3 in the first year to 3 thereafter. The collective restitution
norm also developed in phase. It started at phase 0 in the first year,
developed to a phase 3 agreement in the second, developed to phase 4
(3) in the third, and finally consolidated at phase 4 in the fourth. The
stage of the collective restitution norm was 3–4 in the third and fourth
years.

CLASS ATTENDANCE AND ACADEMIC PARTICIPATION

The First Year

The issue of class attendance was a particularly vexing one. Cluster
had many academically marginal students who had had truancy problems in their previous schools. The attendance rule, decided upon in late
September of the first year, was by the staff's admission a "stopgap"
measure, promising little more than that the most flagrant class cutters
would receive some sanction for their behavior. It was designed to
protect Cluster from falling apart from within ("You don't have any
school this way if everyone can cut anytime they like") or from losing
respect from without ("The headmaster, parents, and everyone else is
going to see Cluster as a playground . . . and in the eyes of the world it
will be nothing"). As important as these conventional concerns are for
organizational functioning; they are not oriented to building personal
relations which are characteristic of a community. It was clear when the
attendance rule was passed that it was only an agreement that students
who cut enough classes would be liable for punishment (phase 3). Once

individuals began exceeding the ten-cut limit, few students publicly expressed their disapproval, indicating that there was no shared expectation that everyone would try to live up to the rule (phase 4).

Greg's Expulsion.[1]

During the spring of Cluster's first year the D.C. recommended to the community meeting that five students be expelled. Only one actually was —Greg. Greg had violated every rule of the school, including fighting, causing disturbances, stealing, and cutting classes. In spite of all these violations about half of the students were willing to tolerate his misbehavior because they liked him and knew he really cared for the school. His caring for the school was manifested particularly in his enforcement of rules that he did not violate. He did not smoke marijuana, and he enforced the rule by making citizen's arrest of a fellow student, grabbing the telltale sack of marijuana and hauling the offending student, Rich, off to the D.C. Rich appealed the D.C. ruling to a meeting of the entire community. which Greg happened to chair. Despite the fact that Greg was out to get Rich, he chaired an extremely fair meeting, allowing all of Rich's friends to speak. Sweat rolled down Greg's brow the entire time as he tried to hold his biases and emotions in check.

Greg finally came up for expulsion for having cut more than ten classes after having been warned by the D.C. In the staff meeting preceding the community meeting, Kohlberg proposed that the manner in which Greg was handled would be a test of the strength of the school's sense of community. Kohlberg suggested that the community could and should accept collective responsibility for him, i.e., that the other students could and should support and pressure him to come to class. The majority of the staff saw it as a different test of the school's strength of community. The students should uphold their rules and expel Greg, or their authority would lose all meaning.

The Meeting

The community meeting began with a representative of the D.C. noting that Greg had already been given a "second chance" and that he still continued to "willfully" cut class. Greg spoke in his own defense:

1. A brief presentation of this case appeared in Kohlberg (1985).

All right, I know I did wrong and I think I should have another chance, and if I do, I will appreciate it, and I will go to class and I will try not to have another disturbance. That's all.

The group very quickly divided on Greg's expulsion. Felix spoke in his defense:

I think that they should help Greg in this school because of what he said and if he didn't want to stay in this school he would just say 'the hell with it' and go back to the other school, so I think he should have one more chance.

Sally countered:

I think that might be best for Greg, but it is not best for the community. It is obvious that Greg thinks it is best for him to be here, but maybe it is not best for the community to have him participate.

Sally's statement became the subject of some controversy as two students cautioned that Greg should only be judged on the issue of whether he had 10 cuts and not on the issue of his past record. Andy (T) disagreed maintaining that their argument was appropriate for a court of law but not for Cluster:

This isn't a court, this is a group trying to be fair, and we don't have to restrict ourselves from thinking about our total experience with a person, and his total experience with us.

Billy asked a critical question which became a prophecy:

Is it fair to Greg just to throw him out of the school with nowhere to go? We need options that would help. . . . We can't just throw someone out of here, without considering what they are going to do when they get older.

After some debate over whether they could keep Greg and still "crack down" on rule breaking, Greg told how he felt about what he did and staying in Cluster:

I know I did wrong but I know I won't fail if you keep me in. I like to go to school and I hope you don't kick me out. It's the only school I ever went to that I like."

William (T) followed with a lengthy explanation of Greg's psychological state at the time he was cutting. He noted that for Greg the community meeting is "everything," the most important thing in his life.

Several students responded to Greg and William (T) by publicly changing their minds and asking for a punishment other than expulsion. Andy (T) then questioned what would become of Cluster's rules if people changed them to fit each case. Simon saw his point but became confused when he tried to reconcile it with the community's responsibility to meet the needs of individuals.

Everybody's different and it seems to me if many people were dissatisfied with the rule, they would do something, and it just doesn't seem like it has happened. [In Greg's case] you are supposed to cater to him because he is different and he has certain needs. . . . I need certain things, everybody in this room needs something different, and it seems to me that we are failing to meet people's needs.

In this exchange Simon was unable from a stage 3 perspective to reconcile the conflicting claims of individuals in the school for sympathetic treatment. He was unable to accept Andy's (T) stage 4 point that only by acting on behalf of the common good could the needs of most group members be met. Andy did not argue that Greg should be sacrificed for the good of the whole. Rather, he maintained that Cluster did not have the resources to meet Greg's extreme needs and that another situation should be found.

At the end of the meeting, the forces of law and order carried the day by a single vote. When the vote went against him, Greg wept. He had an option to reapply in the fall, which he did, but his sense of belonging was gone. He repeatedly and senselessly broke rules and was again expelled. He never returned to the regular school but moved his life to the streets. Three years later he was sent to prison for armed robbery and later was accused of murder.

Analysis

Greg's expulsion is unusual in that Greg never psychologically withdrew from Cluster as other chronically truant students had. Because Greg cared for Cluster, there was some chance of helping him. However, because he presented such an extreme disciplinary problem, only a community with very strong norms of collective responsibility and participation could have undertaken such a task. Unfortunately, Cluster, still in its infancy, was not up to the challenge. In the next chapter we will present an analogous case in a school that was—the A School.

Although Greg's expulsion illustrates that the attendance norm had not developed to its full potential, we should not overlook what development had occurred over the spring. In the meeting prior to Greg's case, the majority of students expressed little concern over the cases of flagrant class cutting. They were more intent upon finding "loopholes" in the assessment of cuts than they were in enforcing their rule. Greg's repeated violations of the attendance and other rules made the futility of their permissiveness painfully obvious. Some began to recognize a need to balance their feelings of sympathy and identification with the individual breaking the rules with a determination to uphold their rules for the sake of order in the community. For example, a student said, "I think that it [not expelling Greg] might be best for Greg, but it's not best for the community. It is obvious that Greg thinks it is best for him to be here, but maybe it is not best for the community."

In spite of this dawning awareness of the need to take responsibility for upholding rules, the majority of students who spoke on Greg's behalf failed to demand that he change his behavior. Borrowing a defense typically employed in earlier expulsion meetings, one student laid the responsibility for maintaining discipline squarely on the shoulders of the teachers:

If you [teachers] can't control your classes, that's none of our business. It's your business. If you can't handle them, I don't think you should be here working. Greg may bother the community but he is also a help to the community too. Not in all ways, but everybody should have fun during classes here or there. And some people are fun, that is just how they are. Even in Latin they fool around. It is just normal, and every semester people get cuts; it makes school fun.

This student viewed the Cluster rules as the majority did in a phase 3, stage 2 way. Cluster has rules but they should not get in the way of "having fun." Enforcement of the rules should not really be a student concern. Control is up to the teachers, that is what they are paid to do. Not all students were willing to excuse Greg's behavior, as we have seen. Some, like Stuart, felt stongly that if Greg were to remain in Cluster he would have to change and follow the rules: "If we do something he has to be willing. If there is a lot of support here then he will support himself." Unfortunately, there were not enough students like Stuart who were willing to make demands on Greg and then offer to help him meet those demands. The stage of the collective norm of helping did not advance beyond a stage 2–3 willingness to do concrete favors for others to a higher-stage concern for taking collective responsibility for rehabilitation.

The Second Year

Modest progress was made on a norm of participation in the second year, which set the stage for more significant developments in the third year. The community meeting discussion of Bob's expulsion reflects this. Bob had been seen in his auto mechanics class (taken outside Cluster) but not in his Cluster classes. He had a poor attendance from the year before and, unlike Greg, showed little interest in Cluster School. Counseling and a parent conference failed. After missing the first community meeting that was to decide his expulsion, he came to the next one under an ultimatum to be present or be expelled automatically.

The Community Meeting

The meeting opened with Bob stating quite simply that he wanted to stay in school until January, when he would be admitted into the occupational education program in auto mechanics. Patty objected, "Why should you *use* this school until January when you are not helping to make it any better? You just use it." Several other students questioned whether Bob really deserved the "privilege" of continuing to stay in Cluster and asked him why he felt he should be given another chance. Simon said, "If he is not helping us now, we are going to be helping him by giving him the satisfaction of something he has never done for us." Bob shot back, "What are you making a big deal for? You don't have to make a big deal!" Students came to the defense of their rule and questioned the propriety of modifying it to suit Bob. One said, "The rules are set up by the students, and if we are going to make the rules, we've got to follow them to the letter. If you don't like the way the rules are, you can change the rules."

Those who argued against expulsion asked for some compassion. Ethan said, "I see why people feel sort of used in this situation because in a way they are right. We were sort of used by them, but I still think to mess up somebody's future, it is not really worth it. I think it would be an honorable move on our part to let him do this." Phil added, "If he is willing to come to school and participate, I don't see why we shouldn't let him do this. . . . he might have something to give if he comes to this school. . . . It's not going to add anything by just kicking him out, but if he is forced to come and participate, maybe it will help people." A motion to put Bob on probation passed easily.

Before a vote was taken on it, another motion was made for a participation rule. It was introduced in an exchange with George, a friend and supporter of Bob's:

BILLY: People say he is not hurting us, but this is a community. Everybody has to work to get this place right, and there are about twelve kids who aren't coming to school. Is that helping us?

GEORGE: You say he doesn't do nothing for the school. How can you say he don't do nothing for the school? Half the people in the school don't do nothing for the school.

BILLY: If you want me to answer that, George, I have a proposal coming up in a couple of minutes that has everybody's name on it who don't belong here. I have a list of about ten kids who never come to community meetings and never do good work. George, you do work, you come in. I am not talking about people who participate in the community and go to classes.

KEITH: I would like to say something like what Billy said, and George too. There are a lot of kids in this school who don't do shit; they come, but they don't do anything and they do about as much as Bob does. And the only other thing is that they are here in the building. I really hate to use an example, but Joe, he doesn't do a thing; he comes and listens to the radio, he doesn't participate. *Maybe there should be a participation rule.* If you don't do shit, then why are you here? There are people who don't do anything at all.

Analysis

Billy's and Keith's proposals did not come to a vote but indicated a dawning awareness of the importance of an academic participation norm. The stage of reasoning behind their proposals is 3–4. Cluster members have a duty not only to be in school but also a responsibility to make a contribution to it. Billy's and Keith's understanding of participation was higher than that of most students. The majority felt participation implied "giving" something to the school, at least by attending it. This sense of participation informed the decision of whether a student should be expelled or allowed to remain in school. The decision itself was made by reconciling the duty of the school to help its members and the duty of the members to help the school. As Simon put it, "His cutting is hurting us because we have to try to help him. But you also realize he has to meet us halfway. If we are going to help him, he has to help himself too." For Simon and other students, taking community time and energy to deal with "problem students" is a way of "helping," which requires something in return. This concrete notion of reciprocal helping is stage 2–3.

The phase of the norm of participation is 4. The pattern in the first-year meetings had been for the teachers to advocate enforcing the rule and the students to plead for leniency toward rule breakers. In contrast, the pattern in the second year is for students to show a willingness to uphold the rules. The students admonish Bob for cutting class, indicating that attendance had become an expectation. For example, Phil says to Bob, "You can't be in school and not come to school. You have to come to class." This practice of asking the rule violator to "shape up" and show commitment to the community, as a condition for remaining in the community, was established during this year and continued thereafter. Although students sustained an interest in enforcing rules, they did not abandon their strong concern for trying to help out rule breakers, as we see in the final decision not to expel Bob for the following reasons: "We have given people chances before. If he is willing to come to school and participate, then I don't see why we shouldn't let him do this [stay in school]."

The Third Year

In the second year expulsion meetings over truancy became alarmingly frequent. Over the year sixteen students appeared before the community and five were actually dismissed. Staff and students searched for other ways to address the attendance policy, and two proposals emerged: one for a social contract that originated in May of the second year, and the other for a no-cut rule that was introduced in March of the third year. The social contract proposal was a staff initiative that failed to win substantial student support. On the other hand, the no-cut proposal had student backing from the beginning and led to the development of a higher stage and phase participation norm.

The Social Contract and Bill of Rights

The social contract proposal consisted of an agreement to abide by the existing rules of the school until they were changed via the democratic process. When the proposal was presented to the community, four arguments against signing the contract emerged. First, a number of students did not think that signing a piece of paper would do any good. "When people sign the contract they [will] just forget about it and break the rules anyway." Second, some students did not think that they could live up to the rules and did not want to sign anything stating they would. Third, a few students thought that the proposal spelled out student obligations but neglected to spell out student rights and faculty obligations. Fourth, many students were opposed to the idea of having to affirm publicly their commitment to the rules of the school. Some reacted by saying that forcing them to make any commitment was a violation of their freedom; others felt it indicated a lack of trust in their goodwill. Because of these misgivings, the staff decided to withdraw their active support for a social contract and to advocate that students ratify a Bill of Rights.

Their attempt to soften the social contract proposal did not meet with any more success. Students, reasoning at stages 2 and 3, did not grasp the stage 5 distinction between fundamental rights and contractual duties and saw the Bill of Rights as a social contract in disguise. They objected not to the content of the bill but to the idea of signing. No dissenting votes were cast when a motion to agree to the Bill of Rights was made. On a separate straw vote a small majority rejected the motion that all be required to sign it. The staff pressed hard over two meetings to reverse the majority. Their advocacy backfired as students grew impatient with a debate that seemed largely academic. One student leader, who had been a most articulate defender of the bill, now urged students to agree to sign simply to "shut people up." The deadlock was broken after an emotional appeal by a usually reserved faculty member, Clint. He said that the resistance to signing the Bill of Rights meant that some were not willing to commit themselves to the school. After sacrificing himself for two years in Cluster, he wondered why he should continue to commit himself if others were unwilling to do the same: "I have been in the school two years. I had to give up something to teach here and I expect the students who belong to this school to commit themselves, to sort of give up, commit themselves, to basic standards."

Meeting time had run out. Everyone was exhausted. The final vote was in favor of signing the contract, and over the next several days almost all students did.

Analysis

The proposals to adopt a social contract and later a Bill of Rights seemed promising in staff meetings but floundered in adviser group and community meeting discussions. Although a Bill of Rights was eventually passed, most students perceived it as a staff issue and as an empty gesture, which wasted a great deal of time. Stage theory can partly help us to understand why staff and students reacted so differently to these proposals. Clearly a social contract and a Bill of Rights are proposals that depend upon a stage 5, prior to society perspective. Most of the students, reasoning between stages 2 and 3, viewed the proposals either as veiled threats, coercing them to follow rules, or as a meaningless externalization of their "goodwill." Because the proposals were abstract and global in scope, departing from the "firefighting" approach to rule making in the first year, many students did not understand why they were necessary at all. The staff, of course, tried to be sensitive to the students' stages and to the problem of relevance. Yet all but Clint failed to persuade the majority. Clint's appeal was based on the stage 3–4 notion that it would be unfair to ask him (or anyone) to make sacrifices for the community when others were unwilling to do the same. Most students clearly respected Clint's contribution to the school and wanted to support his continued presence. The vote to sign the bill thus represented more an affirmation of Clint than a commitment to ratify a Bill of Rights. The conventional appeal swayed the vote but failed to galvanize student commitment to the principles underlying the Cluster community.

In retrospect the staff should have been willing to back away from the social contract issue much earlier. Their inability to address the problem of stage mismatch should have become apparent to them after the initial discussions. Furthermore, they should have also recognized the futility of their strenuous efforts to argue for the proposals most students regarded as representing the staff's and not the community's will. In theory, advocacy must take into account both ideals and the realities of the community. The social contract and Bill of Rights proposals failed to come to grips with Cluster's moral culture, particularly with the limited stage of the collective norms.

The No-Cut Rule

In contrast to the social contract and Bill of Rights proposals, the no-cut proposal (no unexcused absenses from a class) was part of a wider student initiative to do something about improving the academic side of their community. After two and a half years of living with a ten-cut rule, which was more permissive than that of Cambridge Ridge and Latin School, Cluster students supported a dramatic change of policy. The staff was very pleased with the no-cut proposal because they thought it would help to develop the norm of participation by making students' responsibilities very concrete. They felt that a proposal most students would regard as extreme would generate the most stimulating discussion about the purpose of an attendance rule.

The Meeting

Adviser group reports at the beginning of the community meeting expressed general support for the no-cut rule:

MARGE: All we said about that part was that we do need a rule that really supports a lot of participation in the school.

BILLY: We sort of recognized that there should be 100 percent attendance, that there shouldn't be any such thing as the cut rule.

KEITH: We were discussing whether a person who comes to class all the time and doesn't do anything is participating less than somebody who comes some of the time and adds a lot. What we basically decided was that the person who is there is participating, but the person who isn't in the class half the time is really hurting this school because he is seen out in the halls and that gives the school a bad name. And so we thought that people should be there all the time, that there shouldn't be a ten-cut rule, that we should have a 100 percent no-cut rule, and if you cut once you go to the D.C.

When a straw vote was taken on the no-cut proposal, it passed 28–18. A few students opposed the rule because they did not think it could change people's behavior. Other reasons given in opposition to the proposal were that some people "can't deal with it [class] every day" and that the D.C. will be overburdened with cases. Proponents of the motion stressed that students must accept responsibility for their actions. Alvin said that the Cluster community should not always be trapped into dealing with the consequences of cutting but should take preventative measures:

It's just like a diet, it's just like saying I'll go on this diet tomorrow. So if you are going to get strict after, you have to get strict before. If you have a certain amount of cuts, you can say I can cut today and I can cut tomorrow and say something else, which I probably feel is right, but I feel it gives you excuses, because I do that myself. But if you have an obligation to fulfill, then you have to face up to it, and if you don't after a certain amount of time, then I just guess you don't belong here. It is a question of where do you want the discipline to start and when do you want it to start. Instead of putting things off in the future, do it now.

The staff suggested that the practical problem of overwhelming the D.C. with petitions for excusing cuts could be resolved by leaving those decisions up to each class. With this issue resolved, the no-cut rule passed with a better than three to one majority.

Analysis

Passage of the no-cut rule marked a positive change in the phase, content, and stage of the norm. Previous to the no-cut rule, the attendance norm was a phase 4 expectation. The no-cut rule strengthened the expectation by setting the enforcement procedure immediately into play. We code this willingness to reaffirm the norm in the face of violations phase 6. It is characterized by a desire to signify the seriousness of the obligation to come to class. Alvin's analogy between dieting and the no-cut rule illustrates that the intent of the rule was to strengthen student resolve to live up to the community's expectations. Thus students in the third year were willing to accept a measure which would have struck them as overly punitive or idealistic in previous years.

The change from a ten-cut rule to a no-cut rule also reflected a content shift from a norm of order to a norm of community. The old ten-cut rule addressed the negative side of the attendance issue: what sorts of behaviors had to be curtailed to keep the school together? The no-cut rule addressed the positive side: what was necessary to build a better school community? In so doing, the no-cut rule embodied a stage 3–4 community norm of participation.

The Fourth Year

Interest in strengthening the norm of participation continued in the fourth year with the passage of a "participation rule" in March. That rule stated that each core class should draw up a contract, stipulating that in order to pass a course each student must receive a minimal grade in attendance, homework, tests, and involvement in class discussion. There were other decisions made in the fourth year that also underscored a commitment to the ideal of participation. First, students and staff agreed to evaluate their participation as individuals periodically in adviser groups. Second, an admission procedure that entailed interviewing and placing late applicants on probation was established. Third, the no-cut rule, which had proven difficult to enforce, was reaffirmed.

The explusion meetings, which were fewer in number than in the previous three years, focused squarely on participation as the central issue. In one of the two cases, Mitch, who had numerous unexcused absences from school, was required by the D.C. to present a statement in self-defense to a community meeting. That statement underscores the importance Cluster members attached to participation:

Dear Community, I am going to try to make this speech as short and as to the point as possible. In the past I have not involved myself in Cluster with any sort of commitment. I would like to try and do something positive for the school the last quarter. Please try and understand. I have been in ten schools previous to this one. I participated willingly and often unwillingly in these programs. Most of these schools were private, and the last two years I went to boarding school. This year I went to Cluster. I chose Cluster because of the concepts I am interested in. At first I was here every day, but then I had home problems and it was hard to get me out of bed in the morning. I have always been one who pushes to the limit and I see now that that limit has arrived. It is time to tighten up a bit. Usually I straighten out because I don't want to get kicked out, but that is not why I am doing it this time. I really feel guilty about not putting anything into this place, and I would like to try and do something for you in the last quarter. This is no bullshit. I know there are kids who would like to kick me out and slam the door on my ass. But I am asking for one more chance. If you don't think that I have changed sufficiently in two weeks, then you have every justification to get rid of me. Thank you.

Mitch's suggestion that he be placed on probation for two weeks was accepted. What was unique about his suggestion and the discussion which followed was a concern that he not just follow the rules during his probation but demonstrate his willingness to participate through some form of service. Concretely, he was asked to assume special responsibility for planning the annual Cluster retreat.

Analysis

In the fourth year the norm of participation continued at the same phase (6) and stage (3–4) levels attained in the third year, as students worked through the implications of their commitment to participation in the classroom. This concern for participation paid dividends not only in the strengthening of Cluster as an academic community but also in influencing the aspirations of Cluster graduates. By Cluster's fourth year over 90 percent of them went on to college, a remarkable statistic given the high percentage of academically marginal students in the school. Of course we cannot attribute this high percentage to the norm of participation alone. The participation norm was part of a wider democratization process that encouraged students with high aspirations to share their educational values with potential dropouts.

Summary

The cutting rule, a norm of order in the first year, was subsumed under the participation norm, a norm of community, in the third and fourth years. During the second year the content of the norm was somewhat ambiguous as students were only beginning to focus on what positive actions were required for the building of community. Phase development occurred in the first three years from phase 3 at the end of the first year to phase 6 at the end of the third year and remained at 6 during the fourth year.

According to both the meeting and interview analysis, there was no significant stage development until the third year. The attendance norm was between 2 and 2–3 in the first year, and consolidated at 3 in the second year. The stage 3–4 faculty proposals for a norm of participation in the first year became student proposals in the second year and a shared expectation by the third year. This process is roughly similar to what happened in the development of the previously discussed trust norm, although for that norm the process occurred more quickly (from the first to the second year).

RACIAL INTEGRATION

The First Year

In Cluster's first year the problem of racial tension was only directly dealt with twice for very brief periods of time. The first occasion came in January during a discussion about equalizing the sexes (there were almost twice as many boys as girls). At this meeting a black student noted that the ratio of black to white students was a far more important issue. "You shouldn't talk about equalizing as far as boys and girls. You should equalize races. How many blacks do you see in this room? Now if you can get some black girls that's OK with me." Black students made up 20 percent of Cluster's student population, which was representative of the proportion of blacks in Cambridge. However, some black students expressed their discomfort during that meeting at being a minority in such a small school. The staff let the issue drop in part because they had not prepared for it and in part because they felt uneasy about opening a Pandora's box of sentiments on this volatile topic. The racial issue surfaced a second time during a discussion at the end-of-the-year retreat, when students were asked to vent their feelings about the school. Once again black students complained of feeling uncomfortable. When asked for recommendations, they proposed that Cluster hire a black teacher, a suggestion the faculty, who had been searching for a black faculty member, wholeheartedly supported. That black faculty member, Ben, joined the staff midway through the second year.

The Integration Issue in Perspective

Before turning to a detailed discussion and analysis of the major Cluster community meeting discussions of racial integration, let us underscore an essential point about the significance of the integration issue. More of Cluster's promise and appeal as the first just community experimental school lay in the fact that its student body was a microcosm of the racial and social class tensions present in Cambridge and in the wider society. When Cluster began in 1974, the Boston City School System began its first year of court-enforced busing. The goals of integration and quality education for all seemed as far away that year as they did twenty years earlier after the *Brown* v. *Board of Education* case. The busing controversy forced a reexamination of the crucial tenet in *Brown* that integration, defined in its most concrete or empirical sense as black and white students attending the same school, was necessary for guaranteeing blacks an equal educational opportunity. Placing students in the same school does not guarantee that they will attend the same classes (if classes are tracked) or that they will interact in the hallways or lunch tables. The problem with efforts to integrate schools since *Brown* has to do with the way we understand integration. To integrate means more than to mix, it means to make whole and harmonious. There is no genuinely human integration without a union of minds and souls. The Cluster staff was committed to this full sense of integration and tried in a variety of ways to help it to develop.

The sequence of integration meetings hardly constitutes an unqualified success story. Nevertheless, we claim that real progress was made. One indication of that progress may be found in the sequence of topics discussed in these meetings. During Cluster's first two years community meeting discussions about integration focused on admissions. During the next two years of the school the focus changed from admission into the school to life within the school, from integration in terms of a numerical ratio to integration in terms of the quality of social interaction. We hope that the reader will see in the integration sequence a continuation of the pattern of norm development described in discussing the stealing and attendance issues. First, the group responds to a social problem with the creation of a rule or policy that meets the minimal demands for fairness or social order but which falls short of being a norm of community. The admissions policy represented such a solution. It provided for the admission of more black students but failed to deal with tensions between blacks and whites. Second, after some period of frustration, motions based on a deeper change of attitudes and a deeper valuing of community are put forth. Here we see the shift from norms of fairness and order to a norm of community. In the third and fourth years a genuine norm of integration began to form, grounded in the valuing of a common community. While students acknowledged that they had difficulty liking everyone, they felt that in a community they should try to relate in ways which displayed not only respect but positive regard and goodwill.

The Second Year

The first sustained discussion of racial relations in a community meeting came in October 1975. The meeting's agenda called for a decision on a motion to adopt a policy of reverse discrimination and admit six black students before admitting the white students on the waiting list.

Black students banded together in support of the proposal for three major reasons. First, many felt that Cluster's image reflected the life-style of the white, upper-middle-class, "hippy" students. The hippy faction in the school wore their hair long, dressed in tattered undershirts and patched jeans, and delighted in displaying a playful but needling attitude toward whoever and whatever symbolized the conventions of the parent high school or society. Both working-class black and white students called these students "freaks," and had great difficulty accepting their presence in the school. This is how one student put it in an interview:

If you are ever around and see the people running around the hallways, and they jump on the casings of the door and think they are a statue or something, and they sit there and they got their clothes ripped up to the kneecaps and they wear shirts that belonged to an old man in 1920. You don't want to see those people in the school, because you can't learn and look at those people at the same time.

Black students—who maintained many more friendships and contacts with students outside Cluster than did the white students—were particularly upset and embarrassed by the identification with these hippy students.

Second, many black students felt that the votes taken often reflected the interests of the white majority and a disregard for the interests of the black minority. For example, Greg's readmission to Cluster the semester after his expulsion created great consternation among many black students, who felt he was being given so many chances because he was white and could sway his friends who made up the white majority. Many black students viewed the proposal to admit black students before the white students on the waiting list as a way of equalizing power in the school and "evening up the score."

Third, the admissions issue became a test case for black students to see if white students could be sympathetic to their needs. Wasserman (1977) pointed to a certain feeling of "hopelessness" which existed among many black students because they thought the white students were either prejudiced or blind to their point of view.

The specific problem before the community was whether to be impartial by admitting students in order of their priority on the waiting list or to take affirmative action to create a community for which black students would feel more ownership and comfort. A related issue was whom Cluster should serve. Some faculty and students felt that Cluster with its unique program had a special responsibility to educate the most disadvantaged groups of students in Cambridge.

Staff Preparation for the Second-Year Admissions Meeting

Preparation for this meeting was difficult because the staff had to confront the admissions issue on two levels. On the first level, the faculty had to debate the abstract justice issue of affirmative action and its relation to this case. On the second level, they had to anticipate how this issue would be perceived by the students. Affirmative action policies present philosophical quandaries whenever they are proposed. Equal treatment seems to many to entail color blindness, but given the history of discrimination in this country, color blindness perpetuates inequalities and prejudice. Promoting equality may, therefore, require the preferential treatment of discriminated-against minorities. In dealing with the particular case in Cluster, Kohlberg took the Rawlsian position that being on the waiting list did not give the white students an antecedent right to be admitted to school. Fairness demanded that the point of view of both black and white students be considered and that a decision be made that would favor the least advantaged. He also noted that Cluster School had been established with a special commitment to deprived minorities, that affirmative action was written into the very foundation of the school.

Not all the faculty agreed with Kohlberg's stance on affirmative action. Kohlberg did not ask for unanimity on such issues, nor did he encourage the faculty to suppress philosophical differences in community. He did, however, ask the faculty to put their own concerns on the back burner, as much as this was possible, and to focus on the concerns the students would raise in the community meeting. Kohlberg thought the issue for most students would not be one of affirmative action, but rather one of racial subgroup norms at stages 2 and 3 standing in the way of genuine integration. Among the black students there were those who wanted to enhance black power by increasing the number of "their own kind." Likewise among the white students there were those who were prejudiced against blacks. Among both groups there were students who wanted a more unprejudiced and integrated sense of community. It appeared to the staff that a vote in favor of affirmative action would represent a movement toward a higher-stage valuing of community and hopefully a norm of integration at stage 3.

The Meeting

The community meeting on October 31, 1975, remains one of the most intense and explosive in Cluster's history. Wasserman (1977) praised it as demonstrating the fairness and effectiveness of the just community approach. Bennett and Delattre damned it as exemplifying " 'a hidden curriculum' of instruction in partial justice" and a "tyrannical" disregard for rational discourse (1978:96, 97). Students who had been discussing racial relations in a special democracy class presented the proposal that the six openings in the school be filled by black students. Sally spoke for most of the black students when she said:

You see, I'm one of the people that wants some black people to come in. . . . because it's just like I feel I would be more comfortable with them here. I would feel more comfortable, because I want them here . . . I want to let people come and experience the school who are black.

Several white males argued that if black students wanted to increase their numbers, they should encourage black students to sign up on the waiting list. Patty responded with an expletive and was reprimanded by the chair. Several minutes later she had the floor.

Can I ask you white people something? I'm not prejudiced, but is it going to make that much difference if there are six more black people instead of white? Is it? There's forty-seven of you . . . whities now. There's eighteen blacks! Six more blacks isn't going to make one . . . difference.

In response to the objection that only one black student was on the waiting list, Patty claimed that she now had her own list of black students who wished to enter the school.

A few white students asked why the black students felt uncomfortable in the school. A black student responded:

Well, I'm going to tell you why I feel uncomfortable. Before I knew who was here, I phoned Cambridge Latin and I didn't want to sign up with Latin, so I heard about Cluster and I came down. This is my first year in this school and I don't know who's here. Never in my life have I seen as many of you who have outnumbered me and mine, anyway. OK, then I get to know them. I say, these whites are all right, you know. And my opinions changed, they changed just a little bit, all right? And then I go home and I look, I listen to the news and I see what the whities are doing to the blacks. For what? Because they want to learn. And then I come back here and try to get some of my brothers and sisters into this school so they can be helped like I'm being helped. And what do I hear? No. Because they don't want to hear it. Why can't they just give us eighteen blacks a little personal satisfaction within ourselves to have some more of us so we can be together? All right! (Applause)

The black students gained support from a number of white students who appealed to a communitarian ethic of care. Phil, one of the more articulate white students, expressed what he believed to be the group's feeling:

All the people in this community right now are all saying in some way or another, usually they don't want to say it, but they are expressing feelings that they care about the other people and how their education goes and their working with this community goes. And I feel that the blacks in this community can't work as well and feel as comfortable without more blacks in the community. It's not fair. Everybody knows that everybody in this school, no matter how it sounds now, cares about the other people. Then why can't you allow six more blacks in, so twenty-whatever blacks will be able to get a good education in this school and a good sense of democracy and just everything. And you know, why can't we just let six more blacks in, it would help the whole thing. The whole community, the whole school would be helped by that.

Phyllis, a black student whom we have noted as the eloquent advocate of collective restitution, responded to a question about what should be said to the people on the waiting list if they were not admitted. She replied, "All you have to do is explain to them that it was the best idea to take all blacks this time for the community's sake." As the number of students favoring the democracy class' proposal grew, a small group of white students persisted in their objections. They began muttering derisive comments about the black students, which led to a shouting match in which a group of black girls threatened retaliation. When one of the more contentious white students asked whether the black students meant by their proposal that "blacks are better than anyone else," Patty shot back:

What do you white people think you are? That black people are lower than you? Because all the other times when the black man had to work with the white man and slave for him, what, you whites think you could do that now? You must be crazy.

Patty's friend Jean concluded:

You know, you ain't doing nobody no favors. . . . You are all acting like you're doing us a favor. You know if you want your school, you can take it. . . . Because everybody owns this school. I don't see how anybody could come here and say, "This is my school, I don't want those people in here." You know if all you were in a class, one or two with twenty black kids, how would you feel?

A few minutes later a vote was taken on the proposal to admit six black students. It passed by a large majority.

Aftermath

There was real consistency among student reactions to the meeting. Both white and black students perceived the outcome as a "victory" for the black students. Patty commented on the feelings of the black students after the vote: "We felt together, we felt damn right, we got our point across." Gerri, a retiring white student, corroborated. "People felt like they had kinda like won their little war and had as much power as the white students." Most of the white students said they could sympathize with the black students' feelings of discomfort and were quite pleased to help them. A white student, Ethan, reflected on the fairness of giving priority to those within the community over outsiders:

If you are going to think in terms of abstract fairness, then maybe it was unfair for those six or seven whites who were on the waiting list to be bypassed. But you can't think of abstract fairness, or you can, but when you are presented with the reality of the situation at the school, and the reality that people within the school, a large section of the community, feel strongly that that would help them, then aid the community. The needs of the community come before needs of the people outside the community as far as running the school goes.

In spite of a general agreement that the vote was a gesture of concern for black students, the students interviewed questioned whether this meeting contributed to group solidarity. Some white students confided that whites had made prejudicial remarks about the black and white students who had voted in favor of the proposal. One recounted:

After I got done voting that I wanted them to be there, I walked outside and a lot of people called them nigger and called me nigger lover. And I just turned around and said, "Try to put yourself in their shoes. How would you like it if the shoe was on the other foot?"

Also students felt that although the meeting may have increased cohesiveness among blacks, the gap between black and white students had actually widened:

It seemed like the black students became a little closer, but that white and black students now became just a little more separated from the school. There still is a connection (between black and white students), but I don't think it is as close as at the very beginning of last year.

A pressing question raised by a student in the middle of the October meeting was left unanswered. He asked, "I just want to know—if we could solve this we'd be all set—why people feel uncomfortable in the school, why black people feel uncomfortable with all these other people?" This question reemerged in another admissions meeting held in April 1976. During this meeting black students helped white students to understand their role as a minority and explained why they felt uncomfortable in the school. While black students still favored preferential admission, they now argued that Cluster was such a good school that the community should be generous enough to help black students who wanted to come in:

I don't think there is a black person in this room or in this school, when they walk into a room of all white students they never feel uncomfortable. But that is not the point. The point is . . . that this school is really something and everyone should get into it, and more black people should be able to get into it because it is really good.

Several students proposed that Cluster's population should represent other minorities in addition to blacks. The community voted to pursue a policy of active recruitment of all minorities. This policy was partly successful, for by the beginning of the third year, the proportion of black-to-white students was almost equal, and in the fourth year several Hispanic students had entered.

Analysis

As we noted in the introduction to these meetings, the norm of integration that developed in the second year is best classified as a fairness norm. The overriding student concern was to determine whether the request made by the black students for more of their own was a fair one. The thrust of the proposal from the democracy class was not to bring black and white students into a more harmonious relationship but to acknowledge the interests of the subgroup of black students. We do, however, see ambiguous references to a communal norm of caring. For example, Phil advocated admitting six black students "because everybody knows that everybody in the school . . . cares about the other people." Even this norm of caring borders on a fairness norm of respect for others and their legitimate interests and a communal norm of selfless giving to others. Recall that Jean explicitly rejected the patronizing notion of admitting black students as "a favor," and Patty questioned whether white students' objection to the proposal was based on feelings of racial superiority.

Given the racial animosity which surfaced in the meeting and the pressure that both black and white students exerted on their peers to vote along racial lines, the community meetings on admissions served to work out a truce between factions rather than bring them together. The decisions made in the first and second meetings gave a clear signal to the black students that although they were a minority in the school, they could exert a significant influence. Jean's question, "Who owns the school?" was effectively answered. Cluster was not to be a "white school" that condescended to include blacks, but "everybody's school."

From the point of view of the collectivization of Cluster's norms and the phase of the community value, this feeling of "ownership" that the black students gained was important. Because they were a minority, black students were unsure that the democratic process could respond to their interests. The admissions meetings convinced them that they were genuinely members of the school, capable of being heard and exercising power. While the affirmative action decisions helped black students to feel a part of the community, they should not be regarded as unambiguously furthering the collectivization of a norm of integration. The meetings had the immediate impact of increasing solidarity within the black student subgroup. Some white students felt this took place at the expense of the solidarity of the whole community. Yet the question must then be raised, "Solidarity on whose terms?" In our opinion the black students correctly sensed that unless they solidified their presence within Cluster, the school might assume an identity which would *de facto* prohibit other blacks from entering the school and make their own continued membership in the school quite difficult. Cluster could have become a "white school," like the A School or S.W.S. In those schools attempts to pass affirmative action programs repeatedly failed because white students believed that a small minority of blacks would feel uncomfortable in such "white environments." Because minority enrollment in Cluster could have gone either way in the fall of the second year, the affirmative action decisions were very significant.

In assessing the phase of the collective norms raised in these meetings, it is helpful to consider each norm discretely. Insofar as an integration norm is developing, it is a norm related to that of caring for others in need. In the October admissions meeting the phase of the caring norm appeared to be 3. Although Phil, in particular, assumed that everyone in Cluster lived up to this norm, his assumption was contradicted. For example, another student said, "I think that a lot of people in this community don't really care, everybody's shooting on everybody else." While Phil and some students thought of caring as a generalized expectation, a significant number of students saw it as a distant ideal, at least when issues of race were concerned. The fact that some white students were called "nigger lovers" for supporting the proposal indicates not only the low phase of the caring norm but the existence of what we call a counternorm, a peer group norm at odds with the collective norms that the staff were seeking to form with students. This counternorm presented a far greater obstacle to strengthening the phase of the norm of caring than individual student opposition or apathy.

The April community meeting transcript and the ethnographic interviews, administered at the end of the school year, indicate that the norm of caring developed to phase four. The counternorms that had perpetuated hostility disappeared. In addition, black students retreated from their position that affirmative action was necessary because they were uncomfortable. Rather, they acknowledged that a spirit of caring was a generally held expectation at Cluster which they wanted to extend to outsiders with special needs.

The stage of the collective norm of integration appears to have been stage 2–3 in the October meeting and to have progressed to stage 3 by April. In the October meeting many black students voiced their concerns in terms of a stage 2 demand for the satisfaction of demonstrable, concrete wants and needs ("We should have more blacks because we want them and feel uncomfortable without them") and for the equalization of power ("Who owns this school?"). The white students who sided with them did so for stage 2 reasons (to get along and to avoid fights) and for stage 3 reasons (out of sympathy for their discomfort). During the second admissions meeting almost all black students expressed a stage 3 concern for helping white students understand their feelings and for sharing the benefits of Cluster membership with disadvantaged blacks. Most of the white students responded quite positively at stage 3.

The Third Year

Questions of how integrated the Cluster community was and how integrated it should become were squarely faced in the third year. They surfaced when the only black faculty member, Ben, complained before a community meeting that his core class had become so large that it was unmanageable. Admission into the core classes was done on a voluntary basis that year, with students supposedly selecting teachers who indicated they would best suit their learning style. After unsuccessfully trying to persuade members of his class to transfer, Ben had no recourse but to seek the aid of the community. Ben's class presented a problem in addition to size; it was predominantly black. Paul, a black student who was not in Ben's class, took center stage by charging that he knew that many of the black students in Ben's class were there just to be with their friends and to have a good time. He challenged them to admit the truth about it. When they did not respond, he called out their names and said: "I know all you want to do is fool around and talk about basketball. I knew that if I wanted to learn I'd have to go to another class where I wouldn't be with my friends and could concentrate on my work." Paul's charges were greeted by forced laughter and loud denials. Yet a decision was made to discuss the matter further at a later date. In the meantime, Ben's class promised the community that they would "shape up," if Ben allowed them all to remain. He agreed to do so on a provisional basis.

The Meeting

A few weeks later Ben returned to the community. Nothing had changed. Several suggestions were offered, such as asking for volunteers to switch out, giving Ben the right to decide who should be in his class, or having a lottery to determine who could stay. Kohlberg interjected that he thought from the previous meeting that the problem went further than the size of Ben's class; it involved the question of racial division among the core classes. Ben agreed: "The issue is integration and diversity in classes and not so much my class." Frank, a white student in Ben's class, objected. "I don't want to break up my group when they are just getting it together." Ben retorted, "That's the whole thing we have to do. Some people don't want to break up groups, and that doesn't necessarily deal with a community-like attitude." Tom, a white hippy student, sided with Ben:

I think we have a good group and a good class, but I think I am missing out on a lot of people's opinions. I think we have a very diverse group of people here with some very different thoughts in their heads, and I think that we could all learn from each other a lot. We will never learn from each other if we are separated into separate little groups. Ben's class has people who think about the same. And Andy's [T] class has another group of people who think really differently, and if we mix them together we will come out with a learning experience that will just be incredible.

Tom then proposed that Andy's accelerated, all-white class be merged with Ben's:

So the formal proposal is that the two groups merge and then break into two groups after that, but keeping as one basic core class, referring to each other, and people could move back and forth in the classes, as things work toward a working out, but hopefully they will split into two groups of equal size.

Tom's proposal was defeated in the straw vote and he withdrew it toward the end of the meeting, claiming that he had only intended that it be "a tool for discussion." He then launched into an eloquent personal plea for a community that could bring together people with very different values:

I feel this way: I don't hang out with a lot of people in this room right now, I don't know if I could have a meaningful relationship with them, I don't know if that could happen. A lot of things have gone on in past years so that that may never happen. But I think we have the courage to make it happen. I think that we have the power to become one group and really break away those barriers and get to be friends with everybody in the community.

The issue dragged into the next week without a solution. Students felt torn not only by peer group loyalties but also by the conflict between the educational advantages of dividing the group according to learning style and achieving integration. Tom reported that his adviser group advocated both academic excellence and integration but that the core classes should concentrate on education. Patty added: "We also talked about that. In core classes too much is based on moral development and we need more education. . . . In English here we don't do stuff. . . . We don't learn basic U.S. history here." Faculty members pointed out that education meant more than learning grammar and history. Andy (T) put it this way:

You are taking what I would call a very narrow view of the ideal education. Education is not just nouns, verbs, and adjectives. Education is also learning to get along with your neighbors. You don't do one or the other, you do both.

A few students felt that to expect people with very different life-styles to become friends was unrealistic. Simon thought it was like wanting to mix "cats and dogs":

Each group was brought up in different places, and we can't take a person that grows up in his own style and make him go into somebody else's style and vice versa. . . . That would be like taking a dog and a cat and putting them together. They are going to fight. I think you can't press on people to make friends with who they don't want to, because that won't work.

Simon explained how difficult he found it to adjust to the "freaks"— "people taking their shoes off and picking their toes." Several students responded to Simon by saying that he was not being considerate in his comments; and he clarified what he meant, saying that he believed people should "respect" each other, but he did not think they should have to be friends. The issue was finally resolved with a vote that black students in Ben's class voluntarily withdraw in order to better integrate other classes.

Aftermath

During the next community meeting, core class rosters were reviewed and everyone was satisfied that a racial balance had been achieved. This led a faculty member to address the group: "I think we are to congratulate ourselves; this is one of the few times we brought a real problem to the school and solved it." Not only had the group managed to diversify classes, but there were also signs that racial barriers were being broken down. Throughout the remainder of community meetings that year, black and white students sat with each other, and there were few occasions in which either black or white students voted as a block. Two of the white students, who had been thought of as "freaks," got haircuts and wore more conventional clothes as a conscious gesture of their sincerity in trying to overcome some of the subcultural barriers in the community. Finally, when students went on their end-of-the-year retreat they agreed to have activities in which everyone would mix with each other, and they did.

Analysis

These community meetings and the moral atmosphere interviews show that among students who had been in the school for over a year, a stage 3–4 collective norm of integration was developing. Members of the school were expected not only to "get along" in the sense of avoiding negative behaviors but to communicate about their differences and to build relationships. While all of the students we interviewed thought of racial integration as at least an ideal for the school (phase 2), few students actually saw it occurring or even fully expected that it could occur given the diversity of life-styles in their group. A black student expressed this phase 2 sentiment in her interview: "That's what it is supposed to be—'friends'—but students don't feel that." In the community meeting we found a similar view, best exemplified by Simon's statement that integration is like putting a "dog and a cat . . . together." Nevertheless, the fact that students did switch classes indicated a willingness to try to overcome barriers. Here is how Patty explained why she switched: "Everybody said that I should . . . and they thought it would be democratic. I thought it was a good idea, a way of trying to get to know people and break up the cliques."

The Fourth Year

The successful resolution of the class size problem in the third year did not end tensions between blacks and whites in the community. In the fall of the fourth year, as in the beginning of previous school years, black and white students gravitated toward separate homerooms and adviser groups, and many spent their free time in segregated friendship groups. Knowing that there were distinct "turf" areas and cliques in the school disturbed the staff and some students. The staff were agreed that this division should finally be confronted because they believed that the past discussions about socially balancing the school and classes made discussion of informal integration a real possibility. At the same time, they recognized that some students would feel uncomfortable discussing clique patterns. Their willingness to go ahead was part of their more general policy in the fourth year of having Cluster School address concerns of the community that lay outside formal rule making. Confronting the problems of cliques and turfs presented an opportunity for members to examine their valuing of community and their commitment to racial integration.

The discussion of cliques broached new territory but did not advance the stage or the phase of the norm of integration beyond what had been achieved in the previous year. However, because of the difficulty in resolving the clique problem, students became more reflective in community meetings and in their interviews about the nature of racial and ethnic group differences and why they appeared to be intractable.

Summary

Our analysis showed that Cluster's integration norm shifted in content from fairness, as nonprejudice, in the first year to community, as care, in the second year and afterward. In the second year student statements indicating the phase of the integration norm were bimodally distributed between phase 2 and phase 4. In the third-year community meeting analysis the phase of the norm of integration appeared to slip somewhat to a bimodal 2–3 distribution. However, note that the stage of the integration norm developed in the third year from 2–3 to 3–4. What appears to have happened is that as students entertained a richer conception of integration in the third year, they perceived it as more of an ideal or an agreement than as a realistic expectation. Recall that in the second year students focused less on internal problems of racial relations than on whether they should have an affirmative action admissions policy. In the third year they faced for the first time a concrete problem concerning racial cliques within the school. By the fourth year there was some slight phase progress on the stage 3–4 norm of integration to a bimodal phase 3–4 distribution. This indicated that most students felt that they had made some agreement as Cluster members to build an integrated school.

The phase of the norm of integration did not develop as far as the trust or participation (attendance) norms at Cluster. Although students accepted the ideal of an integrated community, cliques based on race and social class stood in the way of attaining that ideal and discouraged many students from trying to reach out. The reader should not lose sight of the fact that in spite of the difficulties in developing a strong integration norm, the students did hold a norm of nonprejudicial respect for others at a high phase from the end of the second year on. In the third and fourth years of the school they focused on the much more elusive issue of informal peer socializing. This is an area of community life in which it is impossible to legislate. Even with a resolve to remediate the clique problem, it is a most difficult ideal to translate into action. Voluntarily switching the core classes and agreeing to racially mix student cabin assignments on the retreat were attempts in this direction in the third year. During the fourth year these efforts continued.

ALCOHOL AND MARIJUANA USE

Probably no other issue divided the adolescent society in the 1970s from its teachers as much as the use of drugs—and particularly the smoking of marijuana.[2] We found the division not only at Cluster, but also at the A School, S.W.S., and the Murray Road Alternative School in Newton, Massachusetts, and suspect it exists in almost all schools. It is not a clear-cut division, for not only are there adolescents in each of these schools who oppose the smoking of marijuana, but there are also teachers whose opposition is not to the use of drugs per se, but to their improper use during school. Nevertheless, the battle over "pot and alcohol" seems a constant feature of contemporary high school life.

Our interest in this issue derives from the way it affects not only questions of order, but also questions of community. The battle over pot extended throughout the first four years of Cluster, coming to a head usually at the time of retreats. The first retreat during the first year was preceded by a meeting at which a discussion about drugs led to a serious division of opinion between marijuana users and nonusers. When the faculty threatened to cancel the retreat, a rule against drugs on the retreat was adopted. But no sooner did the retreat begin than there were reported violations of the rule. The faculty called an emergency community meeting in which there was a good discussion about community, but little commitment to get tough on drug use.

After a number of drug-related incidents, including a student's being caught smoking by the principal of the high school, a working agreement about drugs did evolve. It became clear to almost everyone that the open

2. This discussion borrows in part from a previously published chapter by Reimer and Power (1980).

use of drugs—which after all broke the rules of the state and the larger school—would generally endanger Cluster's existence and particularly put the teachers in the nasty position of having to enforce the law against the students. Thus a rule against drugs in school was adopted, and those students who flagrantly violated it were punished. However, many students implicitly interpreted the rule to mean that they were obligated to be discreet about, rather than cease using, drugs. While this implicit understanding helped to avoid open conflict, no strong (phase 4) normative expectations evolved during the first year.

The Second Year

In October of Cluster's second year staff and students went on a retreat. They had made a special agreement to abide by all school rules, especially the drug rule. But the first night of the retreat students from one of the cabins broke out some liquor they had stashed away. Soon the noise and antics roused the staff, who caught one student running around squirting a fire extinguisher and others throwing firecrackers. The next day an outraged staff called a community meeting. They decided to encourage the students to handle this incident themselves and so avoid being cast as prosecutors. They hoped they could get the guilty students to "confess" and then involve the whole group in working out a suitable punishment.

The Meeting

The community meeting began with Andy (T) charging students with "being extremely disrespectful and rowdy." He zeroed in on an incident in which a student threw a firecracker into a room in which he and other teachers were sleeping. He then asked students to give their versions of the events of the prior night. At first, the students in the cabin admitted there was liquor in the cabin but denied that any drinking was going on. Felix, the student who threw the firecracker into Andy's room, excused himself by saying that he just threw it there for kicks. "If I had known that . . . someone was going to get really upset about it, I never would have thought about it." Clint (T) focused the issue by recalling why Cluster had decided to have a drug rule in the first place.

When we discussed the drug rule we thought it would be kind of OK if someone went out into the woods and drank a can of beer as long as I was not affecting anybody and as long as nobody knows that I am drinking. But last night was an entirely different situation. ... Felix would have shot that firecracker no matter who asked him not to. And that proves to me that the community was affected by his action and to my mind he has to pay.

Andy advocated following the prescribed punishment for breaking the drug rule by calling up the parents of those drinking. Some of the accused students objected that the punishment was too severe because their parents might "pull them out of school" and that it was unfair to single them out for punishment while others who broke the rule remained undetected. Kevin summarized their arguments:

Felix [the student with the firecracker] feels it isn't fair to the accused people, even if they were getting drunk, for people of this community to vote to punish them when assorted other people in the community got drunk and high. So we, the rest of the community, some got high, and we are going to judge whether those people should get punished or not, and we should see that's not fair ... and one proposal is that there be an alternative punishment because Felix and Keith and Erin felt that if their parents come in they will be out of this school. If their parents came into the community and found this out and knew all about this situation, they would be pulled out of school. And school means enough to them so that they really don't want that. So you won't be just voting on whether they broke the drug rule but whether they should be in school.

Billy suggested a compromise: students who confessed getting drunk or high to the community should be given a lesser punishment:

If they admit, if they can come up here and tell you that they did get drunk or were high that takes a lot of guts. ... when you know your parents could come up and could be thrown out or have your ass beaten or all this complicated stuff with your parents, I think they should get a lesser punishment if they have the guts, if they have the heart to stand up here and tell everyone that they were high.

Nona stunned the group by responding to Billy's challenge: "I want to say that I didn't bring alcohol up here, but I drank it last night." This impressed the students. Clint asked Felix to do the same. Felix bargained: "A lot of people ain't going to say that they did it because they don't want their parents up here. If there is an alternative punishment besides parents coming up here, I bet you will have everybody saying it." He turned this into a motion which carried the straw vote easily. Immediately after the vote was taken, Felix spoke up, "Now that you are not going to call my parents, there ain't no sense in my lying no more! . . . I am saying that I was drinking." Following Felix's confession, each student in the cabin who was seen drinking or partying with those who were drinking was asked whether or not he or she drank. All but two students admitted to drinking.

At the next community meeting adviser groups presented a number of alternative punishments, such as giving all the students caught drinking a cut, requiring attendance at an AA meeting, and having them clean Cluster classrooms after school. Yet the majority of students favored modifying the punishment they had originally stipulated in their rule (that a parent conference be called for the first offense) by having a parent conference for *all* Cluster members. At this general meeting the drinking episodes could be discussed without bringing up particular names.

Patty objected to this as "picking apart" the Cluster rules. She asked, "What happens the next time we go on a retreat and people drink?" There was some discussion of whether those caught drinking on this past retreat would be expelled on their second offense as the rule stipulated. A further question was raised whether the drug rule should be changed for the future to eliminate parent conferences. Alvin responded to this vacillation by siding with Patty.

I was thinking myself about the history of decisions we have made about important issues, and every time we made a rule, that was like forethought, so if someone did something, we would have the punishment for that particular thing. But almost in every instance we set aside a rule when that punishment came, when the person did the crime, and we made a punishment for that person, so that was sort of like afterthought, where everything is put aside and we are always behind ourselves in everything we are doing. I myself am tired of the idea of having the rules bent and putting ourselves behind and also making our ethics sacrilegious to what we believe in, so I want the rules not to be bent, even if they are right or wrong and not have the idea of bending them in every situation.

Karl supported Alvin's position with a contractual rationale for upholding the rules. "I agree with what Alvin said, only I think that it is important enough to be put into a motion and vote on it. I don't know if I can make a motion now and discuss this, but I think a general consensus is that everyone wants to follow the rules that are written, and we should, as a school, we all made up these rules."

Bob agreed with their point, although he felt strongly that parents should not be called up: "I agree that we shouldn't bend the rules and we shouldn't put them aside. But I don't believe that my parents should have to come up because some parents, like I said before, parents don't get along with their children that well. If I brought my parents up here, they might just make things worse."

Karl sympathized but stressed the need to work through the legislative process to change the rules: "We should follow all the rules as they are. If we don't like them, then we should change them, but we have the rules. Bring them up in adviser groups and change them if you don't like them."

The meeting concluded with a decision to have a general parent conference and to require that the guilty students paint two of Cluster's homerooms "to give something back to the community."

Analysis

The phase of the drug norm became 4, that is, most students expected others to live up to the rule. William's (T) adviser group reported that before, the rule had not been "taken seriously," but that "now, we realize and internalize the feeling that we are going to take our rule seriously." This is the best expression of this phase. During these meetings support for enforcing the drug rule was based on a concern between stages 3 and 4 that the community's rules be upheld out of a respect for the community's authority and the prior agreement all had made. Alvin's Durkheimian-like appeal to the "sacredness" of the rule was the best example of this: "I myself am tired of the idea of having the rules bent and putting ourselves behind and also making our ethics sacrilegious to what we believe in."

In spite of the development of the drug norm, the end-of-the-year ethnographic interview analysis revealed that there was some covert smoking at lunchtime. This bad news was mixed with some good news:

many of the Cluster founders had given up smoking for the sake of the community—and the smoking was pretty well limited to newcomers to the school. One of them, who daily violated the drug rule and was not shy about discussing it, was Patty. Arguing from a stage 2 perspective, she wanted the drug rule to be changed. Nevertheless, she acknowledged that she was only speaking for herself, that the community actually supported the norm.

I didn't pay any attention to that [drug rule] because I get high in school, and I didn't even know what they were talking about. They have to change that rule because if you're coming to school high that's your business as long as you don't bother anybody. . . . But I guess they [Cluster students] don't feel that way.

The failure of some of the new students to uphold the drug norm should not obscure the progress that had been made since the first year, when blatant drug use disrupted classes and threatened the reputation of the school. In addition to the strict, no-drugs norm, an alternative norm developed permitting only discreet marijuana use. It later came to be known as the "be cool rule." Although only a small subgroup of students followed the "be cool rule" in the second year, a majority did in the third. We would characterize the "be cool rule" as a stage 2–3, phase 4 norm. It is a mixed stage 2–3 norm because it combines a pragmatic stage 2 concern for avoiding punishment and a stage 3 community-oriented concern for not upsetting others, particularly the teachers, or damaging the reputation of the school. The strict no-drugs norm and the "be cool rule" eliminated all public incidents involving drug use, and the issue of drug use did not arise for almost two years, until preparations for the third-year spring retreat.

The Third and Fourth Years

The issue of drug use surfaced during the Cluster retreat in the third year, when it became public knowledge that the students directly responsible for losing the dock had been high. Staff members expressed surprise that smoking had been going on behind their backs, while many students maintained that in spite of the dock incident the "be cool rule" had worked pretty well. In the fall of the fourth year several Cluster students were caught smoking marijuana, and token punishments were administered with the greatest reluctance. Students and staff frankly admitted the drug rule had become "a joke," and a proposal was made to replace it with a participation rule. That proposal, which enjoyed considerable student support, addressed the problem of getting high but left the decision of whether to smoke up to the discretion of the individual. What they wanted was the "be cool rule" without the hypocrisy. They saw nothing intrinsically wrong with marijuana use. Moreover, many thought smoking a joint together could serve the positive function of overcoming social barriers, particularly of race, and thus promote community. The staff and a number of students supported a linkage between the drug issue and community building but came to the conclusion that community values could only be upheld if drug use were prohibited. When the fourth year ended the community was at an impasse. The old rule was still on the books, but it lacked the force of a collective norm. Thus the drug norm, which had peaked at phase 4 during the second year, steadily declined over the next two years and ended at phase 1.

Nucci offers an interpretation for Cluster's failure to maintain a drug norm, based on Turiel's distinction between a moral norm and a convention. He argues that since drug use was a convention, an educational approach focused solely on moral development would be inadequate. Nucci is not criticizing the just community approach per se. His major contention is that it is limited and requires a supplemental approach.

There is evidence that a unitary approach to social rules that places convention within the moral domain does not have an equally beneficial effect in students' appreciation of social conventional and moral standards. . . . Geiger's (1978) study [a study showing links between conventional development and disruptive school behavior] suggests that an approach to classroom management and values education that effectively caused adolescents to construct coordinated conceptions of conventional norms would have a positive effect precisely on those conventional behaviors unaffected by the just community approach to moral education reported by Power and Reimer (1978). (1982:7)

While Nucci's insights help us to grasp the subtleties of the drug problem, we do not agree with his conclusion that the just community approach was inadequate for dealing with it. We believe that certain so-called conventional norms like drug use can take on a moral status insofar as they influence the establishment and maintenance of the social bonds necessary for community. In the following chapter, when we discuss the A School, we will present a more successful just community resolution to the drug issue.

Summary

The drug norm began in the spring of the first year as a phase 3, stage 3 norm of order. The content norm started to shift the second year as respect for the drug rule became associated with respect for the authority of the community. In the third and fourth years the drug norm was perceived as a community norm of participation. As we noted, the phase of the drug norm was highest in the second year, phase 4, and then declined in the third year to 3 and finally to 1 in the fourth year.

The finding of a regression in the norm concerning drug use does not violate our expectations for cultural development as we described them in the last chapter. Phases are a measure of student commitment to uphold collective norms. As our presentation of the discussions of the drug issue illustrates, the Cluster "founders" were the strongest and most effective supporters of the norm. They understood why drug use and participation do not mix from their experience during the first year of Cluster, and they had the benefit of many community meeting discussions on the drug rule and its enforcement over that year. Many of the students who entered the school during the second and third years never really discovered why there was a drug rule in the first place, as there were no community meeting discussions of drugs until the very end of the third year. Unfortunately, in the fourth year, with most of the founders having graduated, there were few student advocates for an effective drug rule, and the staff was forced to begin anew to build peer support.

The stage of the drug norm developed from 3 in the first year to 3–4 in the second and remained at stage 3–4 thereafter. Curiously many of the most vocal opponents of the drug rule clearly understood it in stage 3–4 terms. Their opposition was based in part on the libertarian grounds that the rule violated their rights and in part on a lack of willingness to make a sacrifice.

CONCLUSIONS FROM COMMUNITY MEETING AND ETHNOGRAPHIC INTERVIEW ANALYSES

We present an overview of the stage and phase assessment of the collective norms in table 5.1. This table shows quite clearly how norms

Table 5.1.
Modal Stages and Phases of Collective Norms

Issue	Year	Collective Norm	Content	Stage Community Meeting	Stage Interview	Phase Meeting	Phase Interview
Property	1	Property	Fairness	2 (Faculty proposals)	2	3	1–2
	1	Trust	Community	3 (Faculty proposals)	—	0,1	0
	2	Trust	Community	3	3	4–5	4
	3	Trust	Community	—	—	4	4
	4	Trust	Community	—	3	4	4
Attendance	1	Attendance	Order	2–3	2–3	3	3
	1	Participation	Community	3 (Faculty proposals)	2–3	1	3
	2	Ambiguous	Order/community	3	2–3	4	3 (2)
	3	Participation	Community	3–4	3	6	6 (4,7)
	4	Participation	Community	3–4	3–4	4–6	4 (7)
Racial relationships	1	Nonprejudice	Fairness	2–3	2–3	2	—
	2	Caring/respect	Community/fairness	3	2–3	4	2 (4)
	2	Integration	Community	2–3	—	2–4	—
	3	Integration	Community	3–4	2–3	2–3	2 (4)
	4	Integration	Community	3–4	3–4	3–4	4 (2)
Drugs	1	Drug rule	Order	3	2–3	3	3 (4)
	2	Community authority	Order/community	3–4	—	4	0,3,4,5
	3	Participation	Community	3–4	2–3	3 (4)	2 (3)
	4	Participation	Community	3–4	3–4	1	0 (1)
Collective restitution	1	—	—	—	—	—	—
	2	Collective restitution	Community	3–4	—	3	—
	3	Collective restitution	Community	3–4	—	4 (3)	—
	4	Collective restitution	Community	3–4	—	4	—

NOTE: The numbers in parentheses indicate that 25 percent or more of students' perceptions were scored at this value.

developed from faculty proposals in the first year to stage 3–4 and phase 4 norms by the fourth year. The table also indicates that there was fair agreement between the community meetings and the ethnographic assessments. The scores used in both assessments were arrived at by rating individual statements and calculating the modes for each category. The only systematic discrepancy is that the collective stage scores tend to be slightly higher in the community meeting analysis. This discrepancy may have occurred because the students who articulated collective norms in community meetings may have been more advanced in their stage of reasoning than the average student.

In conclusion, all of the hypotheses raised at the end of the previous chapter were confirmed:

1. Cluster's norms were progressively collectivized. Generally this collectivization process began during the first year, when the rules were being made.
2. The content of the collective norms shifted during the second and third years from norms of substantive fairness and order to norms of community.
3. Phase development was generally sequential. The exceptions from the community meeting analysis were minor (only by one phase), and the ethnographic interviews supplied the intermediary phases in most cases. The one case of regression did not violate our hypothesis.
4. Stage development was similarly sequential, and there were no examples of regression.
5. There was some overall consistency in the pattern of development across norms. Generally, the norms were between phases 0 and 3 in the first year and 4 thereafter. Similarly, the norms tended to be stage 2–3 in the first year, 3 in the second year, and 3–4 in the third and fourth years. However, there were interesting differences among the norms. For example, the drug norm regressed in phase and the other norms developed in phase and stage at different paces.

HISTORICAL POSTSCRIPT: CLUSTER'S FIFTH YEAR AND ITS IMPACT ON THE WIDER SCHOOL

Cluster School, as an alternative high school, lasted only five years. Then, instead of remaining an administratively separate alternative school, it became a "leadership program," renamed K-100. Several factors, external and internal, contributed to this reorganization. Externally, a new headmaster of Cambridge Rindge and Latin pressed for a greater consolidation of alternative programs within the parent high school. In a time of tight budgets he threatened to cut back on Cluster's staffing. Internally, an inability to meet recruitment goals for two consecutive years led to serious questions about the future of Cluster, especially given the prospect of reduced staffing. Although the number of students joining Cluster was dwindling, the problems they brought to Cluster (both in terms of discipline and learning) seemed to be adding up. Understandably, the staff were reluctant to accept a worse faculty-student ratio with this situation. Rejecting the options of continuing Cluster with fewer staff or closing it down, they reconstituted it as a leadership program with a more manageable population of students and fewer staff.

The K-100 program went into effect in the fall of 1980 with 45 students, many of whom had been in Cluster, and two of the Cluster faculty members.[3] The major institutions of Cluster, the community meeting, the D.C., and the adviser groups, were retained, as was the guiding philosophy of the school—Kohlberg's just community approach. The core curriculum of English and social studies was revamped along the lines of Fenton's "civic education" programs. Fenton had been on sabbatical in 1974–75, working with Kohlberg in developing curricula and moral discussion formats for moral and civic education. He was impressed with the potential of the Cluster School's just community approach, but he felt that the approach could never be widely disseminated if it remained within the framework of a separate alternative school. Accordingly, he developed a civic education format that functioned for two periods a day. His model eliminated the organizational and fiscal complexities of establishing a separate school, and left the program free of the onerous connotations of "alternative school." The Cluster staff welcomed the greater inclusion within the parent high school that the Fenton model offered. They felt that being in an alternative school had isolated them from their peers, and weakened the positive impact Cluster may have had on the larger high school.

The K-100 program continued to deal with many of the same issues we have discussed in this chapter. One noticeable difference from Cluster

3. This postscript was composed with the help of K-100 faculty members Betsy Grady and Phyllis Brethols.

was that the racial and social class composition of the student body changed such that it was largely white and middle class. For a while the program maintained "open slots" for minority students while turning down actively interested volunteers. One particularly conflictual community meeting was held when a middle-class white applicant, Danny, appealed to the community to be admitted on the grounds that as a senior, it was his last chance to experience K-100:

... everyone is the same, our blood is the same color. I'm a senior, leaving this year, and this is my last chance to make a contribution in high school or in general ... and to be a member of a group like this. ... I have a lot of experiences to offer.

A white male student presented a rebuttal based on stage 4 consistency:

We're not rejecting Danny because of anything personal ... we're being honest. We've made a decision with good judgment—affirmative action —about letting people in. Do we let someone tug at our hearts and then let them in on the basis of friendship? ... That's where the conflict is ... it's drawing the line somewhere and explaining to that person hoping he understands.

Another student, a white male, introduced another consideration— that the practice of affirmative action was not really unfair to Danny:

I really don't think we can make our decision on the basis of whether or not Danny will be a good community member or not. He's a great kid, but I haven't heard him say today that if he didn't get into the program it would be unfair to him ... so that when I balance affirmative action versus the consequences to him, my feeling is that I'm going to be secure (in my decision) and affirmative action is too important! I thought I might be moved by his plea, but now it's not unfair for him not to enter the program.

Interestingly, the black students in K-100 did not all uphold the affirmative action position against Danny:

... it's unfair to keep him out while other people are taking up space in the program ... why can't we trade off?

... I feel having him in would be an asset for us, he could help us and we could help him, and it wouldn't affect affirmative action . . . he's shown special interest.

The proposal that Danny be admitted for membership to the K-100 program was defeated, 19–13, on a roll call vote. The next year the extreme affirmative action policy of keeping spaces for minority students changed, partly as a result of this meeting.

The use of alcohol and marijuana at retreats from time to time surfaced as a problem, but the students took more responsibility for enforcing the drug rules than was true in the Cluster School. In 1984 at a retreat in a Vermont farmhouse, five boys, all new members, drank beer and offered it to other students. All the students, but not the staff, were awakened, and those drinking were confronted with their violation of their agreement. In a community meeting with staff the next day, the offending students were put on probation for the rest of the semester. The K-100 students, then, dealt with drugs and alcohol at a higher phase than was true of the Cluster School, perhaps because of the more homogeneous nature of the student body and the smaller size of the program.

Judging from these discussions, K-100 retained the just community emphasis of Cluster School, although Kohlberg no longer regularly consulted with it. This is further supported by interviews with students who stressed the ideas of community and democracy:

It's a working community—we're working toward it . . . toward having trust and respect for one another.

K-100 really is a community. People have rights and can bring up issues of concern to the attention of the community—and people listen to what you have to say, and therefore make you feel like a real person. You get to make your own decisions and feel like a "being."

The teachers, who were also interviewed, emphasized similar themes. One said: "We try to represent a true community of shared responsibility between teachers and students. The academic part is certainly important, but so is the social. The idea is to make the program both challenging and pleasant in the context of fairness."

K-100 ended in the spring of 1987 but the model continued as Elsa Wasserman, the former counselor at Cluster, was appointed an assistant principal of Cambridge Rindge and Latin High School. She was asked to carry forward the work she had begun ten years earlier when she was recruited by the superintendent to use her Cluster experience to find ways of building a greater sense of fairness and community in the large high school. Her efforts and those of a second Cluster faculty member had led to the institution of a Fairness Committee, a Teacher/Adviser Program, a Student Service Center, and a multicultural awareness project (Wasserman and Garrod 1983). In the coming years, Wasserman will establish programs that will further involve students in school governance along the lines taken in Brookline High School's Democracy Project, which we describe in chapter 10.

6

The Scarsdale Alternative
High School

with Judy Codding

In this chapter we turn to the Scarsdale Alternative High School (the A School), the second school to adopt the just community approach. After briefly highlighting the events that led up to the decision by A School members to become a just community school, we will discuss their responses to five key issues: drug use, individual rights, faculty intimidation, cheating, and expulsion. As our readers will recall, two of these issues, drug use and expulsion, were addressed in Cluster with limited success. The other issues never evoked much interest nor received any sustained attention there. Thus this presentation of the A School allows us to complete the description of the just community approach and of the culture of democratic community that we began with our focus on Cluster.

Scarsdale, located in Westchester County, New York, is about a twenty-mile commute to downtown Manhattan. It is a very affluent suburban community with about 20,000 residents in the school district. The high school is dominated by a concern for high achievement and annually places among the top schools in the National Merit competition and in admissions to prestigious colleges. Like Cluster, the A School began when a group of teachers, dissatisfied with the regimentation and highly competitive atmosphere of the regular high school, persuaded the super-intendent to convene a joint parent-teacher administrative committee to explore the feasibility of establishing an alternative school. After a year of planning, the A School opened. Its goal and programs were typical of what had become an alternative school movement in the late sixties and seventies. Emphasis was given to student responsibility in directing and evaluating their own learning; the resources of the New York metropolitan area were utilized; a variety of alternatives to didactic classroom instruction were offered; and the formalities of scheduling and disciplinary practices were relaxed.

Unlike Cluster, the A School has its own building and provides a complete standard college preparatory curriculum, with additional courses such as marine biology, anthropology, and William Faulkner. While students are permitted to take courses in the regular high school, few have actually done so. One of the most unusual features of the A School is its Career Internship Program, in which students spend a month away from school exploring a future career possibility of their choice. A School students over the years have worked all over the country and abroad in the offices of congressmen, lawyers, businessmen, and university professors and in schools, hospitals, and social work agencies.

THE TRANSITION TO THE JUST COMMUNITY APPROACH

The A School was democratic from its inception in 1972. A two-hour community meeting was held each week, with the students and faculty each having one vote, although the faculty had the right of veto. As in S.W.S. and most alternative high schools with some form of democracy, attendance at these meetings was originally voluntary. This was in keeping with the laissez-faire and individualistic orientation that inspired the establishment of the school. Furthermore, a compulsory attendance rule hardly seemed necessary, since few students skipped the meetings.

By the middle of the A School's third year, attendance began to rapidly slide. This signaled to the staff that relying on a completely voluntary policy threatened to undermine their vision of student participatory democracy. At that point students and staff began to split into rival factions—a "community participation group" and an "individual freedom group." The "community participation group" won the passage of an attendance rule; however, true to the core ideology of the school, the rule did not provide for sanctions. Attendance continued to wane.

The following year direct participatory democracy was replaced by a representative group, the Governance Committee, but little changed. The students complained that the meetings were dull, and the continuing exhortations about their "civic" responsibilities to the school had little impact. After two frustrating years with the Governance Committee, the principal and two teachers began looking into the just community approach. They also became familiar with cognitive developmental psychology and Fenton's (1977) moral discussion techniques, and they quickly piloted a moral discussion course, "Ethical Issues in Decision Making." When the three attended the Harvard Institute on Moral Development and Moral Education in the summer of 1977, they discovered that Kohlberg's diagnosis of the free school malaise applied with full force to the A School and that the just community approach offered a viable way of resolving their tensions between the individual and the community.

One year later the A School was formally declared a just community school. In contrast to the Cluster staff, the A School faculty was well prepared. Their commitment to the approach and to Kohlberg as their consultant (he was at this time "easing" out as a consultant to Cluster, which was in its fifth year) was free of the reservations expressed by the Cluster staff. Of course, the A School staff had the additional advantage of building on Cluster's experiences. Given their prior training, the hindsight gained from Cluster, and an unusually cooperative and capable study body, the A School was virtually an ideal situation for exploring the upper limits of development that the approach could foster.

The only real drawback was the homogeneity of the student body. There were no students from minority or lower socioeconomic groups. Most students were fairly well adjusted to school, and few had serious disciplinary problems. While the similarities in background characteristics contributed to a certain cohesiveness, they nevertheless restricted the range of points of view expressed in the meetings and the kinds of issues that could be discussed and worked through. For example, although discussions were held on affirmative action, they remained a largely speculative exercise without the conflict and passion which surfaced in the Cluster meetings.

THE BIRTH OF A JUST COMMUNITY: THE DRUG RULE

The birth of the A School as a conscious just community came, as did the birth of Cluster, around the issue of drugs and alcohol at a school retreat. Recall that during the fall of Cluster School's first year, everyone democratically agreed not to use drugs or alcohol as a condition for going on a community building retreat. When a teacher discovered the rule had been broken, a democratic meeting was immediately held in which a number of students shared the faculty's disappointed expectations. The emotional catharsis of this reaction resulted in an enhanced sense of community among rule breakers and rule upholders alike, and was the impetus to move forward to make a drug rule for daily class after the return from the retreat. An experience similar in a number of ways occurred at the Scarsdale Alternative School in the fall of 1978.

From the very beginning of the A School's existence, students and faculty started the school year by going on a three-day retreat. The major purpose of these retreats has always been the same: the building of a sense of community. However, the perennial issue of drugs and alcohol on the retreat was handled by A School staff and students in a significantly different manner before 1978 and the establishment of the just community. Previously, faculty members reminded students of the Board of Education policy regarding drugs and alcohol on any school-related function. Teachers simply asked students to agree with the rule, the clear implication being that if the community did not go through this *pro forma* vote, they could not have the retreat. At the retreat, faculty members were "on duty" in the dorms and patrolled the grounds in some attempt to remind students of the considerable responsibility the adults felt and, it was hoped, the students shared. When the faculty met informally during the retreat, teachers would speculate as to whether so and so was high. Some students clearly were, but only in the most obvious cases was a student confronted for breaking the rule. The consequence was to send the student home immediately. After returning to school, there was little, if any, discussion about the rule being broken. Individual offenders were dealt with individually. There was no attempt on the part of the staff to establish a norm that breaking the drug rule on the outing was a violation of the community and its democratic agreement.

During the moral education summer course at the Harvard Graduate School of Education, the staff decided to make the establishment of the drug rule for the retreat the first test of the just community. As a result, the community meeting discussion prior to the retreat, as well as the discussions after it, were significantly different from what had typically taken place in previous years. First, the faculty took a clear and strong stand as to why the community needed to establish a drug rule for the retreat. No longer was the issue presented as "our all having to live with the rules of the Board of Education or the State of New York." Rather, teachers spoke personally about the uneasy feelings they had always seemed to have on previous retreats. They spoke about not wanting to be police and about the necessity of sharing responsibility for upholding and enforcing rules that the community made together. These kinds of faculty remarks sparked some students into speaking about a similar kind of uneasiness they had felt on past retreats. Some revealed their feelings of resentment when others had broken a rule in their presence. Others reported how the breaking of the drug rule on past retreats undermined the very trust that the retreat was supposed to build and jeopardized the whole idea of a democratic school. Was it not a farce, they argued, if we go through the whole long process of deciding rules together only to discover later that some students never felt bound or obligated by the community's rules?

After an hour of personal and sometimes emotional discussion, it was clear to the faculty that they had opened up an important area for all members of the community. For the first time in these pre-retreat discussions, a few students openly and honestly advocated the right to get high. Some students who were eighteen years old brought up the point that they could legally drink if they wanted to. The faculty and a few students directed the issue away from the legalistic arguments and more toward what members of a community could expect from one another. One strand of argument went that if you made a rule, saying you were going to live by it, then you ought to follow it through. You would be "letting down" the community to do otherwise. Elaborating on the need for consistency between making and upholding rules, another strand of argument focused on the stage 3–4 concept that chaos would result if individual dissenters felt no obligation to abide by a majority vote.

After much honest discussion, the community passed a rule forbidding the use of all drugs. However, the discussion was not complete. A second and difficult issue arose about who was going to enforce the rule. Most students could not conceive of turning in a friend. They wanted teachers to have the sole responsibility for enforcement. A few other students were primarily concerned with the obligation to maintain the integrity of the community. They said that one should turn in a friend who broke the drug rule. In an effort to clarify the issue of responsibility and ownership for the newly made rule, a faculty member suggested a roll call vote in which each student would be called on to respond to the following questions: "Will you abide by the drug rule on the retreat?" "*Should* you turn in violators?" and finally, causing considerable squirming and discomfort on the part of many students, "*Should* and *would* you turn in violators?" Thus the faculty was asking for a vote not only on a norm against drug use but on a high phase of enforcement of that norm.

As they would often do in the future, the staff advocated sharing responsibility for the enforcement of the norm in the name of justice as fairness, implicitly using Rawls' (1971) contract procedure that the decision should be made without knowing one's role in the community, teacher or student. Every student except one answered yes, they would abide by the drug rule on the retreat. It was then decided that the lone-dissenting student could not go on the retreat unless he would agree to abide by the rule. As to the other two questions, having to do with enforcement, thirty-two out of seventy-five students said that they felt they should turn in violators, and twenty-eight said that they felt they both *should* and *would* turn in violators. Thus the meeting established a collectively shared norm against drug use for the retreat but failed by a sizable margin to establish a phase 7 student commitment to enforce that norm by reporting violators.

The Post-Retreat Meeting

The meeting after the retreat began with Kohlberg reviewing the vote taken before the retreat. Then he asked what had actually happened on the retreat. One student said things had improved from the year before:

Well, it was better than last year. People felt much stronger about their commitment to the community.

After some other positive reflections, David blurted out that the retreat was far from perfect:

I know that there was smoking on the retreat, and I think that some people might not have smoked because they were scared, not because they felt obligated to the community.

Kohlberg, seizing this opportunity to concretize the issue of student enforcement, asked how students would feel about naming names. Two students replied that while reporting might ideally be the right thing, it was unreasonable to expect students to turn in their friends:

I know I should, but I didn't vote that I should and would turn in people because I knew my loyalty to my friends was just too strong.

Yeah, me too. Ideally I shouldn't but I couldn't. How would you feel if someone were to turn you in?

Kohlberg pursued the issue of enforcement by comparing two community rules, mandatory attendance at community meetings and not using drugs:

It seems as if the problem of enforcement is still unsolved. Do people see a difference between enforcing the rule about attendance at community meetings and the drug rule?

Kohlberg, of course, knew that community meeting attendance was fundamental to the very existence of a democratic school in a way that the drug rule was not. Nevertheless, he wished to call attention to the fact that both rules involved participation.

Two students pointed out how different the rules were, but did not see any value in the drug rule.

The attendance rule brought us together, but the drug rule separated us because of this concern about telling.

Right, the vote was basically selling out so that we could go on the retreat; the attendance rule was an extension of our own values of community.

Kohlberg then asked whether students were not avoiding the uncomfortable task of dealing with the admitted violators of their rule. They continued to excuse their unwillingness to reveal any names, but a few expressed their disappointment that some would democratically make a rule that they did not intend to follow. The meeting, seemingly at an impasse, then broke for lunch.

The afternoon session began with Kohlberg suggesting that the consequences be spelled out for the rule breakers. He thought that the lack of clearly defined consequences had contributed to the stalemate of the discussion. A proposal was made that the consequence for breaking the drug rule on the outing was loss of the right to vote for the remainder of the orientation week. This was seen as a serious consequence, because during that week important matters were to be put to vote. The vote was taken, with 62 in favor of the proposal and 5 opposed. The stage was now set for people to admit they had broken the rule and say what they felt they should say.

After a period of silence to allow people to gather their thoughts, there was discussion about whether rule violators should confess or whether other people have the obligation to report them. Rod, obviously upset by people breaking the rule, encouraged confession: "I'll respect people for speaking up if they broke the rule, but I won't respect you for what you have done."

After a few minutes Tina admitted to smoking and then hastily left the meeting to go to work: "I did it, I smoked on the outing. But I can't explain now. I have to go to work. This meeting has already run past time."

People asked her to stay and explain herself more. Clearly some were upset with the way she had hurled her confession at the community but then had been unwilling to see it through. As Tina was leaving, a number of students were talking with one another, trying to decide whether or not to say they had broken the rule.

Nellie came forward: "I smoked. I went out with Jim late at night. I feel very guilty now, but at the time I saw no reason why it was really wrong."

Then Jim spoke for himself: "I partied once on the last night. It was very late, everyone was asleep. I didn't really believe people felt so strongly about it."

At this point several students and one staff member talked to Jim and Nellie about their offense in an effort to be supportive and understanding while at the same time impressing upon them the seriousness of their offense.

HARRY: Why did you bring up the pot in the first place? That's what bothers me.

JIM: I don't know. I'm not sure, I think I was testing myself.

DICK (T): I admire you for your guts in admitting it. How do you feel now?

JIM: I feel a lot more relaxed. Dick said that one of the main reasons why pot was wrong on the outing was that it put barriers between people. Well, I didn't see anything so wrong with smoking at 2:30 in the morning with Nellie. I didn't see how we were affecting the community.

MARTHA: But what time it was doesn't eliminate the agreement we made. I respect you for speaking up, Jim, but do you feel about rules here that you can break them if you feel you can get away with it?

JIM: I didn't think about the rule.

JERRY: I understand, but I don't think your actions were justifiable. I lost some respect for the community when I heard that some people had broken the rule.

After a short break to ease the tension, which had mounted again after the lunch break, several more students confessed. It was well past the normal time for dismissal. Some time was given for reflection, and then the meeting was adjourned.

Commentary

With the confrontation, emotion, and pain around confession, this meeting represented a step forward in the development of the sense of community and the collective norms of the A School. This development may best be seen by focusing on how the phases changed. Before the retreat, there had been a vote taken that nobody should use drugs and that people should but would not necessarily enforce this rule on others. The phase of this norm appeared to be phase 4, that is, most students expected that everyone would follow the norm. This was great progress over previous years when the rule was a mere formality and the phase of the norm never got higher than 3. The retreat proved that the expectation was a naive one; and members of the A School clearly expressed their disappointment that the rule was not followed, which we register as phase 5. In the wake of this disappointment, students found a new resolve to uphold their norm. The norm advanced to a sixth phase, as students who had broken the rule confessed and others took the personal responsibility of expressing their disapproval and persuading everyone to follow the rule in future. Incidentally, there was some evidence that their efforts to persuade were, in fact, effective. At the end of the community meeting Jim and Ron, who had confessed but not admitted to doing anything they thought was wrong, seemed to have a change of heart:

JIM: I believe in honesty. I know you are going to say if you believe in honesty then why did you do it. It's true my actions were hypocritical; what I did was wrong.

RON: I don't know. I'm starting to feel guilty. It's difficult to explain, but not every rule is like God's rule—divine from above. It's not like I got struck by lightning.

The emotional intensity of the postretreat meeting, in which feelings of anger, guilt, and defensiveness were expressed, left the students concerned about the propriety of encouraging confessions and confrontations in community meetings. There are really two issues here: first, whether strong outbreaks of emotion have a place in community meetings, and second, whether confidentiality ought to be maintained in handling the enforcement of discipline. These two issues were discussed in a follow-up meeting at the A School. There were mixed reactions to the first issue, but by and large students felt that it was appropriate to experience or express intense emotion when it was relevant to the community. Janet said it well:

I think a lot of good came out of the confrontation meeting because I know really people don't suppress these emotional feelings. So if they don't come out in our meetings, they will come out as either a displaced hostility or something that happens. I think to be able to express your emotions in a meeting is showing that you have some faith in people. And it is also saying that I feel comfortable enough to show what I am feeling.

There was less agreement that rules should be enforced in public. Even more than their counterparts in Cluster, the students in the A School held a strong norm of privacy, a norm that leads to the counselor's ethic that deviations from the rules of the school and the wider community should be dealt with in privacy to spare students the embarrassment of having their transgressions known. Kohlberg and the A School staff took a different position. While they agreed that personal problems should be kept confidential, they advocated a norm of publicity for violations of the rules and norms of the school. They felt confession indicated that the violator was a good community member who cared. The many statements by students supporting the confessors' self-esteem and approving of their honesty, courage, and concern for the community proved their point, as did the decision on a relatively light penalty (loss of one's vote for a week) for those admitting to a deviation. The drama of community confrontation and reconciliation helped, as it did in Cluster, to provide powerful emotional support for a sense of community. Experiences like this helped the A School to progress on the institutional valuing scale from level 3, intrinsic spontaneous valuing, to level 4, intrinsic normative valuing.

Gradually students accepted a norm of publicity, and in the following years the practices of confrontation and confession continued. Although students continued to discuss the phase 7 issue of reporting norm violations, and although the majority of students came to agree to such a policy in terms of what they *would* as well as *should* do, few saw any need for reporting, since the norm of confessing violations was so strong. In an ethnographic moral atmosphere interview administered two years after the first postretreat confession meeting, a first-year student in the A School explained that it was unnecessary to report students for violating the drug rule because "if they break it they *will* confess it." When asked why she was so sure that the rule breakers would confess, she said, "I don't know, they just do. All we do is just ask that those who broke the rule admit to it, and they always do. I'm not sure I understand why. I just know that they do." This student describes the practice of confession as a social fact. Although she lacked appreciation for its historical development, she did express a widely held view that confession was an obligation and that most would confess. Confession, then, was a phase 4 norm in itself, as well as being an indicator of a high-phase drug norm.

PERSONAL FREEDOM IN A DEMOCRATIC COMMUNITY

In this section we will take up the second important issue which emerged in the A School's history as a just community school—the tension between individual freedom and the demands of community life.

We noted that prior to 1978, the A School in most respects had adopted the free school ideology with its emphasis on laissez-faire individualism. After the discussion about drugs on the retreat the students sensed that a very different approach to life in the A School was being proposed. While the majority responded to the appeal to curtail their use of drugs during class time and school functions, they were unsure whether they could obligate the minority who did not wish to agree to make that sacrifice. Most thought that whether students smoke or drink was up to them, there was nothing inherently evil in those actions. Following the analysis provided by Turiel (1983) and Nucci (1982), we can say that they clearly treated societal prohibitions about drug use and underage drinking as conventions. What made the issue problematic was that although they regarded smoking marijuana and drinking as morally neutral in most contexts outside of school, they felt that such acts were incongruous with the strong, normative ideal of community that Kohlberg and the faculty were advocating. The critical question then became whether this normative ideal of community was itself justifiable.

The first occasion for working this out came the week following the postretreat discussions, when the A School set out to make a new drug rule for school time. The students understood that any new rule they made would have to include some student responsibility for enforcement. Thus it would be very different from the rule they had had in previous years that signified at best an ideal, but not an expectation for a behavior. A more serious phase 6 drug rule would clearly infringe upon the liberty of a vocal minority in the school who did not accept the rule to begin with.

The Drug Rule: An Infringement on Individual Liberty?

After the postretreat discussions A School members turned to the problem of making a rule pertaining to the use of drugs in school. By now students had become very reflective about what it meant to make a rule. One issue was its practical enforceability and the second, more basic issue was the right of the group to make rules that restricted the personal freedom of some members of the group. This second issue had been discussed in core (adviser) group meetings and was consequently taken to the community meeting. A student, reporting on the conclusions of his core group, introduced it quite simply: "It might be nice to think that everyone thinks that they shouldn't come stoned to school, but there were people who thought that it was their right to come to class in whatever condition they wanted."

Another student, Janet, defended the right to come to class stoned. She observed that some students can function well in school, even if they are high, and concluded that there is no good reason why there should be a *general rule* against it. In saying this, Janet was essentially proposing that the teachers handle each case on an individual basis, which is the way it had been done in the past at the A School.

Janet's position was similar to that of several of the Cluster students who opposed making a general drug rule on the same grounds; namely, that some students could carry their liquor and drugs and some could not. In the A School, however, students more readily saw the reasons against the "individual differences" approach to drugs. They saw that from a stage 4 point of view of procedural fairness or impartiality they could not penalize some students for drug use and let others go free.

When Janet said that you should deal with it class by class, and if the teacher wants to he can say something to the class, I don't think that is appropriate. I think a drug rule is something that should be a school-wide expectation that students cannot come to class stoned. If we don't have a rule, it puts the person not getting stoned in a difficult position. People might not know whether they should really object to people being stoned, whether they have the right to tell the person that they don't like it when they are stoned. So I think we should all decide how we are going to deal with this.

I think that it is known here that we all respect your rights to do what you want to do on your own time, but I think we sometimes approach issues with an attitude of protecting this right; I don't think that it is a right that should be regarded as protected.... I also don't care if a person can function perfectly. There are some people it really doesn't affect, but I think in school you should be on a common ground with all people around you. And just the fact that some are stoned and some are not puts you on a different ground.

They also saw with the help of staff advocacy that from a community point of view it was important to have a collective norm (a norm at a high degree of collectiveness) outlawing drug use because it affected the students' ability and motivation to participate.

I don't want people stoned in my class. I don't feel that people can handle it. I tend to feel that people either get overly giggly or they withdraw, and either of those things is not what I want in my class.

In the first year of the A School as a just community, then, students were advocating a drug norm at a higher level of collectiveness, phase, and stage than was perhaps reached at any time in Cluster School. At the same time, however, the Scarsdale students articulated a reason against having a drug rule, largely absent in Cluster—the idea that the minority had rights that should not be violated even by majority vote. In general, our research suggests that this very strong notion of individualism, individual rights, and the relativity or dubious validity of majority rules is articulated by students who reason at stage 3½ or are in transition from a stage 3 acceptance of group norms to a stage 4 awareness of a need for rules to resolve disagreements between "moral" or "decent" people in order to build a system of cooperation.

The whole issue of making the drug rule led to a great deal of theoretical discussion about the meaning of the term "rights" or "having a right." A common attitude to the issue was taken by Jim, who said: "I don't believe that people should get stoned in school. I believe that they have the right to do it if they want to, but I don't believe that they should. But I do believe that it is their right, their prerogative."

As we have noted, a common reason why A school students viewed coming to school high as wrong was that it prevented participation in class and the larger community. The question, then, was not whether the drug rule served to promote the welfare of the majority but whether a rule good for the majority should be imposed on the minority, who felt they had a right to use drugs.

A partial way out of this dilemma was enunciated by Laura. Laura took the contractual position that the A School was a voluntary community and that participation in a voluntary community rested on every member's agreement to abide by the majority rules or to act in terms of the welfare of the majority. In other words, she was saying that even though people should have the personal right to choose, they should not be allowed to exercise it at school. Laura put it this way: "I can kind of look at it as if the person has an obligation to the class and the community not to be stoned, and therefore, being part of that class, they give up that right to be stoned. I guess I would like to hear what people think of that."

It is obvious that students were struggling with not wanting to deny individuals their personal rights but at the same time not wanting to allow certain actions. They felt that recognizing the right but denying its exercise was a way out of the dilemma.

Some students were obviously confused about the meaning of the notion of having a right and mistook it for having the free will to choose and perform an action that is generally considered wrong as long as its consequences are accepted, as we can see in John's comments in this community meeting segment:

JIM: I would just like to say that people also have the right to break the law, and that is why they have the choice.

MARTHA: And the right to be punished.

STUART: You don't have the right to break the law.

SALLY: I would like to know the meaning of the word "right." What is a "right"? Define it; what does that mean? What do you mean when you say people have the right to break the law?

JOHN: They have a choice of breaking the law and paying the penalty. It is just like saying someone can murder somebody if they are willing to pay the penalty.

SALLY: No, we do not have the right to murder somebody. How would you like it if everybody felt that they could come to class stoned, and everyone was sitting in class giggling and laughing because they were all willing to pay the penalty? That is not right.

In the course of this discussion Sally clarified the meaning of rights by making the distinction that people do not have a moral right to do something that hurts others even if they are willing to pay the penalty.

Further discussion of rights and civil disobedience with regard to the law and the political state did not help students to resolve the particular question the rights and obligation of participation within a voluntary democratic and moral community. In the United States there are very few positive demands or obligations of participation. Even voting, the most basic expression of membership in a constitutional representative democracy, is only a right, not a duty. In the discussion of the "right" to use drugs, progress was made only when students began to clarify the distinction between rights and duties in a legal state, and rights and duties in a participatory moral community. A participatory moral community requires moral responsibilities beyond those demanded of the state or the society. At the same time, a just community must recognize respect for individual rights as strongly as does the constitutional state, especially the right to liberty of conscience.

It is quite clear that this discussion began working through a very basic philosophic issue for the alternative school. Does the majority have the right to restrict the rights of individuals who are in the minority in the school? The resolution did not come through a blanket acceptance of the notion that the majority does have the right to limit the rights of the minority. The resolution had to do with the clarification of what it means to have a right. What are the conditions under which minorities have rights that the majority cannot infringe upon? What are the conditions under which the majority can make a rule that the minority must accept as limiting their rights? This is where distinctions were drawn between conventional and moral obligations and personal and moral rights. In the just community school the majority cannot, in general, limit personal and moral rights. In the just community school the majority cannot, in general, limit personal rights of students; it can only limit them where the personal right cannot be held to be a moral right because it violates the more essential obligation to participate in a voluntary community. Smoking pot is not a basic right like freedom of speech but is rather a personal habit that can be restricted for the sake of the community and the individuals in it. As Joe put it in the meeting: "If we have an obligation to participate in class, then we don't have a right to be stoned."

The Enforcement of the Drug Rule

Once the students resolved that they could justifiably make a drug rule that had moral force without violating the rights of the minority, they returned to the more concrete task of making a rule. Debate centered around whether the drug rule should have sanctions or simply be an expectation. The general sentiment of the community was that they wanted to have whatever had the most force behind it. The community concluded that a rule had more force because expectations are more easily broken. As Rob stated:

The difference between a rule and an expectation is a very important one, and I think in order to avoid the same mistake that we made last time, we have to decide what the difference is. In my opinion it is that there is a big difference between a rule and an expectation in the sense that we all know that we should abide by a rule but expectations are easily broken. Whereas with rules it is sort of an inner struggle inside yourself. Even if you know you are not going to get caught, you are breaking a rule and you have to be held accountable for that whatever the consequences later may be.

Rob is saying that a vote for the rule makes the lofty aspiration of internal control easier by making the individual publicly accountable.

The distinction between rule and expectation clarifies what we mean by the phase of the norm. In table 4.4, phase 4 was called the phase of expectation. At that phase students recognized a shared commitment to live up to the norm. Nevertheless, they refused to commit themselves further by agreeing to a rule that they would have to enforce. The notion that making the prohibition of drug use a rule entailed a greater commitment to uphold the norm, which would raise its phase to 6, is implied by Hugh:

I think that a rule would force this community to deal with something that is very difficult. I don't think there is a person here who would say I want to be able to come to class stoned and I think that I have that right. I don't think that anyone would take that position because that seems like an impossible position for me to defend. Yet the thing that this community has a hard time doing is saying that this expectation—that people should not come to school stoned—is something that needs to be codified. By making it a rule, it would put responsibility on other people, and somehow we have a difficult time drawing the line with that. I believe it is important that we draw the line by saying that I don't think we should be able to come to class high and believe it strongly enough to make a rule on that. We have a hard time putting expectations and rules out onto others. To some extent there has been a kind of individualism operating which says, in a sense, that everyone has the right to do their own thing and who am I to impose a majority rule? I hope to cop out, take the easy way out, and say, "Well let's just leave it at the expectation level." It is too easy for people to do it, and they will do it all year long because that doesn't hurt so much.

Hugh's statement provides a neat summary of the entire discussion to this point. First, he noted that no student would claim a right to come to class stoned. We have seen that at the outset of this discussion a good many students did, in fact, claim this right; so we may assume, if Hugh was accurately representing the state of the question in the group, that the discussion has had a considerable impact on student opinion. Nevertheless, Hugh detected some lingering "individualism" that inhibited students from imposing the majority will within the form of a rule. This led him to chide the group for "copping out" and considering a weaker commitment to upholding the norm as an expectation. Hugh indicated later that he would be willing to go as far as reporting a fellow student for being stoned but that such a step was contingent on a drug prohibition being made into a rule. In his view passing the drug rule would signify a shared commitment to norm enforcement.

Recall that in the Cluster School discussion there was a very different relationship between a rule and an expectation. The "fire fighting" strategy in Cluster's first year led to a number of rules which were not expectations, that is, rules which we coded as phase 3 agreements. The goal in Cluster School was to raise the phase of the rules from 3 to 4. With regard to the drug issue, that meant trying to go from a "be cool rule" to a genuinely shared expectation that drugs would not be used. Part of the problem in advancing the phase had to do with a stage 2 confusion about the concept of a rule. Cluster students were willing after considerable discussion in the first year to agree to a rule, which meant agreeing to accept the consequences if they were caught. However, they were quite reluctant in their third- and fourth-year retreat discussions to agree to a stage 3–4 "promise" that they would not use drugs. Unlike the A School students, they did not think that making a drug rule entailed either a promise to uphold the norm (phase 4) or a commitment to enforcement (phases 6 and 7). Thus most Cluster students did not experience the same lack of consistency as did the A School students between democratically making rules and refusing to uphold them.

The A School finally passed a drug rule that resolved for a time their ambivalence about the majority making a rule that would obligate all. As we noted, this represented a crucial development in the phase of the drug norm. It also represented a development in the degree of collectivity of the drug norm from degree 12 to degree 14. Most students did not think that this decision would entail the loss of a sense of individuality or of personal choice, although they realized that they would have to put the community's needs before their own in making decisions which affected the school.

The success that the A School had in developing a drug norm appears almost spectacular in comparison with Cluster's experience. Within the Scarsdale School System the A School's virtual elimination of drug use on retreats was regarded as a remarkable achievement, since trips away from school had been abolished in the large high school because drinking and marijuana use had gotten out of control on class trips. As we see it, one essential difference between the drug norm in Cluster and the A School was that upholding the drug rule was the first and one of the few opportunities the A School students had for making a personal sacrifice that would symbolize their commitment to the school. Another difference was that marijuana use provided one way of breaking down Cluster's social and racial divisions, divisions which did not really exist in the A School. Finally, the moral reasoning of the A School students was on the average a stage higher than that of the Cluster students. No doubt this gave them an advantage in sorting out rather complex conceptual issues around the rationale for the drug rule and its enforcement.

STAFF ADVOCACY AND INTIMIDATION

In an article published in the *Moral Education Forum*, Ed Zalaznick, an outgoing senior, criticized the A School faculty and Kohlberg, the consultant, for what he called "moral intimidation." In his view this was the major issue throughout the A School's third year as a just community, and he cited a number of intense community meetings to prove his point. His concern was not simply that the faculty had the power to get their way but that they exerted too much influence on students in their application of moral education theory:

The feeling of being pushed toward "higher stages" was very intimidating to many students. They perceived that every issue was presented with a "right" and a "wrong" side and that there was tremendous pressure to choose the "right" side, despite what they really thought. . . . Teachers must be sensitive to how they approach the process to avoid "preaching." After all, the teacher figure is respected by the adolescent; and having the students accept these ideas merely because they perceive them as the teachers' "bag of virtues," is not effective. This I saw happening in our school especially with a big shot Harvard professor in addition to the entire staff supporting certain ideas which they called better. With the notion that there exists a hierarchy of reasoning and values in the air, the idea of better and worse is always on the minds of students. . . . This turns discussions into battles of who's right and who is wrong based on stages. (1980:31).

Zalaznick's remarks highlight differences between Cluster School and A School students' reactions to their respective faculties. In Cluster, students rarely experienced this subtle form of faculty pressure because few of them worried about how the faculty thought of them or how they measured up according to Kohlberg's theory. The only time Cluster students rebelled against the theory of moral education was when some perceived it as encroaching upon the time they thought might best be spent mastering the "basics" of reading and grammar. They did complain from time to time about being bored by long-winded faculty speeches, and in the fourth year they held occasional "student only" meetings because they thought they could operate more efficiently without the faculty continuously requesting further discussion. Cluster students, then, while sometimes feeling "bothered" by the faculty, never felt the psychological pressure to please the faculty that Zalaznick identified in the A School students.

In an interview with Kohlberg which was appended to his article, Zalaznick distinguished between the faculty's influence and indoctrination: "We were never indoctrinated in the sense that someone would come up with, 'this is the situation, and this is the most fair thing to do, and can you all see that now.' It was more like 'we have this focus and we're gonna work on it and so let's talk about the issue with that in mind,' so we all had to teach ourselves the experience" (p. 34).

He also admitted that, insofar as the students tried to make their decisions as fair as they could, they accepted the teachers' efforts to promote higher-stage thinking:

When you talk about teaching morals, I would assume you meant teaching a higher stage, a higher perspective of justice . . . you know, a more universal concern. Well, I think there was an attempt to teach that, and, if it was agreed upon by everyone, that we would try to be universally just in all our actions as possible, and that the teachers would stimulate discussion to get the most universally just decisions out of the group as we could come up with . . . .

We all wanted to guarantee that we could strive to be fair; that there would be no breakdown where teachers could suddenly usurp power and do something underhanded or unfair and so we decided that everything that we do should be done with the priority of fairness and democracy . . . and majority rule went along with that. . . . So in a sense, we really arrived at a just community on our own. . . . When we were given alternatives and we talked about the different ways our school could be set up, it turned out to be a Just Community School. (pp. 34–35)

Zalaznick went on to describe how the intimidation issue was finally resolved. He noted that the faculty brought the problem up in a community meeting. They tried to defend their position by shifting the focus of discussion from Kohlberg's psychological theory to the moral, philosophical question of what guidelines should be used in making decisions together. The students agreed that principles of universal justice should not only inform their substantive decisions but also should support and protect the democratic process itself. With that as a foundation they judged that the just community approach and its use of a psychological stage theory were in accord with their moral, philosophical convictions.

While the faculty were reasonably successful in justifying the just community approach and in sharing ownership of it with the students, they did not fully alleviate student feelings of pressure or, as Zalaznick called it, "moral intimidation." As this issue evolved over the next two years, some students expressed a concern, not so much for the faculty's use of a psychological theory, but for their strong advocacy, which they saw as choking off student initiative and self-direction. For example, in an essay on the school written for one of his classes, Sam noted that the faculty had become "a well-organized voting block that almost always speaks with one voice." One consequence of this, in his view, was that students were hesitant about expressing differing opinions: "S.A.S. students tend to accept faculty proposals as the *status quo*, and a student proposing an alternative to a faculty proposal is always fighting an uphill battle. . . . This [1981–1982] has been a record year for unanimous and near unanimous votes. And it has been a year devoid of the type of struggle present in the past."

For Sam the stifling of student thought was further promoted by an appeal to community, which he characterized as a "crutch," preventing well-thought-out individual decisions, and as a "justification for going along blindly with the majority." Finally, he objected that the faculty had placed too much emphasis on advocating specific policies rather than on creating a process in which students could develop their own decision-making capacities. As he put it, "Education should teach an individual how to make choices, not what choices should be made." Sam, then, is claiming that in some sense the A School democracy was becoming indoctrinative. He makes the distinction frequently made by

Kohlberg that moral education should emphasize the development of moral reasoning, not conformity to a bag of virtues.

In our view, although students disagreed about the seriousness of the intimidation problem in the A School, it was one which is in some sense endemic to the just community and one to which we must try to respond. While in the opening chapters of this book we have presented a positive case for developing a moral education approach in which there is a place for faculty advocacy in the name of community, we do not wish to abandon the concern present in Kohlberg's earliest educational writing for developing the autonomy of the student and avoiding didactic approaches that can become indoctrinative. The best way for the faculty to achieve such a balance is to make sure the issue of intimidation is publicly discussed on a regular basis, as the A School faculty has done.

CHEATING AND RESPONSIBILITY

In introducing our method for assessing the moral culture of schools (chapter 4), we presented a series of Cluster School meetings that illustrated the development of the norms of trust and collective responsibility in response to incidents of stealing and property loss. We now wish to report an analogous development of a trust norm in the A School against cheating. Scarsdale students come from well-to-do homes, and family and community socialization provides firm norms against stealing. Since 1978, when the just community approach was inaugurated, the only episodes of stealing in the A School involved the disappearance of a few students' sandwiches from the communal refrigerator. While stealing was not an issue in the A School, another form of injustice was— cheating.

Cheating has been central to the study of student moral behavior since Hartshorne and May (1928–1930). Hartshorne and May found that cheating was situation specific and that the risk of detection was one important situational factor influencing the likelihood that cheating would go on. Another important situational factor involved a classroom, or what we would call a "moral culture" effect. Hartshorne and May's findings led Kohlberg to question the tradition of postulating fixed character traits or virtues, like honesty. Instead he found that stages of justice reasoning have an influence on cheating behavior after reviewing a range of studies indicating a monotonic decrease of cheating with the increment of moral stage. These studies point to the relevance of a personality variable contradicting the skepticism of the original Hartshorne and May research. On the other hand, we believe that Hartshorne and May were basically correct in identifying situational factors as the major determinants of cheating. As we noted in chapter 1, while Blatt (1969) was successful in stimulating upward movement in stages of moral reasoning through dilemma discussions, he did not find a corresponding decrease in Hartshorne and May's cheating tasks. Perhaps this was because the relatively small development in moral judgment was offset by the more powerful effects of the setting.

Although Kohlberg found a monotonic relationship between moral stage and cheating behavior, he postulated that that relationship was mediated by a judgment of responsibility. He came to that conclusion by observing that almost all students, whatever their stage of moral judgment, think that cheating is wrong. Nevertheless, the lower their stage, the more likely it is that students will offer excuses. These excuses involve quasi-obligations that make cheating permissible on lower-stage grounds.

For instance, stage 3 subjects feel they must uphold the expectations of parents that they receive good grades and expectations of friends that they be helpful. Stage 4 students are more likely to be sensitive to the unfairness to noncheaters of cheating and to the trust and implicit contract with the teacher for not cheating. Like stage 3 students, however, their refraining from cheating at stage 4 will depend upon making a judgment of responsibility not to cheat in the particular situation. If almost everyone else is cheating, responsibility to a few honest students and to the teacher is weakened.

In summary, responsibility judgments translate deontic judgments of rightness (it is right to do X) into obligations for the self (*I* ought to do X). Although responsibility judgments appear to develop with the stage of deontic moral judgment, we believe that responsibility judgments at any stage may be promoted through a positive moral culture. More specifically, we believe that all individuals are inclined to go along with the norms of their peer group, and thus it is important to develop group norms that are moral.

Developing a peer-supported norm against cheating is more difficult than doing so against stealing. Collective norms against stealing develop readily because peers are clear victims of unfairness in stealing. In the case of cheating, those most concerned or victimized seem to be the teachers. Peer group norms typically support and protect cheating in an atmosphere in which students are a "we group" distinct from the teachers, a "they group." Strong collective norms against cheating can usually only develop if the peer and teacher groups are seen as parts of a common community with norms that are fair to teachers as well as to students. This is, in fact, what happened in the A School.

The Meeting

In the spring of 1982 Judy Codding, the A School's director, held a core group (the A School's equivalent of Cluster's advisory group) meeting in which students talked about cheating in school and the moral atmosphere that made it acceptable. In response to her opening question, "Is cheating widespread at the alternative school or at the high school?" Wilson answered affirmatively: "It's very common at the high school; there's the opportunity to cheat and get away with it. Teachers can't really keep their eyes on every student. There's a feeling your friend is going to help you if you don't know the answer."

Here Wilson describes not only the situational risk factor identified by Hartshorne and May, but also the existence of stage 3 norms of friendship and affiliation that constitute peer "counternorms" to honesty. As we noted in the cheating situation, not only peer norms but parental expectations act as quasi-obligations that prevent judgments of responsibility to do "the right thing."

Another student from Judy's core group, Rod, explained this: "I got a lot of pressures from my parents, and in the ninth grade I was saying, 'OK, it's your first year of high school, you have to do well,' and I was just cheating because I wanted to do well and I wanted to make my parents happy." Going on to describe how other students acted, he said: "I just know there has to be in other people's minds that parental pressure 'I have to do good on this test or my Dad is going to kill me.' That's how it was for me, so I cheated."

Rod described the moral culture of the high school as almost supporting cheating: "At the end of the test people would be walking up to hand it in and say, 'Hey what's the answer to number 8?' You sit there and tell the answer right in front of the teacher and nobody really cared and it helped you out a lot."

In experimental cheating studies we discussed earlier, it was shown that one important situational predictor of cheating behavior is whether or not adults seem not to care about cheating. If adults do not express strong expectations for and trust in students' honesty, then conventional stage subjects, like Rod, are not sensitized to having a responsibility not to cheat. Cathy corroborated the idea that in the high school teachers did not seem to care about cheating, and that made it "allright." She said, "I was in the French class at the high school, and the teacher walked out and we had an open discussion about the test until she came back." Even teachers who tried to stop cheating ran the risk of having their vigilance backfire. For example, Jill thought that by being mistrustful, some teachers dared students to cheat: "At the high school they assume you're going to cheat. The teacher says, 'Don't cheat,' and it's almost like inviting it. They'd say, 'Keep your eyes on the test. I don't want any eyes wandering around.' And so it's always a challenge, let's see if we can beat this teacher."

Pam raised a different point. She noted that cheating begets cheating in a competitive atmosphere: "I'd think the atmosphere at the high school was that everyone around you is cheating; it pressures you into it, because they're going to get a ninety and you're going to get an eighty. It's a lot of pressure to be like them and to get a good grade too." Pam excused cheating, not because she thought it was right or moral, but because of the pressure to keep up with other students who cheated to get high grades.

For other students, the atmosphere of the high school was such that it desensitized them from making a deontic moral judgment of rightness at all. As Jane put it, "When I was in the high school I didn't make generalizations about people cheating at all. I cheated for myself and never gave it too much thought." Other students made justice judgments that cheating was not unfair to other students. "It never seemed to hurt anyone else." "It wasn't a matter of making someone else pass or fail; you are just doing better."

Most students in Judy's (T) group agreed that cheating was less frequent in the alternative school even without a formal democratic norm about cheating, because of smaller classes and greater trust between teachers and students. Nevertheless, they admitted that cheating still occasionally occurred, especially with regard to copying homework.

Two cases of cheating in the A school had precipitated the above core group discussion. A math teacher discovered that one student had cheated on his exam, and a group of four students were reported to have cheated on an English essay test. In both cases students were first brought before the Fairness (Discipline) Committee. The Fairness Committee strongly recommended that the community have a discussion on cheating and that they develop rules and consequences about it.

The issue of making a rule against cheating was relatively noncontroversial when it came before the community meetings, since most of the students thought that cheating was unjust. Nevertheless, discussing a rule against cheating led students to consider making a judgment of a responsibility not to cheat.

As stated by one student: "It really bothers me to have cheating going on because it's intruding on my rights. If there's cheating, for the people who do work hard it makes them seem like they're not working hard because others are copying papers and get the same grades and do nothing. If there was a rule which said we realize cheating is wrong and it's your obligation not to cheat, it would make everyone feel the obligation." This student sees cheating as unfair and violating the rights of other students who work for their grades, a common form of conventional (stage 3 and 4) justice reasoning. To translate this reasoning into a judgment of responsibility or personal obligation, however, requires community agreement.

Other students gave reasons against cheating not in terms of fairness or justice but in terms of community valuing. Joe said, "It goes with being in a community. Ending cheating is a good direction for our community, it's for the benefit of our community." Speaking for "the community," Joe proposed a communal norm against cheating. Judy T., the director, advocated a shared norm against cheating by facing the problem of peer counternorms directly and invoking the need of a collective norm of trust for the solidarity of a community that included teachers and peers.

Cheating is an issue that can really divide our community, students against teachers, in terms of cheating. There are students who join the teachers' ranks, but it sounds like on this issue that it's we and you, because obviously teachers don't participate in cheating. David, you were asking for reasons why in this school it should not occur, where it happens so much in the high school. It's because that it's fundamental to our school that there's trust within the community. You know my attitude when I give a test. It's based on trust. I would hate to mistrust people in the community, and when people say it's not so bad cheating on a little test because you won't ever take it again and it's not relevant to your later life, it ignores a decision about trust which can divide the community.

While making a rule against cheating was soon agreed upon, the question of how to enforce this rule was extremely controversial. The teachers proposed that not only they but the students had the responsibility to enforce the rule by confronting those they saw cheating. As we noted in connection with the drug issue, the A School faculty were concerned that the students share in responsibility for the enforcement of agreed-upon norms. In our theoretical language, they were determined that the norms should reach phase 6 or 7, that is, that students be willing to persuade others to desist from rule violation or to confess having violated the rule or, if all else failed, to report the violator. The rationale for the faculty's expectations that students confront one another over cheating was that teachers and students belonged to a common community and that it was not fair to the faculty to leave it to them to be the police or enforcers of a rule arrived at democratically. As stated by one of the teachers, Mike:

Is it fair in a democratic school to make these rules and then shuffle down to the teacher's corner for their enforcement? There are certain rules that we make and the problem of who finds out about violations of them and who enforces them doesn't arise. But others that are hard to enforce like this one, I would say if we can't enforce it together we can't make it together. We don't own it. It's all our responsibility to deal with the cheating problem. If John sees someone cheating, why is it any different from my seeing someone cheating?

This effort of the staff to make students responsible for enforcing the cheating rule obviously contradicts peer norms of friendship and trust, which are very powerful. While it is easiest to conceptualize these norms at a third stage of caring as mutual aid, caring and trust are basic to fourth-stage concerns about solidarity in the school community and fifth-stage concerns about the prerequisites of any human relationship.

No matter how students justified these peer norms, almost all of them felt some dread at the prospect of reporting a peer. For example, Jill said: "For someone to turn somebody in who they saw cheating, I would just go through a lot of pain. It would be personal hell." Tammy recognized the emotional difficulties of reporting but thought it was the responsible thing to do in a community: "At first, I felt like I didn't want all that responsibility, but I think we do have a lot of responsibility to each other, a responsibility to the community and in a way to each other." Judy articulated more clearly Tammy's justification for confrontation. She pointed out that in a just community students have some responsibility for the character of their friends. "I think that sometimes we confuse what it means to be a good friend and that sometimes the best way you can show your caring and friendship is to show this responsibility and help your friend to act more honestly and not to violate the trust of the school."

Many students saw the rightness of confrontation in this light while, nevertheless, acknowledging that it was a very difficult thing to do. Speaking for the group, John said: "I don't think anybody really thinks that cheating is not wrong. I think most people think it's right to turn someone in. But it's really hard to do. We're friends and you don't want to hurt their feelings. It would be easier if this proposal is passed. I won't let myself look away if I see someone cheating." Other students felt making an agreement to confront a friend or a fellow student was asking too much. As one put it, "It would be hard to confront. I think it should be left up to the person, not up to the rule."

Ginny replied with reasoning that is transitional from stage 3 to stage 4, both in terms of her individual moral reasoning and her valuing of the community and its norms. First, she did some role taking and explained that she could report another student who cheated because she would be willing to be reported if the situation were reversed. Then she argued that the community would collapse if individuals decided for themselves whether to commit themselves to the norm of honesty:

I would be able to do it because I would expect her to do it to me. It's not fair to the community because the community would fall apart if people thought they could cheat and others would feel "I can't make that commitment." You just have to harden yourself and say that you have to do it. The community has to be based on honesty."

After further discussion a vote was taken in which a large majority voted for the rule requiring confrontation.

The reader may have considerable conflict about this meeting. Strong teacher advocacy led to a vote for students to confront one another about cheating. Cheating was perceived as unfair, and the norm against it was raised to phase 7 in its strength of institutionalization. By democratic agreement, an honor code against cheating was set up much like that at West Point, the military academy. The price of the code, however, could easily be the weakening of ties of loyalty and trust between intimate friends, and considerable emotional conflict and pain for both members of a friendship pair. The question is whether the enhancement of the "virtue" of honesty and strengthening trust between teachers and students is worth the price.

The Honor Code and Peer Loyalty

To address this question, we shall report an incident which occurred in Judy's core group. Some weeks after passing the rule against cheating and requiring student confrontation, Judy asked how the new policy was going. At that time Jenny, a sophomore student in her core group, revealed that she had cheated on homework since the rule had been made. She explained that if she did not admit to breaking the rule, she could not feel close to the community. At that point several students asked if she had thought about the rule when she was breaking it. She answered affirmatively and apologized: "Yes, I knew I was breaking the rule but I also knew I was not doing well in this class; I was behind. I obviously made the wrong decision to cheat, but I did it and I'm sorry."

After a few others spoke, Jenny took the floor again, obviously quite agitated. She said that she felt frustrated because someone in the group, who she knew had cheated, had not come forward. "I feel like I'm a hypocrite because although I knew I cheated, I'm extremely bothered by someone else in this group who also has cheated and who has not said anything."

Several students asked her what she felt her obligation was. Going back to the community meeting decision, Jenny said, "I know I'm supposed to confront the person who cheated. But the other person who cheated and I don't get along so I just can't do it." Then Judy asked if she would like a friend or someone else to help her confront the person who cheated, and a student promptly volunteered. Jenny declined these offers and then blurted out, "Mary, I wish you would just explain what happened." At first Mary had no comment. She began to cry. Jenny said that she had seen a student in another core group copy from Mary's homework with Mary's knowledge.

Judy asked Mary if she would just take a deep breath and, if possible, respond to Jenny. Mary, through her tears, said, "Please talk softly. I don't want my mother to hear this. She would kill me." (The core group meeting was taking place in Mary's home). Then she explained that Sally and she were best friends and that Sally had not done her homework and just took her notebook. Mary said that she told Sally not to do it but that Sally persisted and she backed down: "You know Sally has a very strong will and personality, much stronger than mine. So although I knew it was wrong I couldn't say no to Sally." Mary continued by saying that she did not want to make an issue out of what Sally was doing and jeopardize their friendship.

Mary then turned on Jenny for reporting her: "I feel terrible about what I did, but you know, Jenny, I'm really angry with you. Why didn't you say something to me first? That's our rule." Before Jenny could respond, John took Mary's side and attacked the honor code agreement. "I voted against the procedure. I believe in the rule but I don't believe in how we've agreed to enforce it. You should never report on a fellow student. We need to be loyal to each other."

At that point, Jenny gave a passionate and personal defense of her action and the rule:

I love this school. I came here as a total screw off. You remember how angry Judy [T] was with me at the beginning of the year. This school has helped me, and I'm going to help make the school a good place. If that means reporting on a friend who breaks a rule, then that person is not much of a friend anyway. I'm going to report on them. If we don't follow the rules we make, then it's a joke. Maybe you just don't care as much about this school as much as I do, John, and maybe I went about reporting on Mary and Sally incorrectly, but I did it for the sake of our school.

The core group focused on how Jenny and Mary should approach Sally about what had happened. Jenny and Mary decided that they would go together and speak with Sally about the cheating issue and that the three of them would meet with Judy on Friday morning. After the core group meeting, Jenny and Mary immediately talked to Sally, and she offered a public apology hours later in the community meeting. Jenny, Mary, and Sally left the meeting feeling closer to each other and to the community. Recall that Jenny felt it would be particularly difficult to confront Mary because she could not count on being listened to and understood by her, since they were not friends. Feeling supported by the group, Jenny resolved her own guilt of silence by identifying Mary as having violated the rule. The supportive atmosphere of the core group allowed Jenny and Mary to go together to talk to Sally, thus bringing Jenny and Mary into closer communication with one another. It also helped Mary to be more honest in her relationship with Sally, who tended to be domineering.

We believe that the preference of the just community approach for open public discussion over concealment and gossip can be justified as not violating privacy. The rules involved are public rules, democratically agreed upon by the community, and the infringement of these rules is a public matter. This norm of public discussion is quite different from opening up personal issues to public scrutiny and criticism. It does not imply constant "big brother" monitoring by teachers and students. Public discussion is restricted to issues of fairness in the school life of the community. Furthermore, unlike moral education models in authoritarian and totalitarian countries, public group discussion is not used as a form of humiliation and emotional ostracism; it culminates in a reaffirmation of everyone's worth to the community and their continued membership in it.

In the episode we have presented, the act of admitting a rule violation was seen by most of the community as a very positive sign of caring for the community. It was responded to by group emotional support and reassurance of the confessors' solid standing of membership in the group. The group felt this way because the rule violators' concern about the community was sufficiently strong to lead to admission of rule violation. In spite of the fact that the confrontation of student with student is a painful, even tearful, emotional process, its resolution can be one of a stronger sense of solidarity both among the friends involved and among the members of the core group and community.

LISA'S EXPULSION AND COLLECTIVE RESPONSIBILITY

In chapter 5, we described Greg's expulsion at the end of Cluster's first year as one of the school's most regrettable failures. We will now describe a somewhat similar case in which the just community approach worked.[1] Like Greg, Lisa was trouble from the moment she entered the school. She was branded as a "terror" in the regular high school after episodes of name-calling and fighting. At her sister's (a solid A School citizen) insistence, she came to the A School hoping to straighten out. During her first semester, there was no visible improvement. She failed three out of four of her classes, was involved in an incident of cheating, was accused of verbally abusing an aide in the regular school, and cut class regularly. After numerous attempts to counsel her and threaten her with expulsion, the faculty gave up. They concluded, as did the Cluster faculty with Greg, that Lisa was a hopeless case, and looked into other programs that might better meet her needs. They hoped to persuade Lisa to leave the A School voluntarily and recommended this in a conference with her and her parents. Lisa, claiming the A School was the best situation for her, adamantly refused, and her parents strongly supported her. The faculty then gave her an option: withdraw from the school on her own or take the risk of being expelled in a community meeting. Lisa decided to take her case to the community.

In the core group meetings each faculty leader presented as a unanimous faculty recommendation that Lisa be expelled. The faculty felt that in all honesty they must be quite clear about their position and left it to the students to decide whether they felt a responsibility for coming up with another solution. We will present one such core group meeting, which took place in a member's home over breakfast. The discussion began with the adviser, Judy, giving some background to Lisa's case, explaining the faculty position and trying to present Lisa's point of view.

A number of students took issue with the faculty's position. When the students asked how it would benefit her and the community to expel her, Judy expounded on the rationale for the faculty's recommendation: "Lisa has taken up an enormous amount of faculty time. She is only one

---

1. This is an elaborated version of the case discussed in Kohlberg (1985).

of seventy-five students. The faculty and school have had little, if any, impact, while at the same time the faculty has had to spend more than its fair share of time on her case."

Several students wondered whether Lisa would be better off if she went back to the high school. For example, Joan said: "I think Lisa needs us. In the high school nobody would care what would happen to her. She doesn't have to report to anyone at the high school, and anyway, Judy, it really doesn't matter if she takes up more than her fair share of time." Some students pointed out that they could give Lisa some help. One student, Sharon, suggested that they form a support group: "We could be a support group to her. We could have a support group for her. Maybe that would help her start to come to class and do better."

Judy encouraged this idea but stressed that the students would have to accept responsibility for following through on it: "That sounds like it would help Lisa, but the notion of a support group is something the students would have to make work. The students would have to accept responsibility for this. I support you bringing it up to the community meeting if you, Sharon, and other students would accept responsibility."

Not all students wanted to help Lisa in school. Some, like Jim, felt that she had taken advantage of the school by being in it without contributing to it: "It is unfair that she is taking up so much of the teachers' time. She has been warned. She hasn't done anything for the school. She doesn't participate in the democratic process, and I think Lisa has taken unfair advantage of us by not participating."

Judy ended core group by asking: "How do you feel about confronting Lisa in the community meeting?" This solicited a variety of responses. For example:

MARY: I would feel rotten. It is like turning against my friend.
BILL: Lisa broke trust. It's like what happened with the drug rule. It is OK to tell her that you're angry. She has to put something into the school. We can have compassion for her yet tell her that we are angry. She has put us on the spot.

The meeting concluded with opinion divided between those who wanted to keep Lisa in the school and give her support and those who felt she was taking unfair advantage of the school.

Community Meeting

The community meeting to decide on whether Lisa should be expelled began with a statement from the student chairperson, noting that while expulsion had been discussed before as an abstract possibility, this was the first time a case had actually been brought to a community meeting for a decision. After representatives from the faculty presented their side of the issue and Judy assured the students that the faculty had agreed to abide by whatever they decided, Lisa was called upon to present her case. She admitted she had a problem with attendance—"Cutting has become addictive to me"—but maintained that she had improved since coming to the alternative school. She requested that she be given one more chance for the remainder of the school year. When asked, "How do we know you'll accept the responsibility? Can you help yourself?" she responded at stage 2 in a manner typical of many of the Cluster students: "My education is at stake. I have to do it. I really want to stay here." A teacher then accused her of having a "nasty attitude" toward the A School staff. She confessed to being "touchy" and overreactive and pledged, "What I can do is just bite my tongue when I feel that I'm going to respond in an unpleasant way."

At that point the chairperson invited members of the group to offer suggestions for what to do about Lisa. The first to speak was Sharon. She elaborated her view that the students should form a support group for Lisa:

To the faculty and to many of the students her rudeness is a personal offense, and, Lisa, I got in a lot of difficulty for a similar attitude. I think, Lisa, you have an authority problem, but to me personal responsibility is the issue. We as a community cannot see Lisa as a problem and just send her back to the high school where nobody cares. Here we have a capacity to care. At her age now her main job is to be a student and a good human being. She needs the support from us. I think the school should put together a student support group for Lisa, we can check on her, be with her, make sure she gets to class. I think helping each other helps the community.

Sharon here proposes a norm of collective responsibility at stage 4. Although members of the A School have never made such a collective commitment to help a student, Sharon appeals to their shared expectation for caring and their shared commitment to community, scorable as at least phase 4.

Sally responded to Sharon's proposal with a reservation as to whether Lisa would not rebuff the students' efforts as she had the faculty's: "I want to believe that Lisa will change and that we as students can help her. But I'm scared that she will just turn on us when we're trying to help her in the same way that she's turned on teachers when they've tried to help."

Her remark prompted Lee to ask the faculty what role they would play if the students decided to help. Judy (T) answered that if the community decided to keep her then the teachers and students would have to share responsibility for the decision. Then she challenged Lisa's classmates to tell how much help they had extended to her once they saw she had stopped coming to class and doing her work. To which a student sheepishly replied, "I guess not very much, have we?"

The discussion turned back to an interrogation of Lisa in search of some convincing indication that she would respond to their help. One student pragmatically concluded, "We have to be realistic; there is no way we can accept responsibility for getting Lisa to her classes. Lisa has to take that responsibility." This led another student to defend collective responsibility as a viable course of action by making a strong appeal to a shared sense of community:

All year long we have been talking about community spirit. Now is the time for action. By helping Lisa we can help ourselves. I take a lot of pride in this community, and I will value the community a little less if we don't decide to keep Lisa and to help her. I agree that it won't work if Lisa won't take responsibility also, but we can help her with that.

To those who wanted assurance that Lisa would not fall back into her regular bad patterns, Stephanie argued that they could change her whole experience of school:

We can show her a better understanding of the school, that it can be both work and fun. I think that we can restore her faith that she can succeed.

Sharon added a realistic affirmation of Stephanie's point.

We have to understand that people who have had difficulty never just have a smooth pattern, that Lisa will probably fall back. But if we have people in the school that she can relate to, that can give her some support, that can help her move forward, they can help her have a better understanding of what is expected of her. You have to trust the school community that we can help.

Judy clarified how this student initiative to help Lisa might represent an untried possibility and then asked Lisa for her reactions:

We, as teachers have been this round, but as a community haven't. We as a faculty failed, we can't sustain it, but if the community can then I think that we as teachers, at least I will support it. But I have a question to Lisa—what is different now?

To her earlier statement that she would shape up out of fear, Lisa added an acknowledgment that others cared for her:

I know that my education is at stake and I have to do it, but I also hear that people care and that's very different.

The issue shortly came to a vote, and an overwhelming majority, including the entire faculty, decided that Lisa should not be expelled but put on probation for the remainder of the year. The terms of her probation included a very careful monitoring of her class work and attendance and a requirement that she not leave campus between the hours of 8 A.M. and 3 P.M. She fulfilled those conditions for the rest of the year.

Analysis

Lisa's case, like Greg's, involves one of the most recurring conflicts a teacher or administrator has to face—the conflict between the special needs of a difficult student and the needs of the school community to uphold its norms and standards. In most schools, teachers and administrators face a no-win choice. If they opt for the needs of a troubled adolescent, they weaken the rules and welfare of the larger group. In Lisa's situation, the option best for the troubled student actually strengthened the group's sense of community and its sense of responsibility for its rules of attendance and participation. This is a key principle of just community theory, which Kohlberg had briefly expounded to some of the staff the evening before the community meeting. Probably quite wisely, the teachers did not buy this solution until they saw it genuinely coming from the students. Observers at the meeting commented on how well students had taken ownership for the meeting and how moved they had been at student concern and responsibility. For us, it was a successful contrast to Greg's expulsion.

In comparing the A School favorably with Cluster we do not wish to suggest that the A School students were simply more caring or softhearted than the Cluster students. As we showed in chapter 5, the Cluster students by the end of the first year had developed a shared phase 4 expectation for caring, which served as a basis for their own collective restitution decision in October of the following school year. Perhaps the critical difference between the two schools in handling their respective expulsion cases was that in Cluster the norms regulating disturbances and attendance, which had become Greg's worst problems, were not as fully developed as were the norms in the A School regulating attendance, class participation, and respect, which were Lisa's major problems. In the A School, students were willing to communicate to Lisa both their desire to be helpful and their criticism of her deviant behavior, since they had developed their commitment to the collective norms of participation and respectful speech to phase 6 (a willingness to persuade others to uphold the norm or to express disapproval at a norm violation). A corresponding development did not occur in Cluster until the middle of the third year.

In this chapter we have presented a sampling of A School discussions that conveyed how the just community approach broke new ground in the development of moral culture. In the A School the drug and cheating norms developed to the highest phase, phase 7, as students agreed to enforce them either by persuading those breaking the rules to confess or by reporting them. Perhaps the greatest achievement at the A School as a community was the decision not to expel Lisa, the worst troublemaker the school had ever had, but to take collective responsibility for helping her to improve her behavior in school. Finally, they dealt honestly and sensitively with issues of minority rights and indoctrination, which touch on the most controversial aspects of the just community approach itself, by courageously airing their differences in community meetings and by attempting to make shared norms protecting freedom of conscience and public expression.

7

S.W.S.: A Second Perspective on Democratic Schooling

In this chapter we will discuss the third of the experimental schools in our study, School-Within-a-School (S.W.S.) in Brookline, Massachusetts. The reader will find many parallels between S.W.S. and the other two alternative high schools, Cluster and the A School. Yet our aim in this chapter is not to underscore the similarities as much as to probe into differences between the approaches to high school democracy taken in the schools. Specifically, we will focus on how Ralph Mosher as a consultant to S.W.S. departed from just community theory in three areas: advocacy, community, and moral development as the aim and guiding principle of democratic schooling. We will begin to develop Mosher's position in these areas first through a brief presentation of S.W.S. history during the four years he served as participant observer there. Then we will draw out the theoretical contrasts between the democratic approach that evolved in S.W.S. and the just community approach.

A HISTORICAL OUTLINE OF S.W.S.

S.W.S., an alternative school that is part of Brookline High School in Brookline, Massachusetts, was established in 1969.[1] Like the A School,

---

1. This account of S.W.S. history is drawn from Mosher's (1978, 1980) two previously published chapters on S.W.S.

its roots were in the discontent and protest of the Vietnam era. It began with a group of students, teachers, and parents proposing to the school committee a plan for an alternative school that would offer a more student-centered approach to education and a more equal and personal relationship with teachers. S.W.S. occupies three classrooms and an office on the third floor of a wing of Brookline High School. It enrolls approximately one hundred students a year. There has been a waiting list for admissions since 1977. The staff includes two half-time English teachers, one full-time math and science teacher, a half-time social studies teacher, and a full-time coordinator and counselor. Most students take at least two courses in S.W.S. and the rest in the regular high school. The content of the courses is traditional and the classes are distinguished mainly by their relaxed atmosphere and in the friendly relationships among students and teachers.

The Advent of Democracy

Until the fall of 1975, S.W.S.'s rules and policies were largely made by the director and faculty with some input from students, who were encouraged to attend staff meetings. Although staff and students were generally satisfied with the substance of these rules and policies, they grew increasingly discontent with the lack of student involvement. In the spring of 1975 a group of students and teachers, who had become familiar with Kohlberg's and Mosher's ideas through the Danforth Moral Education Project, which had started in the Brookline School System that fall, proposed that S.W.S. become a participatory democracy. A ballot vote indicated strong student and staff support for such a move, and the next fall the first democratic town meetings were held. The Danforth Foundation supported Mosher and several assistants as consultants in developing the town meeting (the S.W.S. equivalent of the community meeting) process.

The First Year

Initial town meetings were taken up with detailed discussions about the rules of order, how the agenda should be set, and choosing a chairperson. Of all three alternative schools in this study, S.W.S. evolved the most elaborate set of procedural rules. This reflected not only the students' interest but also Mosher's emphasis on the democratic process. Once students and staff reached an agreement on procedural matters, they turned to the thorny issue of making attendance at town meetings mandatory. Those defending the liberty of the individual outnumbered the proponents of an attendance requirement by a wide margin the first time the issue came to a vote. However, that margin dwindled as successive votes were taken on the issue that year.

The libertarian leanings of S.W.S. members also surfaced in the resistance shown to the consultants' gentle suggestion that disciplinary matters and other sensitive issues ought to be brought to town meetings. The students were more than willing to discuss the abstract principle of respect for the rights of others. They also debated with fervor the right of the high school administration to restrict the freedom of speech of several students in S.W.S. Nevertheless, when cases of student rule violations and disrespect toward faculty were broached, the students were reluctant to take action against their peers. Unlike the Cluster and the A School, S.W.S. had no disciplinary committee or procedure involving the students in rule enforcement. The closest institution to a discipline committee was the A.W.O.L. (Absent Without Leave) Committee, established in the first year to determine whether or not missed classes were to be excused and to offer assistance to those with attendance problems. The A.W.O.L. Committee did not involve itself in whether or how students cutting classes should be punished.

In spite of students' distaste for disciplinary restrictions, they did agree to rules that required all S.W.S. students to take at least two S.W.S. classes and that limited the number of times a student could cut class. Another set of town meetings focused more on "boundary questions" than discipline. Criteria for admitting new students and whether to open S.W.S. courses up to students in the larger high school were discussed.

The Second Year

Town meetings during the second year took up three general issues: the responsibilities of S.W.S. members to the community, student rights vis-à-vis the high school administration, and student participation in the hiring of S.W.S. staff. The issue of students' responsibilities surfaced in the discussion of whether to make town meeting attendance mandatory. A mandatory attendance policy was nearly unanimously accepted in the late spring by the sophomores and juniors, and it was in Mosher's estimation a pivotal step in making S.W.S. a truly democratic community. The mandatory attendance policy brought S.W.S. in line with the practice in Cluster and the A School. However, one significant difference remained. In S.W.S. students were permitted to schedule classes during town meeting time, whereas in Cluster and the A School this was not allowed. Other developments in S.W.S. that spelled out student obligations included the establishment of behavioral guidelines for the S.W.S. parties and discussion about in-school suspensions.

The issue of student rights resurfaced in the second year when the school administration attempted to institute a moment of silence at the beginning of the day as was mandated by school law. The discussion of the topic proved to be highly entertaining and informative although it resolved little. One of the most unusual developments in S.W.S. was the involvement of students in the hiring of two part-time teachers. In Cluster and the A School students were encouraged to make suggestions to staff, but the staff had primary responsibility for making the appointments. This division of labor reflects the just community policy of leaving pragmatic administrative and curricular issues up to the staff. No such policy existed in S.W.S., where the students constituted a majority of an Appointments Committee that screened candidates and made recommendations for final approval. So impressive were the recommendations that in the years that followed, students even participated in hiring a new coordinator and in evaluating staff for reappointment.

The Third Year

During this year students gradually assumed greater responsibility for establishing and enforcing disciplinary expectations. After a number of "incidents" of drug use and food raids occurred on an overnight retreat in the beginning of the second year, the coordinator asked for and received some clear-cut rules for future functions. One student, playing devil's advocate, stated that he would not abide by such rules and asked what those present in the town meeting intended to do about it. He goaded them into insisting on an ad hoc committee composed of two students and one faculty member to deal with rule violators. Later in the year that same student challenged students and staff to make explicit their expectations for membership in the S.W.S. community. They came up with a list that included not only town meeting and class attendance but participation on at least one major committee or an equivalent contribution to the community.

The coordinator precipitated a further development in student involvement in the adjudication of discipline. Toward the close of the school year she announced in a town meeting that she had drawn up a list of students who she felt should be suspended because of their unexcused class cuts among other things. She then dared the students to get involved in the final decision: "Until the community instructs me otherwise, I intend to suspend these students and put them at the end of the waiting list for admission." Although the students trusted the good judgment of the coordinator, they understood the need to establish an institution for the protection of students' rights should she or another person in her position make an arbitrary decision. In defense of this notion of due process, a decision was made to establish a peer review committee, made up of two students chosen at random and the coordinator. Decisions by this committee were subject to further appeal in a town meeting.

The Fourth Year

In many ways this year represented a consolidation of gains made in the second and third years. The policy of mandatory town meeting attendance was reexamined and reaffirmed, as was the policy governing participation in town meetings. Progress was made in the area of enforcement. Prior to this year no penalties for violating the above attendance policies had been stipulated. This changed when members of the Agenda Committee asked the town meeting assembly to respond to a student's flagrant absenteeism from their weekly planning meeting. A proposal that put some "teeth" into the existing policies was advanced: a student who failed to attend a given number of committee and town meetings without an acceptable excuse would be liable for expulsion pending a peer view. It passed by a vote of 35–23, with about 10 abstentions. This vote put democratic participation on equal footing with academic participation in S.W.S., a remarkable achievement seen against the backdrop of the first year.

In subsequent meetings social participation in S.W.S. became the focus of discussion. A number of community building proposals were made for a school fair and a car wash to raise money and for retreats and festivals to socialize and have fun. Many of these were adopted. The most controversial and interesting of all was a faculty member's proposal to reduce the number of required S.W.S. courses from two to one and to mandate that students participate in S.W.S. activities during "F Block," a free period scheduled twice a week at the end of the day. Because of the radical nature of the proposal, a 75 percent majority was stipulated for its passage. Debate lasted several weeks. The initial straw votes strongly supported the proposal as a way of building community at little cost. Then the opposition gained strength as students questioned the wisdom of substituting an academic requirement for a social one and wondered whether imposing "community" would backfire. When the final vote was taken, the proposal was defeated. However, at the end of the school year it reappeared and was passed in a modified version, calling for advisory group meetings in F Block.

THEORETICAL DIFFERENCES

The Consultant as Advocate

As this overview suggests, S.W.S.'s identity as a democratic community developed very slowly over four years in response to concrete needs experienced by the students and staff, who had few preconceived notions about the direction in which they should proceed. Although Mosher could have provided that direction, he quite consciously restrained himself in agenda and town meetings: "Democratic groups must decide their own destinies within certain broad principles. Consultants, especially those who believe they know the shape of that destiny, need to permit the pooled intelligence and experience of the democratic group to operate and grow, even to make 'mistakes' " (1980:292).

In Mosher's view the consultant's choice is between an artificially induced accelerated group change or slow, organic growth. For him to have pressed for a specific objective, for example the adoption of the original F Block proposal, would have meant interfering unnecessarily in the natural dynamics of the S.W.S. group. While Kohlberg was far more forceful as an advocate of the communitarian point of view and of particular policies, he basically agreed with Mosher that consultants must be careful about imposing their ideas and schemes. Thus he distinguished advocates from indoctrinators (Kohlberg 1980:48). Indoctrinators, whether by content, method, or intention, attempt to inculcate a particular point of view without regard for students' moral rationality and freedom. As we noted in chapter 1, advocates operate within the democratic process, appeal to reason, and respect student autonomy in taking stands on matters that have consequences for the community. Certainly we would agree with Mosher that consultants to a democratic school should resist the temptation to short-circuit open and thorough moral discussion of an issue either because they think they can scientifically predict its outcome or because their philosophical beliefs lead them to a particular resolution.

While Kohlberg rejected the indoctrinative role, he did think that the consultant should offer concrete direction for a group. In this sense he distinguished advocates from facilitators. The latter refrain, as far as possible, from having any overt influence on the group. They try to help group members become reflective about their group's goals, norms, and values. Mosher often appeared to lean toward this facilitator role in his concern to respect the integrity of S.W.S.'s democratic processes. For example, Mosher did not insist, as Kohlberg did in Cluster, that attendance at the weekly democratic meeting be mandatory or that students routinely participate on a discipline committee. However, his reluctance to advocate vigorously did not prevent him from supporting proposals for affirmative action, greater student responsibility for disciplinary decisions, mandatory community meetings, and F Block community building. Unlike the pure facilitator, he took a stand on certain issues, but he tempered his advocacy with the belief that the group would do what was best in its own time.

Kohlberg did not share Mosher's faith in the spontaneous development of adolescent groups. His skepticism was confirmed during Cluster's first community meeting, when the students hastily voted to make afternoon classes optional. He chided the staff for holding a "romantic Summerhill Alternative School conception of power to the people—the idea that adolescents were basically capable of responsibility and self-governance if only given the chance" (1980:39). While Kohlberg conceded that such a laissez-faire approach might work with students reasoning at conventional moral stages 3 and 4 in an affluent suburban alternative high school, he thought it would fail in an urban setting with underprivileged adolescents reasoning at stage 2.

Building Community

Mosher began consulting in S.W.S. with Cluster's goal of implementing a parallel application of the just community approach. He noted that after some "on-the-job training" he changed his mind and decided to pursue the broader objective of "school democracy" (1980:280). Although he did not abandon concerns for justice and community, he backed away from Kohlberg's Durkheimian emphasis on moral atmosphere. He offered an alternative approach based on Dewey's conception of democratic community:

Dewey was quick to stress that these political procedures were means for realizing democracy as the truly human *way of living*. Democracy, he argued, is more than a form of government; it is primarily a way of living together. And the democratic community will have two essential characteristics: *the interests its members consciously share will be numerous and varied, and it will have a full and free interaction with other forms of social association.* Thus, a democratic community (whether it be a classroom, school, New England village or a nation-state) will share many common interests which require the individual member to consider the views, wishes and claims of others relative to these common concerns. (1978:75).

This Deweyan approach represented a psychological perspective on how communal relations develop. Starting with individuals who have particular interests, a community forms through interaction as they discover and pursue common interests and purposes. This view carries at least three practical implications. First, it underscores the importance of respecting the spontaneous currents of attraction that move within a group. Second, it makes communication through formal democratic meetings and informal "bull sessions" the key to group development. Third, it leads to the sponsorship of varied curricular and extra-curricular activities that surface and encourage common concerns. For example, at the end of his second year of consultation Mosher observed that S.W.S. could do with more "programs and activities (retreats, parties, athletics, drama, enrichment courses, community action, etc.) that cut across existing cliques and involve students in contact with members they did not know" (1978:98). In essence the original F Block proposal was designed to build community in this way.

In contrast to this Dewian view, which emphasizes the voluntary interactions of individuals, we have envisioned community from a primarily sociological perspective and accordingly we have adopted the vocabulary of collective norms, values, and responsibility to describe and evaluate it. Furthermore, our approach to community building starts with a normative ideal of community and emphasizes making rules and agreements that embody that ideal.

Reimer and Power (1980) picked up on the dangers of an over-emphasis on the normative orientation to community building in describing what they called "the unresolved communal dilemma." They noted that the Cluster staff's advocacy of community was sometimes frustrated because the students felt unable to change their patterns of action accordingly. An illustration of this problem is the way the staff approached integration in Cluster's fourth year.[2] As we noted in chapter 5 the staff advocated the high ideal that students mix during lunch breaks and between classes. The students affirmed this ideal but confessed that they felt uncomfortable about venturing out of their cliques. One black student, Eddie, excused this reluctance to mix as part of human nature. He facetiously asked the staff, "You want me to come here, right, and say, 'Hi Karl, how are you doing, how are you feeling?' Well, I don't care. It is just ridiculous, and you will never get it like that." Eddie referred to Karl, not just because he was white and they did not get along, but because his barefoot, "freaky" appearance was anathema to the black subculture. When a staff member replied, "Why won't you get it like that?" Eddie smiled and said, "If I knew that I could solve all the problems in the world." Eddie may be right. Most of us agree on the ideal of integration, but the key to achieving it depends upon knowing how to overcome ingrained patterns of cultural and social class isolation. Simply saying "It ought to be" will not make it so.

As a counseling psychologist, more attuned to the "is" than the "ought," Mosher provides a corrective to our Kantian proclivity to emphasize duty. His notion of community helps us to understand Eddie and suggests a way out of the communal dilemma. If there were an activity that engaged both Eddie and Karl, perhaps then they could form a relation-

2. A fuller account of this meeting may be found in Kohlberg 1985:53–57.

ship. The challenge is to find one. Basketball was Eddie's favorite sport, but Karl was not athletic. Karl loved the guitar, but Eddie was not fond of music. The only thing they did have in common was that they were seniors in high school and members of Cluster.

That proved to be enough, as we learned. A few months after Eddie said he could not be bothered to say "Hi" to Karl, he became involved in the following exchange with him in a community meeting. Karl came before the meeting because he had not registered for the seven courses necessary for graduation that spring.

KARL: I don't care about graduating, and I'm not interested in high school. I'm only here for Cluster.

EDDIE: If you don't like high school, why don't you take the seven courses so you can graduate?

KARL: I can't graduate this year—it would be too many courses.

EDDIE: Why didn't you take more courses last year so you could graduate this year?

KARL: I didn't think about it, I didn't care.

EDDIE: If you don't care about yourself, we have to care about you for you. What are you here in school for now? What are you going to do after high school?

Eddie and Karl had hardly become friends in the interim between meetings. In fact, Eddie still found Karl to be an enigma. Nevertheless, Eddie cared enough to try to help Karl when Karl did not seem willing to help himself. Eddie and Karl would probably get along better if there were additional interests that could draw them together. No doubt, as educators, we need to create such interests if they are not already present. Yet this example indicates that the common activity of participating in a democratic community may in itself provide a basis for solidarity. Such an activity combines the elements of duty and desires and leads beyond the impasse of an exclusive emphasis on either. In fairness to Mosher and to ourselves, none of us takes a completely one-sided approach to community. In chapter 4 we defined community as value and a source of attraction. Mosher (1978, 1890) cast both of his accounts of S.W.S.'s history as a gradual acceptance of obligations based on a concern for the common good.

Although Mosher's view of community is compatible with our own, S.W.S. students developed a different sense of community from that in Cluster or the A School. Perhaps the best illustration of this may be drawn from contrasting discussions about collective restitution in S.W.S. and Cluster. In the spring of 1978, during Mosher's third year as consultant to S.W.S., a proposal was made that the group chip in to replace a backgammon board that a student, Bill, had lent to the school. The board was discovered missing one day, and almost everyone presumed it had been stolen by someone "downstairs" in Brookline High School. Bill promised that if the S.W.S. members pitched in for a new board, he would continue to make it available for everyone. The town meeting discussion focused on the extent to which members of S.W.S. had an obligation to help Bill. All those who spoke in the meeting acknowledged that it was kind of Bill to share his board with everyone. One student suggested that they pass around a hat for those who wanted to contribute, and this received widespread support. There was considerable disagreement, however, that all should feel obligated to contribute. Possibly the strongest argument opposed to collective restitution was given by the coordinator. She said that if she brought some visual aids to school and they were lost, she would have no right to ask the community to replace them. She reasoned that since she brought those materials to school, she voluntarily took the risk that they may be stolen or damaged. If she expected the community to assume responsibility for her materials, then she would have to ask the community to agree to such an arrangement ahead of time "because we are an individual responsibility school, not a collective responsibility school."

Curiously, neither S.W.S. nor Cluster School defined itself constitutionally as either kind of school. Without any possible appeal to a formal statement of purpose, judgments as to whether a policy of collective responsibility was consistent with the nature of the school rested on individuals' interpretations of the implicitly shared ideals of the schools. Members of S.W.S. and Cluster agreed on the importance of caring for students like Bill, who were "victims." The question was whether to make the act of restitution a voluntary one, based on the goodwill of each individual member, or a mandatory one, based on an obligation derived from a normative ideal of community. The differing decisions made by the S.W.S. and Cluster School members regarding collective restitution reflected the differing views of community. The S.W.S. coordinator held a contractarian view that S.W.S. members had no obligations beyond those to which they had explicitly consented. According to this view, a sense of solidarity may move members of the same group to voluntary acts of sympathy and gratitude. However, there is nothing intrinsic to the notion of community that entails obligations beyond those minimally required by a sense of justice. On the other hand, Kohlberg and those who advocated collective restitution in Cluster argued that in joining a community Cluster members assumed obligations of care. In their view community was both a social reality and a normative ideal.

Moral Development

The third and last issue that we will consider in comparing the approaches taken by Mosher and Kohlberg has to do with moral development as a focus of democratic schooling. As with the other issues, the differences between the two consultants are subtle. Mosher (1978, 1980) freely used moral stages to help elucidate the ways in which students thought about and resolved issues in S.W.S. He also thought an analysis of moral judgment development was key to any kind of evaluation of democratic schools. Nevertheless, he was quite critical of what he saw as Kohlberg's exclusive preoccupation with cognitive, moral outcomes.

In 1978 he warned of an obsession with reason and justice, or what an S.W.S. staff member had called "creeping moral developmentalism":

I believe it would be a mistake to reduce school democracy to a means (albeit a sophisticated one) to stimulate the moral development of students. God knows moral reasoning and behavior are critically missing in our present education of children and adolescents, but morality is not, repeat not, all there is to being human. Our "best" education has promoted idolatry of intellect; idolatry of character or an obsession with justice, "a creeping moral developmentalism," would be similarly myopic. What we have to hold is a conception of a psychology and an education for whole and full human development. (P. 103)

Two years later his tone became harsher as he referred to the moral emphasis of the just community approach as "dehumanizing":

When moral issues occur in their individual or school life they deal with them. . . . But morality does not preoccupy or happen in the "natural lives of these adolescents with the preprocessed or total quality of formal classroom moral discussions. Nor does morality begin to span the rich play of their individual or collective lives. Close encounters of this kind with S.W.S. adolescents made it very clear to me that to be concerned only with their understanding and practice of justice *is* reductionistic and dehumanizing—bad psychology and bad education. (1980:281–82)

The issue, then, for Mosher was not whether moral development should be *a* concern in a democratic approach but whether it should be the *only* concern. He pleaded that democratic educators have a broader scope and aim: the development of the whole person:

A democratic education is one whose aim is the full development of every individual's potential. Its psychology and its education must lead to whole people. It is unfortunate that that term has become clichéd. Rationality, character, ego, social contribution, the aesthetic, a sound body, emotion, work, and soul are integral parts of human being and potential: a ninefold helix that is everyone's birthright. For a variety of reasons including a sufficiency or insufficiency of psychological theory about one or another of these interrelated strands of development, a division of labor or the inability to keep a multivariable model of human growth in mind, we may choose to practice a reductionism in either our psychological research or our educational development. (pp. 302, 303)

Mosher raises the issue of how we are to understand the relationship of one developmental domain, moral development, to other domains and to the whole of the personality. We have no quarrel with the position that the aim of education must include more than moral development. Nevertheless, we think that moral development ought to have a priority over other developmental domains and ought to regulate them. While nonmoral aspects of ego development such as independence, critical thinking, and self-confidence are desirable, their ultimate justification depends upon their relationship to moral goals and activities. Self-confidence is hardly a virtue in a "hit man" nor is critical thinking in an extortionist.

CONCLUSIONS

In this chapter we have presented a brief description of S.W.S.'s history and of Mosher's approach to democratic schooling as it diverged from our own. In chapters 8 and 9 we will have the occasion to evaluate the extent to which these differences in approach led to differences in the outcomes we measured. In fairness to S.W.S., we concede that our measurement strategy proceeded from the pedagogical approach applied in Cluster and the A School. Thus, our focus on moral outcomes, both individual and collective, may well have missed certain aspects of the S.W.S. experience that Mosher would have judged to be quite important.

In spite of differences between approaches, the pattern of the development in S.W.S.'s moral culture is quite similar to that of Cluster and the A School. Norms, like attendance, were built by formal rules to a relatively high degree of collectiveness. Development in the phase of the norms also occurred, as S.W.S. students took increasingly greater responsibility for enforcing their rules.

If we look at the content of S.W.S. norms, we find that while there is some shift from conventional and fairness norms to norms of community, this shift is certainly not as dramatic as in Cluster or the A School. The discussion of Bill's backgammon board illustrates this. In terms of stage development, there appears to be a gradual shift from a stage 3 to a stage 4 understanding of group norms and rules. As students realized that more than good intentions were necessary for the functioning of a democratic school, they legislated in certain areas of their common life and based their reasons for doing so on an acceptance of certain obligations for the welfare and order of the school.

We would like to end this chapter as Mosher would have had it, with a tribute not to the development of the communitarian culture in S.W.S. but to its democracy. Having studied S.W.S. for several years, we came away with renewed confidence that adolescents can with remarkably little adult assistance "learn to govern themselves." Mosher made much the same point in summing up his own reflections on S.W.S.:

After four years of observing the weekly town meetings and assisting the agenda committees, it would be hard for me to say that these students govern themselves any less responsibly or democratically than do teachers, school committees, town meetings, or university faculties that I have known. . . . These students practice self-government with more good human forgiveness of their own frailties . . . and light heartedness than their elders. (1980:293–94)

8

Comparing Moral Cultures: Results and Case Studies

In chapter 4 we introduced our method for assessing moral atmosphere by analyzing community meetings and ethnographic interviews from the first three years of the Cluster School. We continued this analysis in chapter 5, tracing developments in the phase and stage of Cluster's collective norms. In this chapter we will use our method of moral culture assessment to analyze the school dilemmas interview in order to compare the moral cultures of three democratic alternative high schools with their parent high schools.[1]

METHODOLOGY

The School Dilemmas Interview

The standard moral judgment interview and scoring method (Colby et al. 1987) have proved to be useful for measuring individual moral judgment longitudinal changes in a variety of cultural and subcultural settings. The best-known dilemma used in this interview is the Heinz dilemma, which is set in Europe. Heinz must decide whether he should steal a drug to save his dying wife. The nonrelevance of the setting and the hypothetical nature of the standard moral dilemmas help make them a test stimulus having similar meanings to individuals living in various

1. This description of the methodology is an elaborated version of a previously published chapter by Higgins, Power, and Kohlberg (1984).

cultural worlds. Their prescriptive focus on what someone in general, Heinz, *should do* minimizes nonmoral, personality, and situational variations in response, which might be brought out by the question *"What would you do?"* As a result they yield a good picture of moral judgment *general competence,* regardless of variations in personality and situation which might influence *specific* moral judgment *performance.*

In addition to being context-free and hypothetical, the standard dilemmas are primarily dilemmas of justice. They pose a conflict between the rights of one person, for example Heinz's wife, and that of another, the druggist. Alternately stated, they oppose one social norm, respecting property, to another social norm, respecting life. The most adequate resolution of such justice conflicts requires reference to a principle, such as the utilitarian principle of the greater good or the justice principle of equal respect for each person. The principles just cited are those found at stage 5, but each stage has its characteristic rules or principles of choice.

In studying democratic schools, we are less interested in students' general moral judgment competence than we are in how students actually make real-life moral decisions in the context of the moral culture of their particular schools. Thus, we designed practical dilemmas that frequently occur in public high schools and asked students how they would and should resolve them in their own schools. We also asked students how they felt their peers would react to these dilemmas.

The school dilemmas interview is quite similar to the ethnographic interview discussed in chapter 4 and shares with it a focus on students' perception of the culture of their school. We adopted the dilemma format for two reasons. First, we wished to make comparisons among schools. Ethnographic interviews were suited to within-school comparisons particularly in the democratic programs, which periodically returned to a set of problems. However, the content of the ethnographic interviews was too context-bound to allow for consistent across-school comparisons. Our school dilemmas interview provides a more standardized format. Second, we wished to analyze collective moral prescriptions, that is, statements expressing the obligations of community members *qua* community members in the name of the community; e.g., "As members of this community, we ought to do X." The ethnographic interview that we used consisted almost entirely of descriptive questions.

In order to elicit the kind of prescriptive statements we actually found in the community meeting analyses, we went back to the format successful in studying individual moral judgments—to posing dilemmas. The resulting school dilemmas interview had a strong prescriptive focus, while it also tapped practical judgments and the cultural context of the school.

Types of Dilemmas

The school dilemmas are presented in table 8.1. The first is the helping dilemma. From a stage 6 perspective of an ideal dialogue or ideal role taking (Kohlberg 1984) Billy's duty to help Harry may be viewed as a moral obligation. However, for adults and adolescents this dilemma seems to go beyond the ordinary requirements of moral duty. Two attributes of the dilemma seem to affect this judgment. First, the dilemma involves the performance of an action that would promote the welfare of another which seems to carry less obligatory force than refraining from actions which would cause harm to another. Second, the dilemma deliberately excludes bonds of family or affection between Billy and Harry. Generally, we recognize that we have special duties toward our relatives and our friends. However, relationships with co-workers or among students are much more ambiguous. By setting the dilemma in a homeroom and stating that Harry is well known, although not well liked, we raise a question about the moral significance of the relationships in the school. In the democratic alternative high schools, we expected that the bonds of community would lead to obligations of care. In regular, comparison high schools we expected that no such obligations are created. In fact, we expected that some exclusive student cliques might create such pressures as to make a student who helped an obnoxious "outsider" like Harry very uncomfortable. Such peer pressure might from a psychological perspective be thought of as constituting a quasi-obligation *not* to help.

The second dilemma involves a group decision about whether to collectively restitute to a member of the class for the money stolen from her pocketbook by an unknown member of that class. We present this dilemma to students as a follow-up to dilemma 3 about the stealing incident. Unlike the caring dilemma, which may be resolved by a deontic judgment involving role taking or utilitarian considerations, the collective restitution dilemma demands something more—the perception of a

Table 8.1.
The Practical School Dilemmas Interview

---

1. Helping Dilemma

The college Harry applied to had scheduled an interview with him for the coming Saturday at 9:00 A.M. As the college was forty miles away from Harry's town and Harry had no way of getting there, his guidance counselor agreed to drive him. The Friday before the interview the guidance counselor told Harry that his car had broken down and was in the repair shop until Monday. He said he felt bad, but there was no way he could drive him to his interview. He still wanted to help him out, so he went to Harry's homeroom and asked the students if there was anyone who could drive Harry to the college. No one volunteered to drive him. A lot of students in the class think Harry shows off and talks too much, and they do not like him. The homeroom teacher says he has to take his children to the dentist at that time. Some students say they cannot use the family car, others work, some do not have their licenses. One student, Billy, knows he can use his family car but wonders whether he should do something for Harry when the few students in class who know him best say they are busy or just cannot do it. Besides, he would have to get up really early on a Saturday morning, the only morning during the week he can sleep late.

Should Billy volunteer to drive Harry to the college? Why or why not?

2. Restitution Dilemma

Having left her classroom, Mary returns to find a twenty-dollar bill is missing from her pocketbook. She goes to the teacher and reports what has happened. The teacher asks whoever stole the money to return it, but no one does.

Should the students chip in if no one in the class admits taking the money or knowing who did?

3. Stealing Dilemma

When Mary arrived at her history class, she noticed that although the students were all there, the teacher had not arrived. She sat down for a few seconds but then decided to chat with a few of her friends in the hall until the teacher came. She opened her pocketbook, pulled out a letter she wanted to show her friends, and ran out of the classroom, leaving her pocketbook unsnapped and lying on her desk. Tom, a student in the class, looks into Mary's pocketbook and sees a twenty-dollar bill. He thinks about taking the twenty-dollar bill from her pocketbook.

What do you think a student like Tom would do in a situation like this? Why?

Should Mary have been trusting like that in this situation, or should she have been more careful?

Table 8.1. (continued)

4. Drug Dilemma

Before the junior class trip the faculty told the students that the whole class had to agree not to bring or use alcohol or drugs on the trip. If students were found using drugs or alcohol, they would be sent home. The students knew that without faculty approval they would not be able to have their trip. The students said in a class meeting that they all agreed to these conditions. On the trip, several students ask Bob, a fellow student, to go on a hike with them to the lake. When they get to the lake, they light up a joint and pass it around.

Should Bob refuse to smoke? Why or why not?

Probe questions, asked after each dilemma:
1. What would you do if this situation were to occur in your school?
2. Would there be a general feeling or expectation here to do X (to help, to chip in, not to steal, not to smoke)?
3. Is there an agreement or understanding that someone should do X or that it would be a good thing if someone did do X?
4. Do you think there should be an understanding? Would you bring it up for discussion? Have others brought it up for discussion?
5. Would you disapprove or be disappointed if someone did not do X? Would most students?
6. Would you express your disapproval if someone did not do X? Would most students?
7. Would you report a student who did not do X? Would most students?

strong social bond that unites individual members to the group as a whole. Because of this social bond, individuals see themselves as responsible for each other.

The third dilemma asks whether anyone should or would steal money from a purse lying open and unattended in a classroom. Obviously most students would agree that the protagonist should not steal the money for reasons of justice, i.e., because stealing it is a violation of the property rights of the victim. Even though a prescriptive judgment that one should not steal is generally made, it is possible that a practical or "would" judgment to steal could also be made.

The fourth dilemma, about the use of marijuana, asks about a norm of order or a conventional norm according to Turiel's (1983) classification. In this dilemma the prescription of not smoking arises from a particular school rule rather than from inherent moral justice considerations of the violation of rights of other individuals or from a consideration of the harmful effects of marijuana to the smoker. As we noted in chapter 4, one of the goals in the just community schools was to change the content of this norm of order to a norm of community.

The stealing and marijuana dilemmas are followed by questions about students' responsibility to intervene when they see others violating the rules. These enforcement questions present students with a new dilemma: whether or not to report a violation of the rules. We predicted that student "whistle-blowing" would most likely be perceived as either heroic or disloyal, depending upon the moral culture of the school. Since helping and collective restitution are often regarded as supererogatory and do not involves rules, it was inappropriate to raise the issue of reporting after those dilemmas.

Samples and Subjects

The total sample of students given the moral culture dilemmas was 112. The students from the democratic programs were selected to represent the population from which they were drawn in terms of their sex, race, grade, and group role. The interviews were administered after four years of consultation in Cluster and S.W.S. and two years in the A School, when these programs were considered to have attained maturity. The students from the parent high schools were selected to match the democratic school samples.

The Moral Culture Variables

The moral culture variables used in the assessment of the school dilemmas interview are basically the same as those used in the assessment of community meetings and ethnographic interviews. Three variables relate specifically to the characteristics of the norm: degree of collectiveness (table 4.3), phase (table 4.4), and stage. Two additional variables relate to elements: the level of institutional valuing (table 4.1) and the stage of community (table 4.2). We have described these variables at some length in chapter 4, with the exception of the degree of collectiveness of norms. In our original moral culture analysis of Cluster School we identified only two degrees, individual and collective. As we interviewed students in other schools, we discovered that we needed a more sensitive measure. We expanded our dichotomous classification to take into account authority and aggregate norms, which we found were prevalent in the non-democratic parent high schools.

An authority norm is at a higher degree of collectivity than an individual norm because the constituency obligated by the norm is clearly the group and not the individual. It is at a lower degree than either an aggregate or a collective norm because the subject obligating the group is limited to the adult authority. Although students may happen to agree with an authority's normative stance, they perceive an authority norm as deriving from the will of the authority and not the group itself. Authority norms should be distinguished from genuine collective norms. Adult authorities may originate collective norms, but the students so assimilate these norms that they view adult authorities as mediators of the group's own norms.

Aggregate norms are at a higher degree of collectiveness than authority norms because the subject obligating the group is more inclusive; it is the student peer group itself. Nevertheless, because aggregate norms exclude school authorities and run counter to their norms and expectations, they are at a lower degree of collectiveness than collective norms. For example, students report peer pressure to smoke marijuana and drink, to ignore those outside their clique, and not to rat or even criticize fellow students. This peer pressure splits adults and students in a school and even divides students among themselves. A further limitation of these aggregate norms is that the peer pressure which constitutes a quasi-normative expectation does not have the obligatory force we associate with moral norms. Moral norms make an explicit rational appeal to a sense of moral rightness. In a democracy such norms are built through discussion and agreement. Aggregate norms, on the other hand, arise implicitly out of a concern to "fit in" with one's peers by adjusting one's behavioral pattern to fall into an "average" group pattern.

Table 4.3 shows four major types of norms: individual, authority, aggregate, and collective. Each of these includes a few subtypes, which brings the total number of degrees to fifteen. The subtypes reflect minor variations in the way in which subjects speak about the norms. For example, in articulating an aggregate norm a student may or may not be in accord with the wishes of the authority. The most differentiated listing is one for the collective norms. Theoretically the most important distinction among the subtypes is between degree 11, a spontaneous collective norm, and degrees 12 through 15, collective norms in a prescriptive

Table 8.2.

Hypothesized Modal Moral Cultures

	Program	
Variable	*Democratic*	*Traditional*
1. Degree of collectiveness	1. Spontaneous or normative (11–15)	1. Individual, authoritarian, or aggregate counternorm (1–9)
2. Phase	2. Expectation, persuading, or reporting (4–7)	2. No collective norm or ideal (1–2)
3. Stage of collective norm	3. Congruent with or higher than aggregate moral judgment stage (3–3/4)	3. Lower than aggregate individual moral judgment stages (2–2/3)
4. Level of institutional valuing	4. Intrinsic community valuing (3, 4)	4. Extrinsic institutional valuing (1, 2)
5. Stage of community valuing	5. Congruent with or higher than aggregate moral judgment stage (3–3/4)	5. Lower than aggregate moral judgment stage (2–2/3)

mode. We found examples of spontaneous collective norms in the S.W.S. and A School samples. We classify a norm as spontaneous when students hesitate to describe what is expected as obligatory but instead report that most students are naturally motivated to uphold it. Thus they will say students do not *have* to act in accord with the norm but most likely would *want* to act in that way.

Research Questions

The major hypothesis in the study was that the democratic schools would have more positive moral cultures than the traditional high schools. This hypothesis was given greater specification in terms of expected mode ranges of each variable in table 8.2. We derived these expected ranges from the developmental assessment of Cluster School's culture in chapter 5. The ranges for the traditional, parent high schools were derived from the early fall of the first year of Cluster, when the rules of the parent high school were still in effect and there was little sense of community. The ranges for the democratic schools were derived from the third and fourth years of Cluster, when collective norms and a sense of community were developed.

We thought that the individual's moral judgment stage, as measured by the standard moral judgment interview, would be correlated with the individual's perception of the stage of the collective norms and possibly also with their perception of the degree of collectiveness and phase of the norms. It is clear why we would predict a correlation between moral judgment and perception of the stage of collective norms, since both tap a similar cognitive developmental construct. It is not obvious why a correlation between moral stage and degree of collectiveness and phase might be predicted. However, note that the higher degrees of collectiveness entail taking a shared "we perspective" which develops at the third stage of moral development. The phases are more problematic, since they are not connected through a mediating cognitive variable, such as role taking, but are more directly related to attitudes and actions. The relationship between moral reasoning and moral action is a complex one (Blasi 1980; Kohlberg and Candee 1984). Nevertheless, there does appear to be a monotonic relationship between the performance of certain kinds of prosocial behavior and moral judgment stage: the higher their stage the more likely it is that subjects will act prosocially. Because of the possibility of explaining group differences through aggregate moral judgment scores, we included them as covariates in our analysis.

A secondary hypothesis was that the democratic schools would differ slightly among themselves according to differences in student population, history, and approach to democratic community. Specifically, we expected to find S.W.S.'s norms at a modal degree of collectiveness 11, a spontaneous collective, and the Cluster and A Schools' norms at a higher modal degree. Correspondingly, we thought that the modal level institutional valuing would be 3, intrinsic-spontaneous, in S.W.S. as opposed to 4, intrinsic-normative, in the other democratic schools. We also expected the A School's drug norm and Cluster's restitution norm to be at a higher degree of collectiveness, phase, and stage than any of the other democratic schools for reasons that can be found in our historical accounts of the schools in the preceeding chapters.

We did not expect that the traditional schools would differ greatly from each other except in terms of the stage variables, which could be explained by site differences (whether the programs were situated in Cambridge, Brookline, or Scarsdale). The student populations of Brookline and Scarsdale are predominantly at the higher end of the socioeconomic status (SES) scale, while the population of Cambridge includes many more at the lower end of the SES scale. A moderate correlation between the moral maturity score (MMS) and SES is common (Colby et al. 1983).

Finally, we explored the possibility that students' perceptions of moral culture may be related to their gender. The hypothesis of gender differences has been raised quite forcefully by Gilligan (1977, 1982) and others (Lyons 1982; Baumrind 1986). They speculate that females deal more competently with issues of care and responsibility, and males, with issues of rules and social order. Since our dilemmas tap both kinds of issues, it was conceivable that gender differences could be manifested.

Program Differences

Given its robust nature and the interpretability of means of ordinal data, an analysis of variance was conducted for each of the six moral culture variables. The factorial design for each variable was two programs (democratic versus traditional) by three sites by two sexes. A preliminary analysis was done on average variable scores, computed by summing each variable score across the dilemmas and dividing by four, the number of dilemmas administered. The results of this analysis indicated that the democratic schools were significantly higher than their parent high schools on all culture variables (see table 8.3). The modal values for all the variables also fit our qualitative expectations for the democratic and traditional high schools, as outlined in table 8.2.

We analyzed the aggregate standard moral judgment scores and found that aggregate scores for the students in the democratic programs were slightly but significantly (statistically) higher than for the students in the traditional programs. We also found significant correlations between standard moral judgment scores and scores on the perceived cultural variables, particularly those tapping the stage of the norm and the community value. In order to determine whether the cultural variables could be reducible to aggregate differences, we conducted a second analysis of variance with the moral maturity score (M.M.S.) entered as a

Table 8.3.
Differences Between Programs on Moral Culture Variables Across
Dilemmas

Variables	Democratic Programs	Traditional Programs	
Degree of collectiveness of the norms	9.9[a] (12)[b]	3.0 (3)	$F = 230.4$ $P < .001$ $N = 112$
Phase of the norms	3.9 (5)	0.3 (0)	$F = 188.6$ $P < .001$ $N = 112$
Stage of the norms	321 A.C.S.[c] (3)	259 A.C.S.[c] (2/3)	$F = 65.4$ $P < .001$ $N = 112$
Level of institutional valuing	3.1 (3)	1.3 (1)	$F = 96.8$ $P < .001$ $N = 82$
Stage of community valuing	3/4 333 A.C.S.[c] (3/4)	3 265 A.C.S.[c] (2/3)	$F = 28.2$ $P < .001$ $N = 82$
Number Ss	59	53	

[a] Mean Score
[b] Modal Score
[c] A.C.S. = Average Collective Stage Score, calculated by averaging scores on each dilemma and multiplying by 100.

covariate.[2] This analysis also yielded significant F values as a result of program differences for all variables, which we report in table 8.3.

This finding of significant differences with an analysis of covariance is important not only in substantiating a program effect but also in validating the construct of a collective stage. In chapter 4 we attempted to clarify in a conceptual way the distinction between an individual cognitive stage and a collective stage. The data indicate that although an individual's stage does influence his or her perception of the stage of the culture, the stage of the culture itself has some integrity above and

2. The moral maturity score (M.M.S.) is a weighted average score, calculated by combining scores across the three dilemmas and multiplying the weighted average by one hundred.

Table 8.4.
The Moral Cultures of the Six Schools

	Cluster	Cambridge High	A School	Scarsdale High	S.W.S.	Brookline High
Standard moral judgment score	298[a] (3)[b]	282 (3)	344 (3/4)	333 (3/4)	363 (3/4)	321 (3/4)
Degree of collectiveness	8.5 (13)	3.3 (3,5)	10.7 (11)	3.7 (3,5)	10.5 (11)	3.7 (3,5)
Phase	8.5 (4)	3.3 (0)	10.7 (6)	1.4 (0)	10.5 (5)	2.0 (0)
Stage of norm	309 (3)	239 (2/3)	337 (3/4)	290 (3)	342 (3/4)	272 (2/3)
Level of institutional valuing	2.9 (4)	1.4 (2)	3.2 (3)	1.5 (1)	3.4 (3)	1.3 (1)
Stage of community valuing	316 (3)	260 (2/3)	333 (3)	288 (3)	350 (3/4)	252 (2/3)

[a] Mean Score
[b] Modal score. Two numbers separated by a comma indicates a bimodal distribution.

beyond the individual's perception of it. The relationship between individual moral stage and the stage of collective norm can be seen in table 8.4, which presents group means for all six schools in both stage variables. Note that the mean stage of the collective norms (summed across the dilemmas) is almost the same as the mean standard moral judgment score in the democratic schools, while in the parent comparison schools there is a marked drop in the stage of the collective norm relative to the mean standard moral judgment score.

Site Differences

One significant difference was due to the main effect of site. The average stage of the collective norms in the Cambridge schools was significantly lower (265) than in the schools at the other sites (Brookline —293, Scarsdale—318). The finding of a lower stage of the norms at the Cambridge schools was not surprising because the students in the Cambridge schools had lower average moral judgment scores than the students at the other sites.

Differences Among the Democratic Programs

Whether or not the program was democratic made a significant difference on all cultural variables, whether we looked at scores summed across all four dilemmas or at scores on each particular dilemma. Although we did not expect great variations among the democratic programs we did expect to see some between S.W.S. (reflecting Mosher's approach) and Cluster and the A School (reflecting Kohlberg's). The mean scores did not confirm this expectation, as S.W.S. and the A School had an almost identical mean degree of collectivity, phase, and stage scores, and Cluster had lower mean scores on all those variables (see table 8.4). However, the modal stages scores, reported in table 8.4, were closer to our expectation. S.W.S. had a modal degree of collectiveness at 11, indicating that although students identified genuinely collective norms, they noted that the motivation to uphold the norm should follow spontaneously from a positive sense of belonging to the group and not from a sense of obligation. Curiously, the A School students expressed their norms at the same modal level, while the mode of the Cluster students was at 13, indicating that a stronger sense of normative obligation existed at Cluster. The same pattern appears on the modal level of community valuing. S.W.S. and the A School have a modal level of 3, indicating a sense of collective based on shared feelings of positive regard, while Cluster at level 4 manifested a more normative orientation to community and collective responsibility.

Looking at school differences on particular dilemmas, we do find statistically significant differences on the drugs and collective restitution dilemmas, as we had predicted. On the drugs dilemma the A School had a significantly higher degree of collectiveness than either Cluster or S.W.S. ($x^2 = 41$, $p < .001$). In the collective restitution dilemma Cluster had a significantly higher degree of collectiveness than the others ($x^2 = 23.4$, $p < .01$). These findings fit our hypotheses. Although the schools differed on all variables, as we had hypothesized, we only found significance on the above.

Gender Differences

No significant main effects for gender were found in any of the variables. This means that both male and female students had similar perceptions of their cultures when the dilemmas were analyzed together.

The same result was found when we examined the dilemmas separately. Although we found no support for the gender difference hypothesis on these variables, it may be argued that such differences are not likely to appear on a task focusing on a perception of an external social phenomenon, a culture. A more meaningful test of gender differences would be on a task focusing on the individual's own reasoning and sense of responsibility. We will examine the data relevant to this task in the next chapter.

CASE STUDIES: DORIS AND JOE

In order to illustrate how we assessed material from the school dilemmas interview and in order to flesh out differences between the democratic and traditional, parent high schools, we present the case studies of Doris, a junior in Scarsdale High School, and Joe, a junior in the A School. Both students were scored at stage 3–4 on the standard moral judgment interview, and both are fairly representative of modal responses in their respective schools.

Doris, a Scarsdale High School Student

On the helping dilemma, Doris thinks Billy should drive Harry to college:

DORIS: I think he should volunteer, personally, because it's pretty important, and I think someone should do that for Harry just to help him. I feel you should help out someone; even if you don't like them, you should help them. If I were in the situation and had a car, I'd probably drive him if he was really in a bind. He's got no other way of getting there, and it's the right thing to do.

QUESTION: What do you mean by it's the right thing to do?

DORIS: Well, if I were in that situation I'd want a ride. Especially in Scarsdale, it's really an intellectual school and college interviews are really important here.

Doris' response to this part of the interview was scored as stage 3. It is based on an idea of fairness as the Golden Rule: "If I were in that situation I'd want a ride." While this is Doris' personal solution (degree of collectiveness 4), she does not think that there is a genuinely collective norm (degree 11 or higher) at the Scarsdale High School supporting this choice:

QUESTION: What do you think most people in the school would do?

DORIS: I don't think they'd drive them. I think they'd think more of themselves. They have been taught and have grown up thinking only about themselves. They have learned that. I think if it's a friend they could do it; do a favor for a friend. If it's someone they don't like, I don't think they'd do it. They'd think, why should I do this guy a favor, he didn't do anything for me.

In talking about other students in the school, then, Doris does not see any collective norm of helping classmates in general but instead sees a norm of helping only your friends, which is stage 2–3, since it is based on liking and concrete reciprocity. On the degree of collectiveness scale, this student norm of only helping a friend would typically be scored as degree 4, an individual norm because Doris initially depicts it as reflecting students' selfish upbringing. However, later in the interview she states that there are strong, exclusive cliques in school that uphold this friendship norm: "Scarsdale is very grouped into cliques. If you are outside the clique, they don't care about you." Doris' identification of peer pressure to ignore an "outsider" indicates that the degree of the friendship norm is 8; it is an aggregate counternorm and not an individual norm. Since there is no collective norm of helping classmates who are not friends, the degree of collectivity and phase of this norm are 1 and 0 respectively. We would rate the phase of the aggregate norm of only helping friends or members of one's clique at a higher phase, phase 4. Doris' peers clearly expect each other to respect the boundaries of their cliques.

We will briefly summarize Doris' responses to the stealing and restitution dilemmas, since stealing was not regarded as a significant problem in the high school. Doris is personally opposed to stealing, and she thinks that about three-fourths of her classmates are too. Nevertheless, she does not feel that she can trust her classmates with her possessions or even that she could get some kind of an agreement on trust. Doris is opposed to collective restitution and believes her classmates would be as well: "I don't think other people should have to pay for a crime one person did. They're not stealing it as one person. I don't think they should have to pay it back as one person."

Of particular interest in the Scarsdale situation are student orientations to the drug dilemma. In terms of both the "should" and "would" questions, Doris responds by using stage 3–4 reasoning based upon respecting agreements:

QUESTION: Should Bob refuse to smoke?

DORIS: "Yeah, I think he should, because if they made an agreement I think they should stick by it. For the high school . . . I think if there was that agreement, I think they should stick by it. I don't think he should smoke dope, I think he should just not be involved; but if they want to take the consequences . . . I would just say, no, I feel I should stick by the agreement.

Doris then relates that the norm of not smoking on trips is to some extent shared among students, at least insofar as they fear or appreciate their teachers:

QUESTION: Are there expectations for not smoking on your high school trips?

DORIS: To each other and to the teachers, I think there is. I know people who would, but I wish they wouldn't because they are going, if they get caught, they are going to take away privileges for the rest of us. And I think if you're making an agreement with teachers, they are being nice enough to take you up there. I think you should be able to handle it, sticking by the agreement.

We would score this norm as a degree 6 authority norm on our scale of collectiveness, since the sense of obligation to uphold the norm derives predominantly from the will of the teacher and not from the group itself. Note also that this concern for upholding the expectations of the teachers is between a stage 2–3 fear of jeopardizing the welfare of the group (if the teachers find out about violations) and a stage 3 sense of reciprocity in gratitude to the teachers, who were nice enough to take the group on the trip in the first place. The phase of this norm is 2; it is an ideal for behavior, not an expectation. Doris admits a lot of people would think it was "ridiculous" not to smoke and would do it anyhow. She also admits that attempts by students to enforce this norm would be futile and that if she were in this situation she would just "walk away" and "not be mean."

In response to questions about whether she valued Scarsdale High School (S.H.S.) as a community, Doris laments the lack of friendliness and a sense of a common social bond. Her only positive comments about SHS have to do with it being an "intellectual school" that offers an excellent preparation for college. We would score these remarks as indicating a level 2 instrumental extrinsic valuing of the school.

Joe, an A School Student

On the helping dilemma, Joe responds at a stage 4 level that helping is necessary for effective institutional functioning:

QUESTION: Should Billy volunteer to drive Harry to the college?
JOE: Definitely, sure, I think he should.
QUESTION: In your school also, you think you should and would help?
JOE: It's inherently good to help somebody. I think it's just that helping people is a positive thing if you can help somebody, and you should help somebody. There should be a law to help people, I would just go along with that. It's an unwritten code that you do help people here. I mean people are here to work together, and it's good because that's one of the reasons they came here, to work together. People do favors for you. Obviously, that's a good thing. I don't think there should be a written code that a person be mandated to do something; however, I think it is important that there are caring people who would be willing to help. I think it's an important thing to happen. Also, I think it's important to have because it helps run the school. The school functions well if people want to help each other.

In response to the issue of Harry's unpopularity:

JOE: Harry might be putting on a facade in front of his friends and the people in the school. And if Billy gets to know him by driving him, a friendship could be formed. I have a couple of very close friends who are not very popular but they are very caring human beings, and it's possible that he could be misunderstood by his peers.

Joe thinks that students in the A School would help out someone like Billy because he perceives the group to have a strong collective norm of helping.

QUESTION: What do you think about it in the A School?
JOE: I think there would be a good percentage of people that would help out, if they were in his situation.

QUESTION: Do you think your school should have an agreement or understanding that people should help out in this kind of situation?

JOE: I guess it's an unwritten law. It's . . . there is an agreement of, when people come here they all come here to work together. I guess that's just, that's coming out of working together and helping people. Especially if you're not going to be put out of your way that much.

QUESTION: So you're saying there already is like an unwritten law here about this?

JOE: No question about it. People try to help you out many times. There are many students that came up to me at the beginning of the year. I was very, not that I was shy, but I didn't know a lot of people here. There are people that came up to me and just started talking, and if I needed help or things like that they were willing to offer.

In describing the norm of helping, Joe speaks as a member of a community that has an "unwritten law" (a recognition of the prescriptive force of the norm) that people help each other. We code the degree of collectiveness of the helping norm as 13. The stage of the collective norm is 4 because it involves the recognition of a mutually shared agreement in which helping other individuals is seen in the service of creating a community of people cooperating or working together.

The above responses also tell us that Joe values the A School intrinsically (institutional valuing level 4) as a community of people whose purposes include building and enhancing the group. Because he values the school intrinsically and believes others do as well, he feels that community members have and recognize the special obligation of helping each other. His stage of reasoning about community is also stage 4.

Joe's perception of his own commitment to the collective norm of helping is phase 6. Asked whether he would be disappointed if someone could have helped but did not, he responded:

JOE: Definitely, I would be disappointed in that person.

QUESTION: Would you express that disappointment in any way?

JOE: Most probably, yes. However, this is a hypothetical situation. If it happened to be a person that I didn't get along with totally, first of all I might think that that was part of his character, and second of all, if I found it difficult to talk to him before, I probably wouldn't. However, if it was someone that I felt I could go and talk to without any problem, like most of the people in this school, then I would definitely go and voice my opinion. I'd say, yeah, that wasn't really very nice of you. You're being very selfish.

Joe's perception of most other students' commitment to upholding the norm is equally high phase, phase 6:

QUESTION: Would most people here talk to them?

JOE: No question about it. People here are very kind and feeling people who try to help people if they can. And I think they would probably mention it.

Concerning the stealing dilemma, Joe's thinking about upholding property rights is influenced by his perception of a collective norm of trust in the A School:

QUESTION: Would you steal in a situation like this?

JOE: I would not think about taking the money. I would think about closing the pocketbook. I think I should do that. I'm not trusting of groups of people, in general. In this school I would trust leaving some things. If there is a twenty-dollar bill on the table, I think in this community a lot of people would not take it. A lot of people would probably turn it in. I think there would be a minimum amount of people that would take the money, especially twenty dollars from an open pocketbook. A majority would not take it. I think there is more of a trust in our school just because there is that emphasis on morality.

QUESTION: Do you think your school does have an understanding about trust?

JOE: There is an understanding about trust. It's discussed in a lot of our community meetings. There is trust that people will abide by the rules of the community and will not break the laws. There is that trust. . . . There is an unwritten code that you don't take somebody's possessions. You can trust people in the school not to take your possessions. You can't trust everyone in a group of eighty students. There are always exceptions. However, the majority I would trust.

QUESTION: Why do you think that expectation exists in the school, and how can you tell it exists?

JOE: Why it exists. Because we're sort of a community. In some respects we are just an enlarged family, and I would trust everybody in my family. We work as a family, or as a team, or as a community. So I think that's very important. How do you expect people to work together if their trusts are broken by stealing things and things like that?

We scored Joe's perceptions of the norm of trust as degree 13 of collectiveness, a norm that he feels he explicitly shares with most of the other students in the A School. Joe's reasons for the existence and maintenance of the norm of trust are stage 4. They are grounded in notions of what is required for a cooperative community and are similar to his reasons for helping in the caring dilemma.

With regard to maintaining the collective norms of property and trust, Joe perceives that people would report, a phase 7 commitment. He believes the norm should be upheld even though this might require reporting a friend: "I think there is a certain trust in this community, that people would say something."

The idea of collective restitution is a new one for Joe and his peers; neither he nor they perceive it as a collective norm. Joe's ideas are scored level 3 on the degree of collectiveness, the level of no awareness of a collective norm, and no clear opinion pro or con on whether the A School should establish such a norm. The phase is 0 and there is no stage, because although he reasons at stage 3 that chipping in would be kind, he does not perceive restitution as a collective norm.

The A School had the strongest norm against drug use of any of our programs or schools. Joe is a succinct and accurate spokesperson for the group. Initially, when asked about that dilemma, he makes a stage 4 judgment that Bob should not smoke:

QUESTION: Do you think Bob should refuse to smoke?
JOE: No question about it. He should refuse to smoke, and he should try at that time to dissuade them from smoking. It's morally wrong. He gave an oath that he would not smoke pot. And I don't think peer pressure would affect him at all.

He also makes a stage 4 judgment grounded in a concern for community:

QUESTION: Do you think a good member of the school should refuse to smoke?
JOE: Yes, by smoking the pot it would hurt the community. Their trust would be broken, and it might deter the community from making any such important decisions in the future, knowing that they might possibly be broken.

Joe's reasoning is stage 4 because he recognizes that keeping promises and maintaining trust are essential for personal integrity ("He gave an oath") and for the capacity of the community to make decisions ("It might deter the community from making any such important decisions in the future"). Also, Joe's position about drugs reflects a very strong collective norm at degree 13. Joe's peers share his conviction that they are obligated as members of the community not to smoke:

JOE: Most people would refuse to smoke because I think they are all moral people. I think they believe that the community is very important, and it is more important than any kind of peer pressure. It's just a general feeling that people have. It's an obligation to uphold the rest of the community. They believe in it and they believe that breaking the law would be hurting the community, and it's more important to abide by the rules for the community than to smoke pot.

Turning to the phase of the "no smoking" norm, we see that Joe spontaneously says that the obligation to uphold the agreement on drugs includes attempting to persuade the person to stop. If discussion does not work, the norm would obligate him and others to report.

QUESTION: Would you report?
JOE: No question about it. Even if my friends smoke pot . . . I would have no qualms about it.
QUESTION: Do you think most people here would actually report?
JOE: They did. There is a minority that would not though. . . . That's a small minority.

Joe's sense of a majority expectation to report someone smoking is scored as phase 7.
Behind Joe's strong perception and acceptance of a collective norm about smoking pot is his valuing of community:

JOE: The community agreed on a rule, therefore they feel a tremendous responsibility to uphold the law. One of the people who was caught said it was wrong, because "I got caught." When he reflected on the process of the law, he had more of an understanding that what he did hurt the community and that he wouldn't do that again. I think that's very important, that it was inherently wrong to do that. It just wasn't wrong because he got caught. It's more effective if the kids in the community say, "Hey, you really hurt me by smoking pot." I might not think that smoking pot is bad, but we made an agreement and you really hurt me and you really took away a lot from the community.

Here again, Joe is seen as level 4 and stage 4 in his valuing of community. He values the community intrinsically and feels that the community can obligate its members to uphold a conventional norm, like the prohibition of smoking marijuana.

CONCLUSIONS

In this chapter we examined the hypothesis that the democratic high schools would develop different moral cultures from their parent, comparison schools. Data from the school dilemmas interview resoundingly confirmed this hypothesis. On all of our moral culture variables students from the democratic schools rated their schools more highly than did their peers in the comparison schools. Our data leave ambiguous what specific features of the democratic school interventions had the greatest influence on moral culture. The fact that S.W.S.'s moral culture closely resembled the cultures of other alternative schools (at least when assessed globally) was somewhat surprising, since the S.W.S. staff were not committed to a theory of moral community. On the other hand, differences in theory did make a difference on the level of what norms were developed. For example, all the democratic schools developed strong norms of caring and trust. But only in schools guided by the just community approach do we find norms of collective restitution and of reporting violators of the drug rule. These results lead us to conclude that there may be some latitude in democratic approaches to community building, at least with privileged adolescents.

Of course, it is possible that democracy has nothing to do with our results and that program differences may be attributed to school size. Unfortunately, we did not include any small, nondemocratic comparison schools in our sample. The best we can do with the data that is available is appeal to the histories of the A School and S.W.S. before they adopted the approaches developed by Kohlberg and Mosher. In both cases the faculty was discontent with lack of student participation in their schools. Meetings were poorly attended and discipline was left up to the teachers. Chapters 5, 6, and 7 document how positive moral cultures developed *after* the consultation began, and this chapter samples some of the fruits of that development.

If the results of this chapter point to the promise of democratic schooling, they should also call into question the approaches used in the parent schools. Although the parent high schools that we studied are recognized as being among the best in the country in terms of serving the educational needs of their respective student populations, and although they by and large are orderly schools, they fail to generate positive moral cultures. This raises the issue, addressed in chapter 4, of the value of establishing moral community in the schools. From one perspective moral community is a means to an end: it is a way of influencing individuals to moral judgment and moral behavior. From another perspective moral community is an end in itself. The experience of being part of a group of people who take trust, care, and participation seriously is a moral good in and of itself. While we will go on in the next chapter to describe some of the effects of moral community on sociomoral judgment and action, we certainly would not wish to convey the impression that the worth of these democratic schools depends entirely upon indices of individual development.

9

Individual Moral Development as an Outcome of Democratic Schooling

with Marvin Berkowitz

In the present chapter we shall report the findings on yearly individual socio-moral development in three democratic alternative schools and in comparison groups of students in the regular high schools with which the alternative schools were associated. Our basic expectation, derived from the theories of Dewey (1916/1966) and Piaget (1932/1965), was that participation in the governance of a small school community would stimulate the growth of moral reasoning more than would participation in the more traditionally governed high schools. We also wished to examine whether the explicit commitment of a teaching staff to a theory of moral community would lead to a process more effective in stimulating change in moral reasoning than would staff commitment to a school democracy relatively independent of guidance by a theory of moral community. In addition to assessing moral judgment development we examined several other related variables: moral type change, political value development, and practical and responsibility reasoning.

DESIGN

Moral Judgment Development

The original design of our research project called for year-by-year assessment of moral judgment change in three alternative schools, the Cluster School in Cambridge, School-Within-a-School in Brookline, and Murray Road School in Newton, and in the traditional high schools associated with them. We thought that variations in moral judgment changes in these settings might be due to two types of factors. One set of factors would differentiate almost any traditional high school. This set of factors arises from the more informal, friendly, and communitarian relations among students and teachers, and the emphasis on democratic sharing in decisions of rules and school policies. A second set of factors might be expected to differentiate one alternative school from another in their effect on the growth of moral reasoning. These factors include the faculty explicitly focusing discussion on issues of morality and justice during democratic meetings and the faculty cultivating a spirit of moral community. This twin focus on issues of justice and cultivation of moral community defines the just community theory, which through Kohlberg's consultation informed the practices of the Cluster School in Cambridge and the A School in Scarsdale. The Murray Road School was originally selected as an example of a typical alternative school that was not guided by the just community approach. It was a laissez-faire, free school, much like S.W.S. before Mosher's consultation and the A School before Kohlberg's. Murray Road had weekly democratic community meetings voluntarily attended by students and a commitment to informed or spontaneous community. S.W.S. seemed to represent a program between Cluster's just community approach and Murray Road's free school ideology. As we noted in chapter 7, Mosher and the S.W.S. faculty focused less specifically on justice and normative community and more on ego development and democratic decision-making skills.

In the first year of this research project the Murray Road School decided to discontinue its existence as a separate alternative school. Therefore, it was not possible to collect change data in an alternative school which had no orientation to moral development or just community theory. Any inference about the influence of an emphasis on justice and moral community would then have had to rest on possible differences on moral judgment change between the Cluster School and S.W.S. Such a comparison would have been very clouded because of the great differences in populations of students in the two schools. The students in S.W.S. came primarily from upper middle class and professional homes and were intellectually and academically advanced compared with students in the Cluster School. The majority of students in Cluster School came from working-class backgrounds: more than 50 percent of them fit into the two lowest status groups on the Hollingshead scale; 44 percent of the students were black. A large proportion of Cluster students had difficulties in intellectual and academic achievement.

Because of the difficulties in separating program orientation (moral community versus democratic problem solving) from differences in student characteristics, we welcomed the opportunity to collaborate in 1979 with the study of the A School in Scarsdale, New York. The A School provided a student population comparable to that of S.W.S. The students came primarily from white, upper- and upper-middle-class families and were academically advanced. In participating in the Scarsdale Alternative School study, we were able to collect data from another alternative school that did not orient to the just community theory, the Mamaroneck Alternative School in Mamaroneck, New York. The students in this school were white and of mixed backgrounds, upper middle, middle, and some working class.

In summary, then, our data base comprises moral judgment change on two schools oriented to the just community theory, Cluster School and the A School. It includes one alternative school with no theoretical or systematic focus on democratic governance, the Mamaroneck Alternative School, and it includes one alternative school evolving its own theory of democratic governance somewhat distinct from the theory of just community, S.W.S. In addition, moral judgment change data were gathered in each of the regular high schools to which the alternative schools were attached; these include Cambridge Rindge and Latin High School, Brookline High School, Scarsdale High School, and Mamaroneck High School.

The Cognitive Prerequisites for Moral Development

While we expected to find moral stage development in the democratic alternative schools, particularly the just community schools, we had reason to believe there were cognitive prerequisites for moral development that might have an impact on our results. Colby et al. (1977), Kuhn et al. (1977), and Walker and Richards (1979) report some evidence indicating that the attainment of basic formal operations, as measured by Piagetian logical tasks, is a necessary but not sufficient condition for the attainment of stage 4 moral reasoning. The implication of their data for our study is obvious: if students have not reached the stage of basic formal operations, this will have a ceiling effect on the extent to which an intervention can stimulate moral development. We were particularly concerned that such a ceiling effect might apply to Cluster School, since so many students there exhibited learning difficulties.

Moral Type Change

We also assessed the moral judgment data for changes in moral type. The concept of moral types has its origins in Kohlberg's speculation that each moral stage had an "A" and "B" substage. He believed that the B substage was more philosophically advanced than the A, specifically that the B substage was a more autonomous resolution of moral conflicts than the A. The notion of "substage" was abandoned when no evidence was found for a developmental sequence of within-stage changes. In its place, two ideal types, A and B, were derived after extensive content analysis described by Tappan et al. (1987). Type B is characterized by its prescriptivity, autonomy, and concern for universality. Type A is differentiated from type B by its susceptibility to claims, such as authority, that are not based on justice.

Schrader (1984) undertook the analysis of moral types for our study in order to investigate the hypothesis that the three democratic alternative schools, especially the two following the just community approach, would promote more change from type A to B than the regular high schools. This hypothesis is based on the understanding that alternative high schools and particularly the just community schools emphasize conditions that ostensibly support type B reasoning: equality, open dialogue, discussion of moral issues, and democratic decision making.

Practical Political Values Development

In addition to the moral judgment interview, our design also called for the administration of the ethnographic moral atmosphere interview to a subsample of Cluster students each year of the study. As we said in chapter 4, when we introduced this interview, its primary purpose was to obtain information about the moral culture of the school. A secondary purpose was to investigate the hypothesis that the school's moral atmosphere had an influence on the development of students' reasoning about political values. We use the term "political" in its classic sense to refer to a moral concern for the good of a city or more generally of an association of free citizens. The specific political values that we assessed correspond to the four content types of norms, distinguished in introducing our method of moral culture analysis in chapter 4: community, democracy (procedural justice), fairness (substantive justice), and order. The values of fairness and order appear to develop similarly regardless of cultural content. In contrast, the values of community and democracy appear to be more susceptable to particular cultural and ideological influences.

Following Vygotsky (1934/1962), we speculated that although the values of community and democracy presuppose cultural transmission, they are not simply internalized but are assimilated by students who reconstruct them through a sequence of stages. In order to test this, we constructed stages of community and democracy to parallel Kohlberg's stages of moral judgment (see tables 9.1 and 9.2). We predicted that, because of the students' unfamiliarity with the political institutions of democracy and community when they first entered Cluster, they would reason about community and democracy at a lower stage than their stage of moral reasoning competence, as measured by the standard moral judgment interview. After a year in Cluster's democratic community, we expected that they would develop their reasoning about the values of community and democracy such that it would approach their moral reasoning competence. In keeping with Vygotsky's theory that ideological concepts are reconstructed in stages, we maintained that such development would be sequential.

We believed that students' reasoning about the universal political values of fairness and order would manifest a similar pattern, although for not quite the same reasons. Research by Leming (1969) and Scharf (1973) indicated that individuals generally perform below their competence in dealing with contextualized moral problems related to their daily lives. The ethnographic interview asks students to relate their understanding of political values to concrete issues occurring in school.

Table 9.1.
Stages of the Community Value

Stage 2:	The ideal of community entails doing the same things together and enjoying common activities. Members are expected to "go along with the group" when everyone's "good time" can be enhanced. Belonging to a community is seen primarily as benefiting individuals in a concrete way. People in the community are supposed "to get along" in the sense that they avoid negative behaviors (such as insulting each other and fighting) and help each other through exchanges of favors.
Stage 3:	The ideal of community entails sharing goals, values, expectations. There is a shared ideal of the group as a good group—a caring, trusting group apart from concrete shared objectives. There is an emphasis on the unity which comes from all members having a common goal and accepting an equal share of the work. There is a feeling that members should be united by strong ties of affection—that the school should be like "a big family." Members should *care* about the school and not just "selfishly" care about themselves. Relationships of members to each other and to the school are values in themselves. Caring of the school involves some concern for improving the school.
Stage 4:	The ideal of community entails an interdependence between individuals and the group as a whole. Individuals contribute to the group through their roles as group members and through their particular talents, experience, personalities. Community is enhanced through diversity if there is a common agreement to live according to a basic commitment to the group. Responsibility to the group comes through having chosen to become and to remain a group member. The unity of community is capable of embracing subgroups which can maintain a certain identity and still be a part of the group.

Given this practical dimension of the interview, we expected an initial competence/performance gap that would close after a year in Cluster. Although we could theoretically differentiate between values relating to a particular political ideology and universal values, we found that in practice we were unable to reliably assess differences between them. Therefore we combined scores on all values to yield an overall political values stage, comparable to a global moral judgment stage.

We advanced two hypotheses about the relationship of the political values stages to the moral stages. The first we have already explained: students reasoning about political values should be lower than their

Table 9.2.

Stages of the Value of Democracy

Stage 2:	The democratic ideal is one in which individuals all have a concrete right to speak as they wish. The major feature of a democracy is that individuals have the opportunity to speak their mind (have "their say") or work to get what they want.
Stage 3:	The democratic ideal entails listening to, taking the perspective of, and having respect for others. Individuals are encouraged to think about what is best for everyone or for other individuals. The "majority will" becomes an authority which expresses what is right and must be respected.
Stage 4:	The democratic ideal entails not only a respectful listening to others but a careful consideration of what they mean and how it will benefit the group. Decisions should be made by considering the "general will," how the group as a whole will benefit.

moral stages at their first time of testing (shortly after being admitted to Cluster) and should be more consistent with their moral stages at the second time of testing (one year later). This is perhaps best thought of as an hypothesis that the moral atmosphere of the school can have a positive influence on politico-moral reasoning performance. The second hypothesis goes further in positing that the moral atmosphere of the school can have a positive influence on moral reasoning competence. One way of testing this hypothesis, using political values data, is to see whether political values development may actually precede and predict moral development. We call this our "leading edge hypothesis," since it implies that the students may first develop their moral reasoning competence in dealing with school-related problems and later, as a function of what Piaget (1967) calls decalage, extend this competence more generally to the content areas sampled in Kohlberg's standard, decontextualized dilemmas. This constitutes an expectation for a reversal of the typical finding that performance-related factors tend to lower moral reasoning. However, note that our expectation for relatively high moral reasoning is in the context of an educational intervention that attempts to stimulate development by providing an "ideal environment."

Practical Judgment and Social Responsibility

In discussing the judgment/action problem throughout this book, we have distinguished between two kinds of interviews: the standard moral dilemmas and the practical school dilemmas. The standard dilemmas attempt to assess moral reasoning competence by presenting hypothetical situations in a remote context (e.g., the Heinz dilemma). On the other hand, the practical school dilemmas are designed to evaluate moral reasoning performance by presenting real-life situations in a familiar context.

In analyzing data from the practical school dilemmas interview, we investigated two hypotheses: that students in democratic high schools would resolve the dilemmas at a higher stage of reasoning than their peers in the comparison schools, and that in so doing the students in the democratic schools would make more responsibility judgments. The first hypothesis is a specification of our more general expectation that democratic schools provide an environment conducive to high-stage moral reasoning in performance-related situations. The second hypothesis makes a new claim that the democratic schools will promote a distinctive orientation to decision making, a social responsibility orientation.

In introducing the concept of a responsibility orientation in chapter 2, we made a distinction between deontic and responsibility judgments. A deontic judgment is a first-order judgment of the moral rightness of a particular action, whereas a responsibility judgment is a second-order judgment of the will to act in accord with what one thinks is right. In addition to expressing consistency between should and would judgments, responsibility judgments may also be thought of as defining an orientation to socio-moral problems. Gilligan (1977, 1982) and Lyons (1983), building on Niebuhr's *The Responsible Self* (1963), suggested that the responsibility orientation is an alternative to a rules and justice orientation. They claim that responsibility judgments emerge directly as responses of a social self in a network of relations with others, not from balancing individual rights through reciprocity and contracts. The view that relationships can have an intrinsically moral quality is somewhat like Durkheim's belief that the sheer existence of a solidarity group creates moral obligations and aspirations.

We accept this notion of responsibility judgments as an orientation to socio-moral decision making, distinguishable from what we will call the deontic orientation. However, unlike Gilligan and Lyons, we maintain that deontic judgments of rightness are embedded within judgments of responsibility, such that judgments of responsibility include (at least implicitly) deontic judgments. The criteria and rules that we used to define and score judgments of responsibility are given in table 9.3. We

Table 9.3.
Criteria for Judgments of Responsibility

---

1. Concern must be shown for meeting the needs of others or enhancing their welfare that goes beyond not harming them and respecting their rights and legitimate claims.
2. Conscious consideration must be given to the involvement of the self in an action or in the welfare consequences that an action has for others.
3. An evaluation of one's personal moral worth (an aretaic judgment) must be at the basis of decision making. There is an anticipation that performing or failing to perform an action will reflect upon and influence character.
4. Justification for performing an action must be based upon the intrinsic valuing of relationships of friendship, family, or community.

NOTE: Responsibility judgments must meet at least one of these criteria.

claim that the experimental schools promote a responsibility orientation because participatory democracy puts decisions in the hands of students, giving them a sense of personal efficacy and accountability, and because the communitarian cultures of these schools provide a strong sense of interpersonal connectedness.

In addition to assessing the school dilemmas data for program effects, we also assessed it for gender differences. Our criteria for coding the responsibility orientation (table 9.3) were influenced by those developed by Lyons (1982), although the two sets of criteria are not identical. Given the similarity, however, one might expect that we would find a higher proportion of females with a responsibility orientation on the school dilemmas than males.

SUBJECTS

Moral Judgment Sample

Table 9.4 shows the number of subjects in each school interviewed on the standard moral judgment interview each year from 1975–76 to 1979–80 and the number of students followed from one year to the next. The democratic school subjects that constitute the one-year change samples were chosen to be and generally were demographically representative subsamples of the total population samples for each school. The

Table 9.4.
Moral Judgment Sample

	Number of Students Interviewed						Number of Students Followed Longitudinally			
	Total	1975–76	1976–77	1977–78	1978–79	1979–80	Total	One year	Two years	Three years
Cluster School	123	64	74	61	31	0	102	72	20	10
Cambridge Rindge and Latin High School	46	0	0	0	41	25	20	20	0	0
School-Within-A-School	101	0	25	48	42	11	61	58	2	1
Brookline High School	57	0	16	17	40	20	34	34	0	0
Scarsdale Alternative School	41	0	0	0	0	41	41	41*	0	0
Scarsdale High School	47	0	0	0	0	47	47	47*	0	0
Mamaroneck Alternative School	9	0	0	0	0	9	9	9*	0	0
Mamaroneck High School	13	0	0	0	0	13	13	13*	0	0

* One semester follow-up only.

comparison school samples were selected to match them according to grade, sex, and social class.

The Piagetian Tasks Sample. The Piagetian tasks were administered to a subsample of thirty-eight Cluster School volunteers in the fall of 1978.

Moral Types Sample. The moral types analysis was conducted with a subsample of students, who were interviewed twice or more on the standard moral judgment interview in Cluster, C.R.L.S., S.W.S., Brookline, the A School, and S.H.S. For those subjects tested more than twice, only their first two interviews were assessed.

Ethnographic Moral Atmosphere Interview Sample. Approximately twenty students from Cluster were interviewed annually on the ethnographic moral atmosphere interview. Selection of students was done on two bases: that they be representative of the total population, and that they be reinterviewed if they had been interviewed the previous year. The major criteria used to determine whether a student was representative were grade, sex, race, and group role. Generally the moral atmosphere sample did resemble the total population on the above variables. Although no attempt was made to select students on the basis of global stage score, the distribution of stages in the sample generally resembled the population. Of the 53 different students interviewed, 21 were reinterviewed at least once and 4 twice or more.

The Responsibility Judgment Sample. The practical school dilemmas interview was administered to 112 students from the three democratic schools and their parent comparison schools between 1978 and 1979. The democratic school samples were chosen to represent the populations of these schools according to grade, sex, social class, and group role, as we noted in the previous chapter. The comparison groups were chosen from the parent high schools to match the alternative school samples.

MEASURES AND SCORING

Moral Judgment Assessment. Two forms (A and B) of the standard moral judgment interview (Colby and Kohlberg 1987) were used to assess individual moral judgment. Students received alternate forms each year they were in the study. In the Boston area schools, each student was interviewed individually. The interview lasted about one hour and the interviewer wrote verbatim responses as the student talked. In the Westchester (Scarsdale and Mamaroneck) schools the interviews were given in a group setting using a written format. Each student wrote her/his own responses during one hour. The interviews were read immediately, and incomplete ones were returned to students with further probe questions written in to which they then responded. Although written interviews are less desirable, this process did produce reliably scorable data.

All protocols were blind scored as to time of testing, school, and subject. Four Harvard-trained scorers with demonstrated inter-rated reliability of between 75 and 85 percent stage agreement within one-half stage assessed all the Boston data. Two of these scorers also rated the Westchester data. Scoring moral judgment protocols according to the Standard Manual (Colby, Kohlberg et al. 1987) entails the assignment of a stage score to each of the six issues across three dilemmas. The six-issue stage scores are weighted and averaged to get a global stage score for the protocol. Global stage scores either represent a pure stage (e.g., 2, 3, 4) or a mixed stage—2(3), 3(4). Moral maturity scores are calculated from the six-issue stage scores. Even though forms A and B are parallel, form B is somewhat more difficult. For purposes of comparison and calculation of change scores, the moral maturity scores of the two forms have been equated by using the linear transformations provided in Colby and Kohlberg (1987).

The Piagetian Tasks. A battery of four Piagetian tasks was administered: an absurd sentences task; a verbal transitivity task; a chemical combination task; and an isolation of variables task. Tasks 1 and 2 assess *beginning* (level 1) formal operations, task 3 measures *early basic* (level 2) formal operations, and task 4 measures *basic* (level 4) formal operations. Subjects received a pass or fail on each task. All protocols were scored blind by one rater. The tasks were given in small group settings (four to six students) in a written format with a demonstration accompanying the fourth task.

Moral Type Assessment. The moral judgment data were also coded for moral type, according to the coding scheme devised by Tappan et al. (1987). Inter-rater reliability with this manual has been calculated at .71 across forms A and B, using Cohen's Kappa to control for chance agreement. A trained coder with demonstrated reliability blind scored all the moral judgment protocols for moral type (Schrader 1984).

The Ethnographic Moral Atmosphere Interview Assessment. The ethnographic moral atmosphere interview was administered during the spring of each school year for four years. All interviewing was done orally, tape-recorded, and transcribed. The interviewers had been in regular attendance at community meetings during the year.

Material to be scored for each political value is grouped from answers to specific questions about those values as well as from material related to the collective norms expressive of that value.[1] Each value is given a stage score, and a summary political values stage score is calculated by averaging across scores on the four values. All of the ethnographic interviews were coded without knowledge of the students' moral judgment stages. There was 75 percent exact inter-rater agreement on the political value stage and 92 percent agreement within a half stage.

The Practical School Dilemmas Interview. We described the practical school dilemmas interview in some detail in the previous chapter. Although we constructed the interview primarily for the assessment of moral culture, we designed the first few questions to probe for deontic and responsibility judgments. We first asked the subjects what the protagonist should do and why, and then we asked what the subjects thought they should and would do and why. Judgments were scored for moral stage according to stage criteria extrapolated from Colby, Kohlberg et al. (1987). They were then classified as having either a responsibility or a deontic orientation, depending on whether or not they met one of the criteria for responsibility judgment listed in table 9.3.

RESULTS

Moral Stage Change. Table 9.5 reports the data on one-year longitudinal change in the unadjusted mean moral maturity scores for each of the alternative schools and the comparison high schools. Note that table 9.5 is divided into two parts: the Boston study and the Westchester study. Because oral moral judgment interviews were given in the Boston study and written interviews were administered in the Westchester study, separate analyses of the pre- to posttest change scores were conducted for each study. We used an analysis of covariance for each study because it allowed for a post hoc statistical control for differences between the

1. See Power (1979) for a detailed description of the questions and the scoring methodology.

Table 9.5.
One-Year Mean M.M.S. Development by School

	Boston Study			
	Cluster	*C.R.L.S.*	*S.W.S.*	*B.H.S.*
Pre-test M.M.S.	286	282	329	311
Post-test M.M.S.	298	280	332	319
Unadjusted mean change	13*	−2	3	8
N	102	20	61	34

	Westchester Study[a]			
	A School	*S.H.S.*	*M.A.S.*	*M.H.S.*
Pre-test M.M.S.	327	288	301	276
Post-test M.M.S.	341	306	310	291
Unadjusted mean change	14*	18	9	16
N	41	47	9	13

[a] One-semester change data rather than one-year change data between pre- and post-test.
*$p < .05$.

schools' mean pretest M.M.S. scores. Since we found in this and other studies that pretest scores were negatively correlated to change scores, a small mean change score might be significant if the mean pretest score was relatively high. The covariance analysis of the Boston area study indicated only one significant comparison—that between Cluster School and C.R.L.S. ($F = 4.7$, $p < .05$). In the Westchester study the A School was significantly higher than the three comparison schools ($F = 3.8$, $p < .02$).

The results from both studies show that significant mean changes only occurred in schools oriented explicitly to just community theory. Surprisingly, we did not find significant change in S.W.S., in spite of Mosher's influence as a consultant and its relatively developed moral culture. Not so surprisingly, neither did we find significant change in the Mamaroneck Alternative School, a school not at all oriented to the theories of moral development or just community.

The magnitude of change in Cluster and the A School, although significant, is rather small (less than fifteen M.M.S. points). Some moral discussion programs report more change (Higgins 1980). One explanation for the small magnitude of change may have to do with the effects of tenure on moral development. It is possible that the biggest impact of moral education interventions may be during the student's first exposure to them. If this were the case then the small mean change scores we report may be misleading, since change scores from some students' first year of tenure have been averaged with change scores from other students' later years of tenure when development may have tapered off. Looking at Cluster School, where we had two- and three-year longitudinal data, we found that students' first year in the school does appear to be the year in which the greatest moral development occurs. The mean change during that year was twenty-two points (n = 40).

Table 9.6 presents two- and three-year longitudinal moral judgment data on thirty Cluster School cases. Global stage scores are reported using a thirteen-point scale. Note that the change is in the pattern predicted by Kohlberg's theory. There are no skipped stages and few reversals (19 percent of the adjacent time points). The percentage of reversals is less than what Colby and Kohlberg (1987) report in a test-retest study; and it seems reasonable to attribute them to measurement error. Eight of the thirty students listed in table 9.6 entered Cluster with scores primarily or purely stage 2. Only two of these students graduated still using primarily stage 2 thinking (major stage 2 and minor stage 3). Of seven other students who entered with some stage 2 reasoning (major stage 3, minor stage 2), one left still using some stage 2 reasoning. In summary, the Cluster experience appears relatively successful in stimulating development from preconventional (stage 2) to conventional (stages 3 and 4) reasoning. It was somewhat less effective in stimulating development from third- to fourth-stage thinking. Only two of fifteen students who entered at stage 3 or 3–4 developed to a pure stage 4. On the other hand, of the ten who entered at a pure stage 3, five developed to at least stage 3–4, and about one-third (eleven) of the total longitudinal sample showed some development to stage 3(4) or 4 by the end of their tenure in Cluster.

A finding that the just community schools promote moral stage development would not pinpoint what kind of influence the moral atmosphere had on the moral development. In chapter 4 we described moral atmosphere as a very general environmental variable that includes the

Table 9.6.
Cluster Students' Two- and Three-Year Longitudinal Moral Judgment
Stage Development

Subject	Test Year	M.J. Stage	Subject	Test Year	M.J. Stage
01	1	3(2)	16	1	3(2)
	2	3		2	3
	3	3		3	3(4)
	4	3		4	—
02	1	—	17	1	3(4)
	2	3		2	3(4)
	3	3(4)		3	4
	4	3		4	—
03	1	2(3)	18	1	3(4)
	2	3		2	3
	3	3(4)		3	3(2)
	4	3		4	—
04	1	—	19	1	—
	2	3(4)		2	2(1)
	3	3		3	2
	4	4(3)		4	3(4)
05	1	2(3)	20	1	4(3)
	2	3(2)		2	4
	3	3		3	4(3)
	4	2(3)		4	—
06	1	—	21	1	3
	2	2(3)		2	3
	3	3		3	4(3)
	4	2(3)		4	4
07	1	2	22	1	3
	2	3(2)		2	3(4)
	3	3(4)		3	—
	4	—		4	3(4)
08	1	—	23	1	3
	2	3(2)		2	3
	3	3		3	3
	4	3		4	—
09	1	3	24	1	3(2)
	2	4(3)		2	3(2)
	3	3(4)		3	—
	4	—		4	3

Table 9.6. (continued)

Subject	Test Year	M.J. Stage	Subject	Test Year	M.J. Stage
10	1	2	25	1	—
	2	3(2)		2	3(4)
	3	3(4)		3	4(3)
	4	—		4	4(3)
11	1	—	26	1	3
	2	2		2	—
	3	3		3	3
	4	3(2)		4	4(3)
12	1	3(2)	27	1	3
	2	3		2	3
	3	3		3	3
	4	—		4	—
13	1	3(2)	28	1	—
	2	3		2	3
	3	3		3	3
	4	3(4)		4	3(4)
14	1	3	29	1	2(3)
	2	3(2)		2	3
	3	3		3	3(2)
	4	3		4	4(3)
15	1	3(2)	30	1	3
	2	2(3)		2	3
	3	3(2)		3	3
	4	—		4	—

dimensions of ecology, milieu, social system, and culture. We singled out moral culture as the particular focus of our research and proceeded to analyze it principally by assessing norms in terms of their degrees of collectiveness, phase, and stage. Of particular relevance to this focus on moral culture is whether relatively high-stage collective norms (as assessed by following the procedures described in chapter 4) can influence individual moral judgment development.

We tested this hypothesis by first determining through our analysis of community meetings and ethnographic interviews that Cluster's collective norms developed roughly from stage 2–3 in the first year to stage 3 in the second, and to stage 3–4 in the third and fourth years. On that

Table 9.7.

Students' Development to Moral Judgment Stage 4 by Year

Year	1 Step Development (Stage 3 to 3–4)		2 Step Development (Stage 2–3 to 3–4)	
	No. at stage 3	*No. (%) developing to ≥ stage 3–4*	*No. at stage 2–3*	*No. (%) developing to ≥ stage 3–4*
2	12	7(58%)	16	0(0%)
3	13	3(23%)	7	1(14%)
4	10	3(30%)	8	5(62%)

Year	3 Step Development (Stage 2 to 3–4)		Total Number Developing to Stage 3–4	
	No. at stage 2	*No. (%) developing to ≥ stage 3–4*	*No. at ≤ stage 3*	*No. (%) developing to ≥ stage 3–4*
2	3	0(0%)	31	7(23%)
3	2	0(0%)	22	4(18%)
4	1	1(100%)	19	9(47%)

basis, we predicted that student development to stage 4 (or a mixed stage 3–4) would be more likely to occur in the third and fourth years than in the first or second and that development to stage 3 would be more likely to occur in the second through fourth years of the school than in the first. Since we had no pretest data to assess moral stage change during Cluster's first year, we were only able to examine whether the culture may have influenced stage 4 development.

In table 9.7 we present data focusing on moral judgment development to stage 3–4 and 4 during years three and four of the Cluster School, when the collective norms had developed to stage 3–4. We see that during the fourth year of the school the highest percentage of students developed to at least stage 3–4, and that in the majority of these cases the development is quite dramatic—a full stage. Contrary to our hypothesis, the next highest percentage of students developed to at least stage 3–4 during the second year of the school. Upon inspection, we discovered that all of these students comprised a unique group in the school—the founders. They participated in the creation of the school

Table 9.8.

The Relation of Basic Formal Operations and Moral Judgment Stage

Formal Operational Logical Tasks

		Early Basic *Passed Task 3, Failed Task 4*	Basic *Passed Both Tasks 3 and 4*	
Moral Judgment Stage	3	10	4	14
	4 or 3/4	1	7	8
				N = 22

$\chi^2 = 7.08$, df = 1, p < .01.

during the summer of 1974 and were generally recognized by their peers as community leaders.

The Relationship Between Logical and Moral Development. In table 9.8 we present data collected from administering the Piagetian tasks to a subsample of Cluster students, grouped according to their stage of moral reasoning. We found that there was a significant relationship between performance on the two most difficult cognitive tasks and the assessment of moral stage, as either 3 or 3–4 to 4. Looking at the lower row, we see that only one of the eight students with some stage 4 moral reasoning failed the basic formal operations task #4. This supports the hypothesis that logical development to the level of basic formal operations is a necessary condition for stage 4 moral development. The data from the right-hand column indicate that basic formal operations are not a sufficient condition for stage 4 moral reasoning, since four of the eleven students who passed the requisite logical task were scored as moral stage 3.

Table 9.9.

One-Year Pattern of Community Value Stage Development

		Stage at Second Testing					
		1–2	2	2–3	3	3–4	4
	1–2						
	2				4		
Stage at First Testing	2–3			3	5	3	
	3		1		2	4	1
	3–4						
	4						

NOTE: Numbers in each cell represent numbers of students tested twice between years 1 and 2, 2 and 3, 3 and 4.

Moral Type Change. Schrader's (1984) investigation of whether the democracy alternative schools promoted a moral type change from A to B failed to produce any significant findings.[2] A chi-square analysis of moral type by school program on the pretest indicated that there were significantly more type Bs among the sample populations of the democratic schools than there were among those of the traditional schools prior to any intervention effects ($X^2 = 7.13$; $p < .01$). On the posttest, however, both populations were no longer significantly different. A chi-square analysis examining schools instead of programs yielded similar results. No significant change was found in either the democratic or the traditional high schools, although a somewhat greater percentage of students in the alternative schools (63.2 percent) shifted to type B than did their traditional school counterparts (58.1 percent).

Political Value Development. Now we will proceed to examine the relationship between the moral atmosphere and political value development by first observing whether students' reasoning about political values actually develops by stage. In table 9.9 we present one-year change data on the value of community. Of the twenty-three cases presented, there is only one regression and no instance of stage skipping, confirming

2. Dawn Schrader conducted all of the moral types analyses. A full discussion of her findings is presented in Schrader (1984).

Table 9.10.

Difference Between Moral Judgment Stage Scores and Political Values
Stage Scores for One Year of Tenure

Moral Judgment Stage Score *Minus Political Values* *Stage Score*	*−1 to* *−1/2 Stage*	*0*	*+1/2 to* *+1 Stage*
Testing Time 1	12(57%)	8(38%)	1(5%)
Testing Time 2	3(14%)	13(62%)	5(24%)

NOTE: Difference between distributions is significant using Kolmogorov-Smirnov Test.
  $p < .05$

the hypothesis of stage sequentiality. Note that in 74 percent of the cases there was upward change. Data on the other values exhibited similar patterns. In table 9.10 we compare the combined political values stage scores with moral judgment stage scores. At the first time of testing in 57 percent of the cases (twelve of twenty-one) the school values stage is below the moral judgment stage, and in only 5 percent of the cases (one of twenty-one) is it higher. After a year of tenure in the school the gap between scores closes, and in only 14 percent of the cases is the moral judgment stage score higher (see figure 9.1).

In table 9.11 we present data relevant to our "leading edge" hypothesis that school values development predicts to moral judgment development. This table shows that there is a significant relationship between the two. It also suggests that the relationship is in the direction we have predicted, that is, the zero in the lower left cell indicates that political values development may have been a necessary but not sufficient condition for Cluster students' moral development.

Practical Judgment and Moral Responsibility. A chi-square analysis of students' reasoning on the school dilemmas interview shows significant program differences between the democratic and traditional schools on each dilemma (see table 9.12). If we compare the mean score on the practical dilemmas with that on the standard hypothetical dilemmas, we find that they are only slightly different in the democratic schools (practical M.M.S. = 320; standard M.M.S. = 336) and that the mean practical score is considerably lower than the mean standard score in the traditional schools (practical M.M.S. = 280; standard M.M.S. = 312). The differences between democratic and traditional school mean practical judgment scores are significant even after an analysis of covariance.

Figure 9.1.

Contrast Between Moral Judgment Stage Mean Scores and Political Values Stage Mean Scores Over One Year of Development

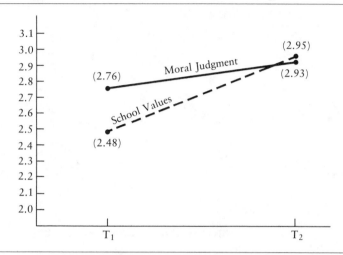

NOTE: Mean scores calculated for students who received both the standard moral judgment interview and the ethnographic moral atmosphere interview in two consecutive years.

In table 9.13 we present a chi-square analysis of the use of responsibility reasoning of each of the school dilemmas for all of the schools. An average of about two-thirds of the students in the democratic schools made responsibility judgments in answering the school dilemmas, while less than one-fifth of the students in the traditional schools did so. The difference between each democratic and traditional school was significant on all of the dilemmas.

These results support our hypotheses that the democratic schools

Table 9.11.

Relationship Between Moral Judgment Development and Political Values Development in the Cluster School

Political Values Development		*No Change*	*+ 1/2 Stage Change*
Moral Judgment Development	No change	5	4
	+ 1/2 Stage Change	0	12

$N = 12$

Table 9.12.

Comparisons Between Democratic and Traditional Programs on
Practical Reasoning by School Dilemma

School Dilemma	Democratic		Traditional		χ^2	df	Significance
	Modal stage	N	Modal stage	N			
Helping	3	55	3	45	20.2	4	p<.001
Drugs	4	53	2	42	40.3	4	p<.001
Stealing	3/4	45	3	42	13.5	4	p<.01
Collective restitution	3/4	23	2/3	16	16.8	4	p<.005

Table 9.13.

Chi-square Analyses of Students Making Responsibility Judgments on
School Dilemmas by School

School Dilemmas	Schools					
	Cluster % (N)	C.R.L.S. % (N)	S.W.S. % (N)	B.H.S. % (N)	A School % (N)	S.H.S. % (N)
Helping*	60% (15)	13% (16)	88% (16)	18% (22)	80% (25)	58% (12)
Drugs**	15% (13)	0% (16)	43% (14)	19% (21)	80% (25)	23% (13)
Stealing***	90% (10)	14% (14)	91% (11)	9% (22)	62% (21)	8% (13)
Collective restitution[a]	60% (10)	— (0)	71% (7)	27% (11)	62% (13)	33% (6)

[a] No χ^2 analysis was conducted because of the low N's and missing data from C.R.L.S.
 * $\chi^2 = 36.6$ 5df p<.00001
 ** $\chi^2 = 36.9$ 5df p<.00001
 *** $\chi^2 = 44.5$ 5df p<.00001

would promote relatively higher stage practical reasoning and a greater
orientation to social responsibility than the traditional schools. We did
not find any significant sex differences contrary to the hypothesis derived
from Gilligan's (1977) work.

DISCUSSION

Moral Judgment Development

The findings on moral judgment development were less striking than what our initial theorizing about the effects of democratic self-governance had led us to expect. One of the experimental schools, the Brookline School-Within-a-School, failed to show any greater moral judgment development than its companion school, Brookline High. The two experimental schools using Kohlberg's theory of just community, Cambridge Cluster School and the Scarsdale Alternative School, did show significant moral judgment gains compared with students in their companion schools, Cambridge Rindge and Latin and Scarsdale High. However, the gains were not dramatic.

There are a couple of reasons we can give to explain why S.W.S. did not show greater change. First, the S.W.S. staff did not explicitly focus democratic discussions on moral or fairness issues. Second the S.W.S. staff did not consciously foster the formation and enforcement of rules and norms for building moral community.

While guidance by moral development and just community theory seems to have been responsible for the moral judgment change in Cluster School and Scarsdale Alternative School, the change was no greater than that found in theory-guided classroom discussions of hypothetical moral dilemmas. The most comprehensive study of moral dilemma discussions in a regular high school context is the Stone Foundation study by Colby et al. (1977). That study assessed change through moral dilemmas discussion in social studies classrooms in schools in the Boston and Pittsburgh areas, and reported an average change of fourteen moral maturity points in nine months. In post hoc analyses classrooms in this study were divided into those in which the conditions for moral growth were present and those in which they were absent. In the classrooms in which the conditions were present the average change was thirty moral maturity points. While the change in the just community schools was not as great as this, it was as great as the change in the kibbutz high school groups that had served as a stimulus to the development of the just community theory (Reimer 1977). Reimer found a fourteen-point mean moral maturity change in the kibbutz high school, stressing the resolution of real-life moral dilemmas through democratic discussion in light of a concern for moral community.

From these studies it appears that if educators were concerned solely with stimulating moral reasoning change, they may opt for classroom moral discussions. Such discussions require far less staff effort and organizational change than the just community approach; and they seem to have the potential for leading to greater average development. However, before recommending moral discussions as a preferable way of promoting moral stage development, we must express certain qualifications and reservations. As Piagetians who think that stage change requires a significant restructuring of cognitive functioning, we believe that there are limits to the rate of stage change that can be stimulated through a school intervention. Thirty points seems to represent an upper limit of average yearly change in high school populations when the data is scored with more recent scoring manuals. Since we have no data for discussion programs lasting longer than a year, we do not know whether it would be realistic to expect that they could maintain such an average over two or more years. It seems plausible to think that after an initial spurt, the rate of moral judgment development may taper off, as we found in Cluster School. The Cluster data show that during the first year of tenure the average stage change is twenty-two moral maturity points, which compares favorably with change resulting from the moral discussion approach. Average yearly change may, therefore, be a misleading indicator of effectiveness in multiyear just community programs without multiyear comparison groups.

A related note of caution in interpreting the significance of the magnitude of moral judgment change concerns whether students have developed nonmoral, cognitive prerequisites for moral judgment development. Walker (Walker and Richards 1979; Walker 1980) presents strong evidence indicating that logical and role-taking skills are necessary but not sufficient for moral development. The data from our study support Walker's findings and those of Colby (1975). Specifically, we found that the low level of many Cluster students' formal operational thinking put a ceiling on their moral development. This suggests that moral intervention programs, whether they utilize the discussion or just community approach, may depend for their success on the effectiveness of a wider school curriculum in promoting logical and social role-taking development.

Two further limitations on interpreting the significance of mean change scores should also be noted. Means do not disclose (a) whether a few

individuals have changed a great deal or a greater number have changed more modestly, or (b) whether change between certain stages (for example, from stage 3 to stage 4) may be more difficult within high school populations than other changes (for example, between stages 2 and 3). Reimer (1977) first raised the issue of the extensiveness of moral judgment change. He found that in comparison with the best moral discussion classes in the Stone Foundation study, more students on the kibbutz changed. The same is true for the students in Cluster. Forty-nine percent of the students in the best classes from the Stone study (Colby et al. 1977) developed at least one-third of a stage compared with 61 percent of the Cluster students in their first year of tenure. Turning to the issue of the relative difficulty of stage transitions, an examination of the global moral judgment scores from all students in our study shows that development to stages 4–5 and 5 is extremely rare in any of the schools, and that development to a pure stage 4 is not that common. This, taken with the result reported for analysis of covariance done on the Westchester data, provides some support for the notion that development beyond stage 3–4 is quite difficult for high school students. These findings have been further corroborated in several longitudinal studies (Colby and Kohlberg 1987), in which it has been shown that the development of pure stage 4 is generally not attained until at least age eighteen, and development to stage 5 is uncommon before age twenty-four. Thus there is considerable evidence indicating that development cannot be accelerated indefinitely.

Our final comment concerns the viability of the discussion approach when compared with the just community approach. By the viability of an approach we simply mean the likelihood that it will become a stable feature of a school. We raise the issue of viability because of our observation that moral discussion classes are easy to start but tend to be discontinued, while just communities are very difficult to start but tend to last. This disparaging comment on the early mortality of moral discussion classes, in spite of the glowing research evidence of their success, calls for some explanation. Most research studies on moral discussion have been one-semester or one-year projects, conducted by a doctoral student or trained teachers knowingly participating in an experiment. We have very little data on discussion programs that were not established specifically as research experiments. What we do know about experimental programs is that after the research on them has ended, they generally stop or they are considerably scaled down. For example, we reported earlier that after the conclusion of the Stone study not one of the trained teachers continued to hold moral discussions. Attempts to keep up teacher interest in moral discussion by integrating moral discussion within the curriculum is a worthwhile goal, but it is not without its hazards. As Higgins (1980) has pointed out, such integration usually entails a dilution of the specifically moral focus of the curriculum. This results in little moral development occurring. At this time, if one is purely interested in promoting moral judgment development, there appears to be no substitute for a specific ethics course based on the discussion method. Such a course requires an explicit curricular commitment that few have been willing to make or sustain. The just community approach requires no less a commitment to the teaching of ethics, but not as a separate course. In addressing the practical concerns of students and of those working in schools, the just community approach can provide the incentive lacking in a more formal philosophical approach.

For the above reasons we are hesitant to abandon our original hypothesis that the just community approach may be the most effective way of promoting moral stage change. Nevertheless, the fact that we only find modest change in the two just community schools and no change in S.W.S. has led us to rethink how the effectiveness of moral education programs ought to be evaluated. We began our research project placing great emphasis on moral stage change as our most important outcome variable. At the time moral stage change happened to be the only outcome variable we could measure. Although we anticipated the development of a method for assessing the moral culture of the school, we thought of moral culture less as an outcome in itself and more as a means to the end of individual moral development. We now argue that moral culture has an intrinsic worth, whether or not it leads to moral judgment change. Furthermore, partly under the influence of our intervention experience and partly under the influence of a more general rethinking of moral action studies (Kohlberg and Candee 1984), we have been led to a somewhat broader understanding of how to evaluate moral education interventions. While we continue to assert the importance of moral stage development, we now recognize other variables related to moral cognition and action, namely moral type, political values, practical moral reasoning, and the presence of a responsibility orientation, as significant.

Before we discuss the results of assessing these new outcome variables, we turn to the issue of the influence of the school's moral atmosphere on moral development. The results we have reported indicate that the moral atmosphere of the just community schools made a difference; however, other explanations are possible. The most plausible rival interpretation of this result is that the development may have been due to classroom moral discussions in the just community schools. We do not have enough classroom observation data to settle this question. Our impression from visiting classes in Cluster and the A School and from talking to teachers is that while moral discussion techniques were used, they were used sporadically. The best case we can make that the moral atmosphere of the just community schools made a difference in stage development comes from our finding that political values development and moral development were closely related, such that there were no cases of individuals developing their moral judgment without also developing their school-related political reasoning. This relationship supports our "leading edge" hypothesis that if a moral atmosphere is effective in promoting stage change, that change should first be observed in the way students resolve school-related issues and later be observed in a more general test of their moral reasoning, such as Kohlberg's standard interview.

As a further test of our hypothesis that the moral atmosphere of the school influences stage development, and as a way of testing more specifically whether the moral culture of the school has an influence, we looked at the relationship between the stage of the collective norms and student moral judgment development. We hypothesized that as the collective norms developed in stage, students reasoning below that level would experience a cognitive mismatch and be stimulated to develop their reasoning to the next higher stage. Our data limited us to focus specifically on development to stage 4. Our community meeting and ethnographic interview analysis established that Cluster's collective norms began to shift from stage 3 to stage 3–4 during the third year of the school and that during the fourth year development continued in this direction. In accord with our predictions, we found that in the fourth year the highest percentage of individual development to at least stage 3–4 occurred. Contrary to our predictions, the second highest percentage was in the second year. However, we discovered that this development was confined to Cluster's founders, a unique group of students in the school. Once Cluster's founders were removed from the second-year sample, the data fit our expectations.

It must be kept in mind that such causal interpretations are quite tentative in studies such as this, in which there is no opportunity to experimentally manipulate explanatory variables. The Berkowitz (Berkowitz and Gibbs 1983) moral discussion study and Walker's (1983) experimental research on the effects of exposure to higher-stage reasoning provide more convincing evidence that cognitive mismatch stimulates development. What our research suggests is that cultural development may create cognitive mismatches between the stage of moral reasoning of an individual and the collective stage of the group norms. When such mismatches occur we think there is a social as well as a cognitive inducement to resolve the conflict at a higher stage.

Formal Operations and Stage 4 Development

The results from administering the Piagetian tasks indicate that the attainment of levels of formal operations is a necessary but not sufficient condition for the attainment of a corresponding stage of moral reasoning. Since only eleven of the thirty-seven Cluster students tested were assessed at the basic formal operational level, we may have some explanation for why developmental gains in Cluster were as modest as they were even when students participated in a moral education program focused on stimulating their moral thinking and reasoning. One implication from this study is that moral educators may have to pay attention to cognitive prerequisites of moral development, particularly when the need for some "remedial education" may already be indicated.

Changes in Moral Type

One of the nonstage variables which we expected would change with experience in the democratic alternative high schools was moral type. Although we found that the percentage of students shifting from type A to type B reasoning was greater in the democratic schools than in the regular high schools, that difference was not significant. The only statistically significant difference between the democratic versus regular schools was on the pretest, in which a much greater percentage of the democratic high school students were scored as type B. This significant pretest difference suggests that students with type B reasoning select schools that they surmise will support their autonomous moral sensibilities (Schrader, 1984).

Political Values Development

In attempting to demonstrate that the moral atmosphere of the school can have an influence on the socio-moral development of students, we first broadened our scope of inquiry beyond the assessment of moral reasoning competence (as measured by the standard moral judgment interview) to include the assessment of a more performance-related variable of how students in the Cluster School reasoned about the following political values: fairness, order, democracy, and community. These values are not all "moral values" (the value of order is a conventional value), nor may they all be thought of as relating to universal features of the social environment. Democracy and community are in our view "ideological" or cultural values that depend upon experiences in particular social settings for their development. In testing the hypothesis that these cultural values are not simply learned but are reconstructed by individuals through stages, we found that most students' reasoning about community and democracy was initially at a lower stage than their moral reasoning competence. After a year of tenure in the school their reasoning about community and democracy developed so that in most cases it was consistent with their competence. We also found that this one-year pattern of development conformed to the Piagetian requirements of invariant sequence, that is, we found only one case of regression and no cases of stage skipping. The regression was only a half stage (from stage 2–3 to 2) and may easily be attributable to measurement error.

Since Cluster students reasoned at about the same stage across all political values, we analyzed their average stage, which we called their political values stage. Although we had some reason to expect that their reasoning about the ideological values may have been lower than their reasoning about the universal, moral, and conventional values of fairness and order, we pointed out that their reasoning on these universal values may also have been low because their reasoning was being assessed in a real-life context and concerned their moral behavior. Additionally, most students were coming from elementary schools that did not encourage them to discuss and deliberate about moral problems arising in school. Our finding that political values developed over a year in Cluster supports our more general hypothesis that the moral atmospheres of democratic schools can have a positive effect on practical moral reasoning.

We will have more to say about the effects of democratic schooling on moral action related variables in the next section, in which we discuss the results of the cross-sectional analysis of practical judgment and social responsibility. Perhaps the most significant conclusion to be drawn from this part of our study is that democratic schools can have a rather powerful impact on the development of politico-moral judgment. We have used the term "political" to describe the values of community, democracy, fairness, and order to call attention to their implication for civics education. If the school is a transitional society between the family and the larger *polis,* then it is crucial that students develop there an understanding of these political values. It is obvious that to become citizens of any society they must develop a keen sense of fairness and appreciation for order. It is no less obvious that to become citizens of a democratic society they must learn how to live democratically. Whether coming to a better appreciation of community is important for civic virtue is rather controversial. In our view a sense of community strengthens the bonds of political association and counteracts perhaps the greatest contemporary threat to our democratic society, privatism.

Practical Judgment and Social Responsibility

We did not undertake a systematic analysis of students' moral behavior for this research. Instead, we focused on variables that we believed mediated between moral reasoning competence and moral action: the stage of practical moral judgment and the responsibility orientation. We assessed practical judgment by posing students with dilemmas that they were likely to encounter at school and asking them how they should and would resolve them in the context of their own school. In accord with previous research, we found a significant gap between moral reasoning competence and practical moral reasoning for those students in the traditional high schools. As we had predicted, but never before demonstrated, we found that the competence/performance gap was almost nonexistent for students in the experimental democratic schools. Results from the longitudinal political value assessment in Cluster corroborate this finding. A second variable, shown to be related to the democratic schools and theoretically mediating between judgment and action, is the responsibility orientation. We described the responsibility orientation as predisposing subjects to make decisions based on an awareness and concern for relationships, the welfare of others, and the public interest. The responsibility orientation not only serves to motivate individuals to do what is right but also informs how they think of their personal response to moral problems. Although we are inclined to believe that the responsibility orientation becomes a "trait variable," our research, confined to the context of the school, does not allow us to conclude this.

CONCLUSIONS

In the previous chapter we examined the effects of democratic schooling in terms of sociological outcome variables, related to moral culture. In this chapter we turned to psychological outcome variables, related to individual moral judgment and action. Our primary attention was given to comparing the moral judgment development of students in democratic and traditional high schools. The results indicated a modest developmental change only in the two democratic high schools with teaching staffs explicitly committed to the just community approach. In exploring other socio-moral cognitive variables more closely related to particular features of the democratic intervention and to moral action, the positive effects of the democratic schools were quite evident.

10

The Just Community
Approach in Prospect

In this book we have proceeded from a practical focus on just community schools to a research focus on their outcomes. We will return to that earlier practical perspective by speculating on how the just community approach might have an impact on secondary education that will reach beyond a few experimental schools. Before looking ahead we first need to review the past: what led us into the experimental schools in the seventies, and what did we learn there?

FROM THE FREE SCHOOL TO THE JUST COMMUNITY

In an extensive review of school climate literature from the 1970s, Epstein (1981) notes that a consensus had formed on the need for new, more responsive school organizational structures and for increased opportunities for adolescent decision making. These were not only the conclusions of educational psychologists but the endorsements of no less than seven national task forces and commissions. While there was a mandate for educational reform that took into account the needs for increased adolescent self-direction and responsibility for decision making, there was little theoretical guidance for how such reform might proceed. Perhaps for this reason the 1970s may be remembered as the decade of failed educational experimentation. Typically, the alternative to a rigid, authoritarian exercise of authority was greater permissiveness.

Open campuses, unstructured time, and free schools lessened the restrictions on adolescents but did not directly foster self-direction or participation. Attempts to share decision making with students floundered, as students often found democratic meetings boring and ineffective (e.g., Bakalis 1976). S.W.S. and the A School started out as free schools, but six years later their faculties recognized the pitfalls of such an atheoretical approach to schooling. The faculty of Cluster School, a latecomer to the alternative education movement, flat out rejected the free school approach.

In our view and the view of the faculties of the experimental schools in this study, the longevity and success of their programs may to a considerable extent be credited to their efforts to ground themselves in the empirical research and democratic theory being developed by Kohlberg and Mosher. This is not to say that faculties from these schools slavishly followed a "cookbook" of directives deduced from laboratory-like experiments or from the armchair philosophizing of Harvard and Boston University dons. Both Kohlberg and Mosher vigorously rejected such models and based their theories and research on experience in the schools. In dialogue with teachers and students they examined the philosophical, psychological, and sociological implications of that experience and revised their approaches accordingly.

THE JUST COMMUNITY SCHOOLS IN RETROSPECT

Kohlberg began his work in the schools with great hope and equally great uncertainty. He knew moral discussions could promote individuals' moral judgment; but he did not know whether democratic communities could be established that would influence judgment and action. What have these years of consultation and research taught us? First of all, we have become convinced of the viability of democratic high schools. This is not to say that democratic governance came easily to staff, let alone to students. How ironic it is that in a democratic society so few of us are prepared to conduct our daily lives in a democratic manner. The good news is that in spite of being superbly "conditioned" for bureaucracy, we can be "retrained" for democracy. In the early days of our projects the staff vacillated between accustomed patterns of paternalism and an "enlightened" permissiveness. The students also vacillated between the luxury of irresponsible dependence and the lure of unrestrained liberty. Eventually both discovered a middle path of democratic authority.

We also learned that giving students a vote did not lead to a "mobocracy" or tyranny of the student majority. The students rarely formed a voting bloc and were quite willing to listen to their elders. As long as some time was given to discussion, we found the decisions students voted upon were on the whole fairer and wiser than those that would have been made without their input. Both students and staff shared our perception.

The research led us beyond an examination of particular decisions to an assessment of how the democratic process influenced school culture, as seen from a moral point of view. As we had hoped, the just community schools did appear to have created a positive cultural alternative to the typical public high school. Our data indicated that the culture of the large public high school actually undermines effective moral education by subjecting students to negative peer group influences and by alienating them from adults. In such a context adult authority tends to reside more in adults' status and coercive power than in their moral persuasiveness. The democratic schools provided an opportunity for staff and students to work together to realize common goals and values. Our measures of moral culture confirmed that students and staff developed shared norms and a shared sense of community over time.

Our observations and research also led us to conclude that the students and staff personally developed through the experience of being members of a democratic community. The students told us that they could see themselves becoming more responsible and better able to stand up for themselves and each other. We saw them becoming more involved in making proposals, organizing committees, and chairing meetings. We saw them speaking with poise and self-assurance at community meetings, Harvard classes, and graduation, where at Cluster the students took turns going to the podium to thank their teachers and offer testimonials to the school. The data on students' moral judgment and political values development, practical reasoning, and adoption of a social responsibility orientation confirmed in a different way the positive effects of their experience. We learned from interviewing teachers that their role had enlarged from giving courses in a particular discipline to educating whole persons. Generally, they appreciated the demands of their new role, although some found that it could become exhausting.

Unfortunately, we did not collect data on how they may have developed as adults and educators through this experience.

Although we did not systematically explore the effects of the just community schools on moral action, we were heartened by the positive results on our measures of practical judgment and the responsibility orientation. The following observations indicated that the schools were more than debating societies, that they had dramatic effects on action: stealing ceased within Cluster just over a year after the school was started; racial relations improved there over four years, and interracial conflict was almost nonexistent; educational aspirations were enhanced, as is evident in the fact that over 90 percent of Cluster's graduates (many of whom were potential high school dropouts) went on to postsecondary education; drug use in the A School virtually ceased; and cheating was also curbed as students adopted an honor code.

Other than moral judgment scores, we have no substantial data on whether the effects of just community schools extend beyond their walls or beyond graduation. We do have some anecdotal information about Cluster graduates who proposed more democracy in their dorms and workplaces. Mosher (1980) cites a study of S.W.S. students by Travers that shows that they were more active in local politics and social justice concerns than their counterparts in Brookline High School (B.H.S.). Whether this finding can be explained by a "selection effect" we cannot say. Clearly more research must be done to determine to what extent these programs produce outcomes that are not context-dependent.

While we believe that these schools have had a relatively favorable impact on most of their student and staff members, there were those who did not seem to profit from the experience. Some of the students who had been alienated before they came to the experimental schools remained that way (Power 1979). Some of the teachers who were initially quite enthusiastic about the ideals of the approach became discouraged by what little they felt was accomplished. Clearly we failed to respond adequately to some students and staff. Nevertheless, the success that we did enjoy, in our view, warrants that we keep trying to improve.

THE FUTURE

In the 1970s advocates of democratic schooling were riding the crest of a wave of educational reform, with its emphasis on social justice and student autonomy. In the 1980s a new wave of reform, emphasizing discipline and preparation for the job market, threatened to submerge them. Given this change in educational priorities, it is perhaps surprising that we can report that interest in the just community approach is growing. In the first half of the 1980s two high schools in the Bronx (Roosevelt High School and the Bronx School of Science) started programs based on the just community approach, and, in addition, a small parochial school in the Boston area incorporated features of it into their ongoing program. Staff at these schools chose the just community approach for somewhat different reasons. In Roosevelt High School, which was one of the most crime-prone schools in New York, they wanted to address the problems of disorder, low achievement levels, and tensions between black and Hispanic gangs. In the Bronx School of Science, which has a highly selective admissions policy and is reputed to be one of the finest high schools in the country, they were interested in the approach as a means of civic education and leadership training. In the parochial school they hoped the approach would boost student and staff morale. These and other more recent additions to the number of just community programs provide some indication that the approach is no seventies fad but relates to enduring concerns about academic excellence and discipline, as well as the development of autonomy and social responsibility.

Although this increase in the number of just community programs is a positive sign for the future of the approach, we admit that our efforts have been focused on small schools and special within-school programs. We do not have pat answers for the many teachers and administrators who, after hearing about the just community schools, ask: "But what does this approach have to say to *my* high school, which is *not* a small alternative school, *not* led by 'democratic-minded' administrators, *not* close enough to the university to take advantage of your consultation, and *not* in possession of the resources to undertake significant staff training?" In order to respond to the challenge that the just community approach may not be relevant to the majority of high schools in this country, we can do little more than refer to a few large high schools in which democratic experiments have taken place and offer our own vision for the future.

Loosely speaking, two models involving students in democratic decision making in the large high school have emerged: a town meeting model with school-wide representatives, and a direct participatory model, centered within semi-autonomous subunits. The first model resembles the traditional student council insofar as it is composed of elected representatives. However, it differs from the student council in that it includes members of the administration, faculty, and support staff (secretaries, cafeteria and custodial workers, etc.), and it deals with more substantive issues in weekly meetings (Power 1985). The second model transforms the old homeroom structure into a just community framework. Instead of "home" being a place where students gather for fifteen minutes of announcements and roll call, it becomes a core community or "mini-school" in which about one hundred students take two classes together and participate in adviser group and democratic meetings. Four to five faculty members are assigned to each core. In addition to teaching in their particular disciplinary specialization, they teach the interdisciplinary core classes, assist in providing guidance, participate in community meetings, and assume pertinent administrative tasks.

The advantage of the first model is its relative ease of implementation, given strong support from the principal or headmaster. For example, in 1981 at Brookline High School, where the model originated, Robert McCarthy, the headmaster, put a town meeting proposal to a school-wide vote after several months of discussion, and it was accepted. The following year elections were held, and town meetings began and have continued (Lightfoot 1983; Kenney 1983; Power 1985). Although a town meeting requires considerable coordination and communication, its small size makes it manageable. Furthermore, it does not demand that existing classroom, discipline, guidance, and administrative structures be changed. The headmaster and other administrators can select those issues that they think are best resolved by a town meeting and leave most to be handled through the regular bureaucratic channels. Of course, town meeting members are free to deal with issues of their own choosing as long as they do not directly involve the curriculum.

From our point of view the town meeting contributes to building a positive moral atmosphere by providing a means of student and staff dialogue and input into decision making on such issues as lateness, littering, smoking, stealing, and vandalism. It also provides an impressive forum for some intriguing debates parelleling those taking place in the state, the nation, and the international community. For example, during the spring of 1982 when budgetary cuts threatened to force teacher layoffs in cities and towns throughout Massachusetts, B.H.S. town meeting members refused to endorse a proposal, cosponsored by the assistant superintendent of the school system, that recommended that private funding be sought for buying computers. Their rationale was simple—if private funds were to be obtained, then the money should first go to retaining staff members. The next year Palestinian and Israeli students locked horns in a town meeting over whether the flag of the P.L.O. should be displayed in the cafeteria along with other flags representing the nationalities of the B.H.S. students. Two years later students and staff protested B.H.S.'s participation in a national scholarship competition that restricted applicants to U.S. citizens. They pressed for a boycott, charging that this policy discriminated against foreign-born students. Because of the rich discussions held in the B.H.S. town meeting and the enthusiasm the meeting engendered among its participants, particularly the administrators, a number of high schools in the New England and New York areas have adopted their own versions of it.

Those working with this representative model quite rightly claim to be developing their own approach and not specifically implementing the just community theory. We are inspired by their courage and resourcefulness, and we expect to learn a great deal more from them in the years to come. There are a number of problems that they must face because of some of the limitations inherent in the representative model. These are problems that are particularly salient to us, coming from our experience in the just community schools, and they shed light on differences between the representative and direct participatory models of democracy:

1. Only an elite of students become members of town meetings. Although a representative structure may teach students how their local, state, and federal governments operate, only the representatives gain actual "legislative" experience.
2. The town meeting "saves the saved." The students who belong to it tend to be recognized leaders. The alienated and marginal students, who need remedial socio-moral education, lack the interest and the social skills to get elected or appointed.
3. The representative structure creates a division of labor that absolves most students from responsibility for the political process. This leads to the view that democratic participation is a nonessential volunteer service and not the principal function of citizenship.
4. Communications between town meeting members and their "constit-

uents" are generally difficult. There are few opportunities for discussing town meeting issues with representatives, and those not in the town meeting are typically not interested in secondhand information.
5. The town meeting alone or with its judiciary counterpart, the Fairness Committee (Wasserman 1979), is not enough to counteract the impersonality of the large high school and the typical split between the adult authorities and the peer counterculture. The diversified curriculum, specialization of personnel, and bureaucratic organizational techniques limit the possibility of building a strong, inclusive sense of moral community in the school.

The core community model addresses these problems by establishing socially significant subunits in which participatory democratic and communitarian practices can be applied. The core community model does not vitiate the large high school. Students can still take advantage of some of its benefits (e.g., greater course selection, better facilities, and more support personnel), while having a "small school" experience. We have found in the school-within-a-school projects (Cluster, S.W.S., and the Bronx programs) that students readily identify themselves as members of those core communities, even though they spend most of the school day outside of them. The major problem with the core community approach is its ambitious scope. The entire staff must be willing to get directly involved in democratic meetings, redefine their roles, and undertake some training. It is more feasible that the second model will be implemented in a piecemeal fashion by establishing one core community at a time. This is what happened in a number of high schools in which a school-within-a-school program was established. In Roosevelt High School in the Bronx, the original just community program was so successful a second one was established for dropout students. Brookline High School is the only large high student in which steps have been taken to involve all students in direct participatory democracy. Occasional discussions are held in all homerooms with input from town meetings about such disciplinary matters as stealing, lateness, and smoking. These discussions generally precede school-wide referenda on changes to be made in the rules listed in the student handbook. The Brookline experience suggests that large-scale implementation of the core community model is possible with the commitment of the headmaster or principal. It also suggests that the two democratic models can complement each other.

CONCLUSION

All great educators from Plato onward have recognized that just communities are necessary for the development of persons of moral character and for the future of a society built on fairness and civic friendship. Our efforts and research represent an attempt in that tradition to discover how schools may be better able to contribute to the socio-moral development of our youth. As we see it, quality of schooling will increasingly depend upon educators responding to discipline and other issues in the school as human problems that require the participation of *all* members of the school for their resolution. The managerial approaches to school administration, with their emphasis on techno-bureaucratic strategies of problem solving, have undermined the ideals of moral education. They must give way to a more self-consciously democratic and communal approach. We are in need of an educational reform far more significant than any we have known, a reform that draws its inspiration not from technological advance but from the moral ideals of justice, democracy, and community on which this nation was founded. In Cluster, the A School, and S.W.S. the vision of reform has begun to take on flesh. They have demonstrated that schools *can* embody in their institutions and cultures our most cherished values and in so doing lead students to understand and practice them. We hope that this volume will encourage and inform future efforts to improve education.

References

Anderson, C. S. 1982. The search for school climate: A review of the search. *Review of Educational Research* 52:368–420.

Armon, C. 1984. Ideals of the good life and moral judgment: Ethical reasoning across the life span. In M. Commons, F. Richards, and C. Armon, eds., *Beyond Formal Operations: Late Adolescent and Adult Cognitive Development*. New York: Praeger.

Bakalis, M. 1976. It works this way for some: Case studies of fifteen schools. Selections. In M. Fantini, ed., *Alternative Education: A Sourcebook for Parents, Teachers, Students, and Administrators*. Garden City, N.Y.: Doubleday.

Baumrind, D. 1986. Sex differences in moral reasoning: Response to Walker's (1984) conclusion that there are none. *Child Development* 57:511–21.

Bennett, W. J. and E. Delattre. 1978. Moral education in the schools. *The Public Interest* 50:81–98.

Berkowitz, M. W. and J. C. Gibbs. 1979. A preliminary manual for coding transactive features of dyadic discussion. Manuscript. Marquette University, Milwaukee, Wisc.

Berkowitz, M. W. and J. C. Gibbs. 1983. Measuring the developmental feature of moral discussion. *Merrill-Palmer Quarterly* 29:399–410.

Berkowitz, M. W., J. C. Gibbs, and J. M. Broughton. 1980. The relation of moral judgment stage disparity to developmental effects of peer dialogues. *Merrill-Palmer Quarterly* 26:341–57.

Blake, J. and K. Davis. 1964. Norms, values, and sanctions. In R. Faris, ed., *Handbook of Sociology*. Chicago: Rand McNally.

Blasi, A. 1980. Bridging moral cognition and moral action: A critical review of the literature. *Psychological Bulletin* 88:1–45.

Blatt, M. 1969. The effects of classroom discussion programs upon children's level of moral development. Ph.D. dissertation, University of Chicago.

Blatt, M. and L. Kohlberg. 1975. The effects of classroom moral discussion upon children's moral judgment. *Journal of Moral Education* 4:129–61.

Bronfenbrenner, U. 1967. Response to pressure from peers versus adults among Soviet and American school children. *International Journal of Psychology* 2:199–207.

Brown, R. and R. Herrnstein. 1975. Moral reasoning and conduct. In *Psychology*. Boston: Little, Brown.

Codding, J. with A. Arenella. 1981. Supporting moral development with a curriculum of ethical decision making. *Moral Education Forum* 6:14–23.

Colby, A. 1975. The relation between logical and moral development. Manuscript. Harvard University, Cambridge, Mass.

Colby, A. 1978. Evolution of a moral-developmental theory. In W. Damon, ed., *New Direction for Child Development: Moral Development*. Vol. 2. San Francisco: Jossey-Bass.

Colby, A. and L. Kohlberg. 1987. *The Measurement of Moral Judgment*. Vol. 1: *Theoretical Foundations and Research Validation*. New York: Cambridge University Press.

Colby, A., L. Kohlberg, E. Fenton, B. Speicher-Dubin, and M. Lieberman. 1977. Secondary school moral discussion programmes led by social studies teachers. *Journal of Moral Education* 6:90–111.

Colby, A., L. Kohlberg, J. Gibbs, and M. Lieberman. 1983. A longitudinal study of moral judgment. Monograph of the Society for Research in Child Development, vol. 48, no. 4.

Colby, A., L. Kohlberg, A. Hewer, D. Candee, J. C. Gibbs, and C. Power. 1987. *The Measurement of Moral Judgment*. Vol. 2: *Standard Issue Scoring Manual*. New York: Cambridge University Press.

Coleman, J. 1961. *The Adolescent Society*. New York: Free Press.

Damon, W. 1977. *The Social World of the Child*. San Francisco: Jossey-Bass.

Dewey, J. 1897/1959. My pedagogic creed. In M. Dworkin, ed., *Dewey and Education*. New York: Teachers College Press.

Dewey, J. 1916/1966. *Democracy and Education*. New York: Macmillan.

Dewey, J. 1938/1963. *Experience and Education*. New York: Macmillan.

Dewey, J. 1960. *Theory of Moral Life*. New York: Holt, Rinehart and Winston.

Dreeben, R. 1968. *On What Is Learned at School*. Reading, Mass.: Addison-Wesley.

Durkheim, E. 1925/1973. *Moral Education: A Study in the Theory and Application of the Sociology of Education*. New York: Free Press.

Enright, R., D. Lapsley, D. Harris, and D. Shauver. 1983. Moral development interventions in early adolescence. *Theory Into Practice* 22:134–44.

Enright, R., D. Lapsley, and V. Levy. 1983. Moral education strategies. In M. Pressley and J. Levin, eds., *Cognitive Strategy Research: Educational Applications*. New York: Springer-Verlag.

Epstein, J. 1981. Secondary school environments and student outcomes: A review and annotated bibliography. *Center for Social Organization of Schools*, Report no. 315.

Erikson, E. 1968. *Identity: Youth and Crisis*. New York: Norton.

Feinberg, J. 1973. The idea of the free man. In J. Doyle, ed., *Educational Judgment: Papers in the Philosophy of Education*. London: Routledge and Kegan Paul.

Feinberg, J. 1980. A child's right to an open future. In W. Aiken and H. LaFollette, eds., *Whose Child*. Totowa, N.J.: Rowman and Littlefield.

Fowler, J. 1981. *Stages of Faith: The Psychology of Human Development and the Quest for Meaning*. San Francisco: Harper and Row.

Fenton, E. 1977. The implication of Lawrence Kohlberg's research for civic education. In B. F. Brown, *Education for Responsible Citizenship: The Report of The National Taskforce on Citizenship Education*. New York: McGraw-Hill.

Gilligan, C. 1977. In a different voice: Women's conceptions of the self and of morality. *Harvard Educational Review* 47:481–517.

Gilligan, C. 1982. *In a Different Voice: Psychological Theory and Women's Development*. Cambridge, Mass.: Harvard University Press.

Gilligan, C. and M. Belenky. 1980. A naturalistic study of abortion decisions. In R. Selman and R. Yando, eds., *Clinical Developmental Psychology*. San Francisco: Jossey-Bass.

Gilligan, C., L. Kohlberg, J. Lerner, and M. Belenky. 1971. Moral reasoning about sexual dilemmas; A developmental approach. Technical report of the commission on obscenity and pornography, vol. 1, no. 52560010. Washington, D.C.: GPO.

Hartshorne, H. and M. A. May. 1928–1930. *Studies in the Nature of Character.* Columbia University, Teachers College. Vol. 1: *Studies in Deceit.* Vol. 2: *Studies in Service and Self-Control.* Vol. 3: *Studies in Organization of Character.* New York: Macmillan.

Hickey, J. 1972. The effects of guided moral discussion upon youthful offenders' moral judgment. Ph.D. dissertation, Boston University.

Hickey, J. and P. Scharf. 1980. *Toward a Just Correctional System.* San Francisco: Jossey-Bass.

Higgins, A. 1980. Research and measurement issues in moral education interventions. In R. Mosher, ed., *Moral Education: A First Generation of Research and Development.* New York: Praeger.

Higgins, A., C. Power, and L. Kohlberg. 1984. The relationship of moral judgment to judgments of responsibility. In J. Gewirtz and W. Kurtines, eds., *Morality, Moral Development, and Moral Behavior: Basic Issues in Theory and Research.* New York: Wiley.

Jackson, P. W. 1968. *Life in the Classroom.* New York: Holt, Rinehart and Winston.

Jacquette, D. 1978. A longitudinal analysis of interpersonal awareness and real-life problem-solving in a group of disturbed adolescents: A clinical-developmental approach. Ph.D. dissertation, Harvard University.

Jennings, W. 1979. The juvenile delinquent as a moral philosopher: The effects of rehabilitation programs on the moral reasoning and behavior of male youthful offenders. Ph.D. dissertation, Harvard University.

Jennings, W. and L. Kohlberg. 1983. Effects of just community programs on the moral development of youthful offenders. *Journal of Moral Education,* vol. 2, no. 1.

Kenney, R. 1983. The creation of a democratic high school: A psychological approach. Ph.D. dissertation, Boston University.

Kohlberg, L. 1966. Moral education in the school. *School Review* 74:1–30.

Kohlberg, L. 1967. Moral and religious education and the public schools: A developmental view. In T. Sizer, ed., *Religion and Public Education.* Boston: Houghton Mifflin.

Kohlberg, L. 1969. Stage and sequence: The cognitive-developmental approach to socialization. In D. Goslin, ed., *Handbook of Socialization Theory and Research.* Chicago: Rand McNally.

Kohlberg, L. 1970a. Education for justice: A modern statement of the Platonic view. In N. Sizer and T. Sizer, eds., *Moral Education: Five Lectures.* Cambridge, Mass.: Harvard University Press.

Kohlberg, L. 1970b. The moral atmosphere of the school. In N. Overley, ed., *The Unstudied Curriculum.* Washington, D.C.: Association for Supervision and Curriculum Development.

Kohlberg, L. 1971a. Cognitive-developmental theory and the practice of collective moral education. In M. Wolins and M. Gottesman, eds., *Group Care: An Israeli Approach.* New York: Gordon and Breach.

Kohlberg, L. 1971b. From *is* to *ought:* How to commit the naturalistic fallacy and get away with it in the study of moral development. In T. Mischel, ed., *Cognitive Development and Epistemology.* New York: Academic Press.

Kohlberg, L. 1971c. Indoctrination versus relativity in value education. *Zygon* 6:285–310.

Kohlberg, L. 1971d. Moral education, psychological view of. *International Encyclopedia of Education.* Vol. 6. New York: Macmillan and Free Press.

Kohlberg, L. 1973e. Stages of moral development as a basis for moral education. In C.

Beck, B. Crittendon, and E. Sullivan, eds., *Moral Education: Interdisciplinary Approaches*. Toronto: University of Toronto Press.

Kohlberg, L. 1976. Moral stages and moralization: The cognitive developmental approach. In T. Lickona, ed., *Moral Development and Behavior: Theory, Research, and Social Issues*. New York: Holt, Rinehart and Winston.

Kohlberg, L. 1978. Preface. In P. Scharf, ed., *Readings in Moral Education*. Minneapolis: Winston Press.

Kohlberg, L. 1980. High school democracy and educating for a just society. In R. Mosher, ed., *Moral Education: A First Generation of Research and Development*. New York: Praeger.

Kohlberg, L. 1981. *Essays on Moral Development*. Vol. 1: *The Philosophy of Moral Development*. New York: Harper and Row.

Kohlberg, L. 1984. *Essays on Moral Development*. Vol. 2: *The Psychology of Moral Development*. San Francisco: Harper and Row.

Kohlberg, L. 1985. A just community approach to moral education in theory and practice. In M. Berkowitz and F. Ozer, eds., *Moral Education: Theory and Practice*. Hillsdale, N.J.: Lawrence Erlbaum.

Kohlberg, L., D. Boyd, and C. Levine. 1986. The return of stage 6: Its principle and moral point of view. In W. Edelstein and G. Nunner-Winkler, eds., *Zur Bestimmung der moral-philosophische und sozialwissenschaftliche Beiträge zur Moralforschung*. Frankfurt: Suhrkamp-Verlag.

Kohlberg, L. and D. Candee. 1984. The relation of moral judgment to moral action. In W. Kurtines and J. Gewirtz, eds., *Morality, Moral Behavior, and Moral Development*. New York: Wiley.

Kohlberg, L., J. Hickey, and P. Scharf. 1980. The justice structure of the prison: A theory and intervention. *Prison Journal* 51:3–14.

Kohlberg, L. and R. Mayer. 1972. Development as the aim of education. *Harvard Educational Review* 42:449–96.

Kohlberg, L. and E. Turiel. 1971. Moral development and moral education. In G. Lesser, ed., *Psychology and Educational Practice*. Glenview, Ill.: Scott, Foresman.

Kuhn, D., J. Langer, L. Kohlberg, and N. Haan. 1977. The development of formal operations in logical and moral judgment. *Genetic Psychology Monographs* 95:97–188.

Lapsley, D., R. Enright, and R. Serlin. In press. Moral and social education. In J. Worell and F. Dunner, eds., *Adolescent Development: Issues for Education*. New York: Academic Press.

Lapsley, D. and R. Serlin. 1984. On the alleged degeneration of the Kohlbergian research program. *Educational Theory* 34:157–70.

Leming, J. S. 1973. Adolescent moral judgment and deliberation on classical and practical moral dilemmas. Ph.D. dissertation, University of Wisconsin.

Leming, J. S. 1976. An exploratory inquiry into the multi-factor theory of moral behavior. *Journal of Moral Education* 5(2):179–88.

Leming, J. S. 1981. Curriculum effectiveness in moral/values education: A review of research. *Journal of Moral Education* 10:147–64.

Levine, R. 1981. Ethnography as science: Knowledge and fallibility in anthropological field research. In M. Brewer and B. Collins, eds., *Scientific Inquiry and the Social Sciences: A Volume in Honor of Donald T. Campbell*. San Francisco: Jossey-Bass.

Lightfoot, S. L. 1983. *The Good High School: Portraits of Character and Culture*. New York: Basic Books.

Lockwood, A. 1978. The effects of values clarification and moral development curricula on school-age subjects: A critical review of recent research. *Review of Educational Research* 48:325–64.

Loevinger, J. 1976. *Ego Development: Conceptions and Theories*. San Francisco: Jossey-Bass.

Lyons, N. 1982. Conceptions of self and morality and modes of moral choice: Identifying justice and care in judgments of actual moral dilemmas. Ph.D. dissertation, Harvard University.

Lyons, N. 1983. Two modes of self and morality. *Harvard Educational Review* 41:325–78.

Modgil, S. and C. Modgil, eds. 1985. *Lawrence Kohlberg: Consensus and Controversy*. Philadelphia: Falmer Press.

Minuchin, P. and E. Shapiro. 1981. The school as the context for social development. In P. Mussen, ed., *Handbook of Child Psychology*. 4th ed. New York: Wiley.

Mosher, R. L. 1978. A democratic high school: Damn it, your feet are always in the water. In N. Sprinthall and R. Mosher, eds., *Value Development . . . as an Aim of Education*. Schenectady, N.Y.: Character Research Press.

Mosher, R. L. 1979. *Adolescents' Development and Education: A Janus Knot*. Berkeley, Calif.: McCutchan.

Mosher, R. L. 1980. A democratic school: Coming of age. In R. Mosher, ed., *Moral Education: A First Generation of Research and Development*. New York: Praeger.

Mosher, R. L. and P. Sullivan. 1976. A curriculum in moral education for adolescents. In D. Purpel and K. Ryan, eds., *Moral Education: It Goes with the Territory*. Berkeley, Calif.: McCutchan.

Neill, A. S. 1960. *Summerhill*. New York: Hart.

Neibuhr, H. R. 1963. *The Responsible Self*. New York: Harper and Row.

Nisan, M. 1984. Social norms and moral judgment. In W. Kurtines and J. Gewirtz, eds., *Morality, Moral Behavior, and Moral Judgment*. New York: Wiley.

Noam, G. 1985. Stage, phase, and style: The developmental dynamics of the self. In M. Berkowitz and F. Oser, eds., *Moral Education: Theory and Application*. Hillsdale, N.J.: Lawrence Erlbaum.

Nucci, L. 1982. Conceptual development in the moral and conventional domains: Implications for values education. *Review of Educational Research* 52:93–122.

Paolitto, D. 1975. Role-taking opportunities for early adolescents: A program in moral education. Ph.D. dissertation, Boston University.

Parsons, T. 1968. The school class as a social system. In *Socialization and School, Harvard Educational Review*, Reprint Series, vol. 1.

Peters, R. S. 1973. *Authority, Responsibility, and Education*. Rev. ed. London: Allen and Unwin.

Peters, R. S. 1981. *Moral Development and Moral Education*. London: Allen and Unwin.

Piaget, J. 1932/1965. *The Moral Judgment of the Child*. Glencoe, Ill.: Free Press.

Piaget, J. 1967. *Six Psychological Studies*. New York: Random House.

Power, C. 1979. The moral atmosphere of a just community high school: A four-year longitudinal study. Ph.D. dissertation, Harvard Graduate School of Education.

Power, C. 1985. Democratic moral education in a large high school: A case study. In M. Berkowitz and F. Oser, eds., *Moral Education: Theory and Application*. Hillsdale, N.J.: Lawrence Erlbaum.

Power, C. and J. Reimer. 1978. Moral atmosphere: An educational bridge between moral judgment and action. In W. Damon, ed., *New Directions for Child Development: Moral Development*. vol. 2. San Francisco: Jossey-Bass.

Rawls, J. 1971. *A Theory of Justice.* Cambridge, Mass.: Harvard University Press.

Reimer, J. 1977. A study in the moral development of kibbutz adolescents. Ph.D. dissertation, Harvard Graduate School of Education.

Reimer, J., D. Paolitto, and R. Hersch. 1983. *Promoting Moral Growth: From Piaget to Kohlberg.* 2d ed. New York: Longman.

Reimer, J. and C. Power. 1980. Educating for democratic community: Some unresolved dilemmas. In R. Mosher, ed., *Moral Education: A First Generation of Research and Development.* New York: Praeger.

Rest, J. 1968. Developmental hierarchy in preference and comprehension of moral judgment. Ph.D. dissertation, University of Chicago.

Rest, J. 1979. *Development in Judging Moral Issues.* Minneapolis: University of Minnesota Press.

Rest, J. 1980. Developmental psychology and values education. In B. Munsey, ed., *Moral Development, Moral Education, and Kohlberg: Basic Issues in Philosophy, Psychology, Religion, and Education.* Birmingham, Ala.: Religious Education.

Royce, J. 1908/1982. *The Philosophy of Josiah Royce.* J. Roth, ed. Indianapolis: Hackett.

Sarason, S. B. 1971. *The Culture of the School and the Problem of Change.* Boston: Allyn and Bacon.

Scharf, P. 1973. Moral atmosphere and intervention in the prison. Ph.D. dissertation, Harvard University.

Schläfli, A., J. Rest, and S. Thoma. 1985. Does moral education improve moral judgment? A meta-analysis of intervention studies using the DIT. *Review of Educational Research* 55:319–52.

Schrader, D. 1984. The development of moral autonomy: A comparison of moral types in traditional and alternative high schools. Qualifying paper, Harvard University.

Selman, R. L. 1980. *The Growth of Interpersonal Understanding: Developmental and Clinical Analyses.* New York: Academic Press.

Sprinthall, N. A. 1980. Psychology for secondary schools: The saber-tooth curriculum revisited? *American Psychologist* 35:336–47.

Taguiri, R. 1968. The concept of organizational climate. In R. Taguiri and G. Litwin, eds., *Organizational Climate: Exploration of a Concept.* Boston: Harvard University, Division of Research, Graduate School of Business Administration.

Tappan, M., L. Kohlberg, D. Schrader, A. Higgins, C. Armon, and T. Lei. 1987. Heteronomy and autonomy in moral development: Two types of moral judgment. Appendix to A. Colby and L. Kohlberg. *The Measurement of Moral Judgment.* Vol. 1: *Theoretical Foundations and Research Validation.* New York: Cambridge University Press.

Tönnies, F. 1957. *Community and Society.* East Lansing: Michigan State University Press.

Turiel, E. 1966. An experimental test of the sequentiality of developmental stages in the child's moral development. *Journal of Personality and Social Psychology* 3:611–18.

Turiel, E. 1983. *The Development of Social Knowledge, Morality and Convention.* New York: Cambridge University Press.

Vygotsky, L. 1934/1962. *Thought and Language.* Cambridge, Mass.: MIT Press.

Walker, L. J. 1980. Cognitive and perspective-taking prerequisites for moral development. *Child Development* 51:131–39.

Walker, L. J. 1983. Sources of conflict for stage transition in moral development. *Developmental Psychology* 19:103–10.

Walker, L. J. and B. S. Richards. 1979. Stimulating transitions in moral reasoning as a function of stage of cognitive development. *Developmental Psychology* 15:95–103.

Wasserman, E. 1975. Implementing Kohlberg's "just community" in an alternative high school. *Social Education* 40:203–7.

Wasserman, E. 1977. The development of an alternative high school based on Kohlberg's just community approach to education. Ph.D. dissertation, Boston University School of Education.

Wasserman, E. 1979. *The Fairness Committee: A Manual for Students and Teachers—a Community Approach to Grievances.* Manuscript.

Wasserman, E. and A. Garrod. 1983. Application of Kohlberg's theory to curricula and democratic schools. *Educational Analysis* 5(1):17–36.

Zalaznick, E. 1980. The just community school: A student perspective. *Moral Education Forum* 5:27–35.

Index